1996

1996

My Backstage Pass to the Wildest Year of Britain's Wildest Decade

Dominic Mohan

HarperCollins*Publishers*

With all my love to Michelle, Gabriel,
Huey, Honor and Lulu.

HarperCollins*Publishers*
1 London Bridge Street
London SE1 9GF

www.harpercollins.co.uk

HarperCollins*Publishers*
Macken House, 39/40 Mayor Street Upper
Dublin 1, D01 C9W8, Ireland

First published by HarperCollins*Publishers* 2026

1 3 5 7 9 10 8 6 4 2

© Dominic Mohan 2026

Dominic Mohan asserts the moral right to
be identified as the author of this work

A catalogue record of this book is
available from the British Library

ISBN 978-0-00-876713-6

Printed and bound in the UK using 100%
renewable electricity at CPI Group (UK) Ltd

All rights reserved. No part of this publication may be
reproduced, stored in a retrieval system, or transmitted,
in any form or by any means, electronic, mechanical,
photocopying, recording or otherwise, without the
prior written permission of the publishers.

Without limiting the exclusive rights of any author, contributor
or the publisher of this publication, any unauthorised use of
this publication to train generative artificial intelligence (AI)
technologies is expressly prohibited. HarperCollins also exercise
their rights under Article 4(3) of the Digital Single Market
Directive 2019/790 and expressly reserve this publication
from the text and data mining exception.

Contents

INTRODUCTION:	**What's the Story?**	1
CHAPTER 1:	**Thatcher**	23
CHAPTER 2:	**Maine Road**	56
CHAPTER 3:	**Blur**	93
CHAPTER 4:	**Euro 96**	124
CHAPTER 5:	**Robbie**	148
CHAPTER 6:	**Spice**	172
CHAPTER 7:	**Knebworth**	203
CHAPTER 8:	**Macca, Townshend, Bowie and Rod**	231
CHAPTER 9:	**Blair**	264
CHAPTER 10:	**End of a Century**	296
	Acknowledgements	313
	Picture Credits	314

INTRODUCTION

What's the Story?

A loaf of bread would set you back 53p. Cigarettes and alcohol? A pint of lager was £1.74, while twenty Benson & Hedges would send three quid up in smoke.

After thirty years of hurt, 1996 was here, the 90s apex and the greatest year of the greatest decade of our generation's lives. The average price of a home was just £53,331 and only 4 per cent of households had internet access, while 16 per cent had a mobile phone. The average annual wage was £17,500.

It was the dying days of John Major's Conservative government. *The Sun* newspaper, where I had just landed an action-packed job as a showbiz reporter, had a cover price of 25p, the *Daily Mail* and *The Times* would cost you 35p some days, the *Telegraph* 40p and the *Guardian* 60p on Saturdays. A TV licence clocked in at £89.50. The interest rate was hovering around 7 per cent and the most popular motor was a Ford Fiesta.

My ticket to see Oasis at Knebworth on Saturday 10 August of that fabled year? Face value £22.50 – with The Prodigy, Manic Street Preachers, The Chemical Brothers,

1996

Ocean Colour Scene and The Bootleg Beatles thrown in. Us lucky enough to be in the melting crowd wore loose-fit jeans and cargo pants, Clarks Wallabees, the three stripes of Adidas and baggy football colours, predominantly those with Three Lions on a shirt, to coin a phrase.

Manchester United did the double under manager Sir Alex Ferguson, winning the recently christened Premier League, while also beating Liverpool 1–0 in the FA Cup Final. The Gallagher brothers' beloved Manchester City were relegated to the Championship. Alan Shearer starred at the Euro 96 football tournament across England that glorious summer and went home to Newcastle United for a then-world-record-breaking fee of £15 million, earning him what was a staggering £34,000 a week, the Premier League average being a humble £3,668 every seven days.

Evenings in 1996 might be spent playing *Tomb Raider* on the PlayStation, or watching a £2 VHS video rental of *Independence Day* from Blockbuster. Tupac was killed, Lewis Capaldi and actor Tom Holland born, Dolly the Sheep cloned. Legoland Windsor opened its doors while, down the road, The Andrew Formerly Known as Prince and Sarah Ferguson divorced. Unemployment was the lowest for five years at under two million.

Palpably, the country felt in purring economic shape, London buzzing with shiny new buildings, clubs and restaurants under revolutionary chefs like Marco Pierre White and Gordon Ramsay. The art and fashionista scene had detonated via Damien Hirst, Tracey Emin, Alexander McQueen and Stella McCartney, and Great Britain felt as if it were truly at the globe's epicentre. Newspapers were

WHAT'S THE STORY?

booming too, *The Sun* reaching its highest ever daily full-price sale in March 1996 just as – unrelated – I joined, shifting 4.78 million copies on Grand National day. (Sales would often peak around pulsating sporting occasions of football and racing, with coupons for free bets and pints frequently serving as something of a circulation Viagra.)

It was a place that, in many ways, still resembled George Orwell's description in his 1941 essay 'England Your England', when he wrote of a nation of coupon-snippers, stamp-collectors, crossword-puzzle fans and pigeon-fanciers, of darts obsessives whose lives revolved around football, the boozer, beer, betting and bawdiness. Not much had really changed – hence the population's love of raucous red tops packed with sport and promotions, inhabited by mischievous and sparkling writers and editors, the pun-loving bon viveurs with passions for footie, drinking and popular culture.

1996 was the momentous year I was appointed as a showbiz journalist for the *Currant Bun*, something of a natural home where I would remain for seventeen years, employed to spot and document the developing trends in British popular culture for *The Sun*'s entertainment column – and beyond. The emerging Britpop bands were groups I was passionate about anyway, had already met and seen live. It was serendipitous: I was in the right place at exactly the right time (a theme that will punctuate this book).

I was handed a precious backstage pass to this magical period, as witness and chronicler of some of its most significant moments, access all areas to its wild protagonists, whether in music, entertainment, fashion, football, art or politics. I was living and breathing the 90s life and had a front-row seat for that insane decade, but it was 1996 that was the period's stunning apex. Oasis at Maine Road and Knebworth, the births of Robbie Williams the solo star and the Spice Girls, the Euro 96 football tournament and 'Three Lions', the rise of New Labour and Tony Blair. I was there for the lot, with front-page bylines, anecdotes you will not believe and mind-blowing memories.

That's why, exactly thirty years on, I am revisiting that glorious year, looking at what has changed (and what has stayed the same) and telling the story of a (perhaps) more innocent, carefree and contented time. I don't think there are many writers better placed to lay out the story of that seismic moment in British cultural history, 1996, the year that encapsulated why we loved our country so much, and the creative earthquake whose aftershocks are still resonating today.

My long professional life as a journalist began in 1990 and I was ringside to observe that knockout moment in time, the sparring, the feuding and the brawling. Three decades on, I will explain the riotous journey to this artistic pinnacle, coming itself three decades after the swinging 60s and a World Cup triumph. I had penned Kurt Cobain of Nirvana's obituary for the *Sunday Mirror* back in 1994 and witnessed close up the emergence of the Britpop bands from the ashes of grunge, alongside the evolution of English football and its entwinement with 90s celebrity culture and the media – my life's passions, rolled into one. And with a pen and reporter's pad in hand at all times, naturally.

WHAT'S THE STORY?

The 1990s was, without doubt, the most important and significant decade of my life to date, with 1996 at its peak. I landed my first job in journalism, moved to London, met the love of my life, landed my dream job, chronicled the birth of Cool Britannia, covered major football tournaments, met prime ministers and Diana, experienced unbearable grief for the first time, proposed to and married my wife; our first child was born three weeks before the dawn of the new millennium.

I have rifled through my old contacts book and gone back to some of the key faces from 1996 to help me contextualise that magical year, speaking with members of, and pivotal figures around, Oasis, Blur, the Spice Girls, Robbie Williams, the England football team, the Young British Artists, the media and New Labour. They have helped me put together what is, if I may be permitted to say so myself, the definitive memoir and cultural autopsy of that year, and the decade itself.

Having lived through that era and knowing many of these figures personally, I wanted to check back in, to ask what it all meant to them – and to Britain. And to help express why that powerful year became the stuff of legend and still matters to us today – culturally, economically and emotionally.

I will forensically scrutinise those mythical twelve months and ask why the cultural detonation happened then and there, what legacy it carries today and whether it could ever occur again, recalling run-ins, late-night encounters and expletive-laden interviews with those who all played a role in making the 90s, and 1996 in particular, the most memorable time of my – and my generation's – life.

1996

There is a particular moment in 1996 that defines and summarises the year in so many ways, a critical congregation of its most influential figures, young and old, who each helped share and define the year.

It had been an arduous trip through British popular culture to get there, with casualties on the way, but in the hallowed halls of Earls Court, where Oasis had slain only months previously, Britpop – until very recently an underground movement – achieved its moment of recognition from the music industry at the Brit Awards.

That bacchanalian evening was to be a night of anarchy, madness and mayhem, of filth and fury, but also a moment of celebration, euphoria and joy at what our nation had become, its bright young hopes and upstarts from the world of music, media, comedy and politics united.

And, as the newly installed showbiz lad on *The Sun* newspaper, I knew that, ahead of the Brits, the brothers Gallagher were, perhaps somewhat unsurprisingly, planning a colossal blowout to top all blowouts – and that is a mighty high bar indeed. Apparently, they would be warming up and pre-loading with champagne at London's Landmark Hotel, close to their management offices, before staggering to the venue. I'd followed the intriguing group since seeing them live at London's Kentish Town Forum two years earlier and was pushing for more coverage of their music and antics within the pages of my new-found journalistic home.

It was late afternoon. I hailed a black cab from *The Sun*'s offices in East London and raced across town where I met a friend who, significantly, happened to be a dead ringer for Manchester United winger Ryan Giggs, for a sherbet in the hotel's low-lit basement bar. A nervy photographer joined us soon afterwards, the band's boisterous reputation preceding them.

Right on cue, the lads and their entourage crashed in with the-then Gallagher girlfriends Meg Mathews and actress Patsy Kensit in tow. That was a Brucie bonus as Patsy had only announced her marital split from Simple Minds frontman Jim Kerr one month earlier. They headed straight for the bar, whence achingly expensive champagne was swiftly procured. We played it cool for a bit before I ambled over and pleasantries were exchanged. A glass of fizz was shoved in my hand and I asked the brothers if we could be permitted to take a photograph of them and the girls, to mark what would inevitably be the biggest night of their careers ... so far. Absolutely, they said – I'd got to them early enough – and a typically modest Noel, who had penned their 1995, now-22-million selling album *(What's the Story) Morning Glory?*, told me: 'We know we will win. There is no one out there to match us right now. We deserve to clean up and that's exactly what we'll do.'

We ushered the giggling foursome into a corridor next to the loos and captured a very rare snap of Liam and Noel entwined with Patsy and Meg. I'm not sure any other such photograph of the iconic quartet has ever been seen publicly. A heavily bearded Liam looked as if he hadn't bathed for several days and was resplendent in a nasty-looking, garish – and now infamous – brown leather parka, which clearly made him sweat profusely, although there were perhaps some other contributing factors at play.

It was clear he was plotting an evening of mayhem – I could see it in his bulging eyeballs. And, as was customary, he would not disappoint.

I thanked them before they headed back to the increasingly raucous bar, but not before City fan Liam simian-strolled over to my panic-stricken friend, who appeared startled as the singer inspected him and snarled, 'What the fookin' hell are you doing here, Giggsy, you United knobhead?' I leapt between them and explained that this was not actually Ryan Giggs, but simply someone who was fortunate enough to share the tousled Red Devil's good looks and cheekbones. I later recalled that Mr Giggs and Patsy herself had been linked only months before, when they attended the *Batman Forever* premiere together in London's Leicester Square, so his hostility made sense. Liam and Giggs would have a real run-in two months later at Manchester's Millennium Club, after the singer told him he was 'shit at football'. Giggs hit back and said Noel was the brains behind the band. It was pretty puerile stuff, but all good copy nonetheless. And that is something Oasis always provided.

Anyway, job done. Picture in the bag. Run-in averted – on this particular occasion. No fisticuffs. And so to the awards. They were pretty eventful too.

This was the spectacular coronation of Britpop and Cool Britannia, as the movement's key protagonists assembled under the crumbling roof of the Earls Court Exhibition Centre in West London for that one and only time. It was the same venue where, as a 14-year-old boy and wannabe writer, I had witnessed my first ever concert, thirteen years

WHAT'S THE STORY?

earlier. My father took me to see the mighty Supertramp and my addiction to live music was ignited from that moment – the first thing I did the following day was to write a review of the gig in my Letts 1983 Schoolboy Diary, something I still treasure today; it was the first of many hundreds of music reviews I would go on to pen.

But, by 1996, the music industry was now a very different world. No place for prog warblers like The 'Tramp that night, but Supergrass, yes. And Radiohead, Pulp, Massive Attack, Robbie Williams and Creation Records Svengali Alan McGee, who had signed Oasis in May 1993 after stumbling upon them in Glasgow club King Tut's. It felt like the revolution was taking place in front of my tired eyes, a transfer of power and changing of the guard, with historic moments such as The Who's Pete Townshend presenting Oasis with their Best British Group award, a symbolic handing over of the rock 'n' roll baton. Oasis would go on to record 'My Generation' as a nod back, and Noel would memorably play with Townshend at an intimate, soul-stirring and rather eventful charity gig. But I'm getting ahead of myself. Much more of that later.

Other luminaries present that tumultuous night included Take That, Annie Lennox, Pet Shop Boys, comedians Vic Reeves and Bob Mortimer (who would perform a vital role later that evening), foreign dignitaries Michael Jackson, Tina Turner, Celine Dion, Kylie Minogue, Jon Bon Jovi, Lenny Kravitz, Iggy Pop and Alanis Morissette, alongside Paula Yates, Michael Hutchence and – awkwardly – Bob Geldof, Page Three girl Sam Fox, members of Queen and a then-unknown girl band of

1996

wannabes called Spice Girls, five months ahead of the release of their debut single. A smattering of footballers and The Lightning Seeds, later of 'Three Lions' fame, were also invited, confirming that music and football were now conjoined worlds in motion.

The hottest name on TV and radio, motormouth Chris Evans, hosted and introduced Leader of the Opposition Tony Blair as 'foot-tapping, pop-loving, he's got nice hair – Tony Blair'. The PM-in-waiting was jeered as he took to the stage to present a lifetime achievement award to a rather sheepish David Bowie, expertly coiffured himself, who admitted afterwards: 'I'm not sure we should pay homage to the past, I prefer to keep reinventing it. But it's a nice place to play my music. It's very nice to be given awards ... I suppose.' Wide-eyed me would, of course, have no inkling then that I'd go on to interview the Thin White Duke many times (and Blair too, actually) and this was classic Bowie: dry, witty and always looking forward.

The nervy Labour leader told the uncertain crowd: 'It's been a great year for British music. A year of creativity, vitality, energy. British bands storming the charts. British music back once again in its right place, at the top of the world. And at least part of the reason for that has been the inspiration that today's bands can draw from those that have gone before. Bands in my generation like The Beatles and The Stones and The Kinks. Of a later generation: The Clash, The Smiths, The Stone Roses ...'

Some compared his appearance to an am-dram attempt at portraying a statesman. Blair escaped lightly though; at the ceremony two years later, his bruiser of a deputy John

WHAT'S THE STORY?

Prescott was soaked with a bucket of water thrown by a member of tubthumping new age crust-merchants Chumbawamba. He was a chap called Danbert Nobacon, but his real name is Nigel and he struck two metres from where I was seated, sploshing my new Paul Smith suit. Oh, the anarchy.

Speaking of Blair, a rather wobbly-on-size-six-feet Noel chirped from the stage: 'There are seven people in this room who are giving a little bit of hope to young people in this country. That is me, our kid, Bonehead, Guigs, Alan White, Alan McGee and Tony Blair. And if you've all got anything about you, you'll go up there and you'll shake Tony Blair's hand, man. He's the man! Power to the people!' This was one of the key moments in the evolution of the Cool Britannia movement, a blurring of the lines between music and politics. Noel may have once implored us: 'please don't put your life in the hands of a rock 'n' roll band', but here was a songwriter at the height of his powers trying to influence the forthcoming general election.

According to the man who signed him, Alan McGee, Noel had necked three tablets of ecstasy and was 'off his tits' when he spoke from the stage. Still ranting, the songwriter would later tell the assembled media in the crowded press room: 'The one voted for by the fans means a lot. Anything voted for by fans is special, anything that's voted for by idiots, corporate pigs, means nothing to us.' The Brits publicity team turned a whiter shade of pale.

Actress Patsy Kensit said that crazy night was the beginning of the tabloid storm that would engulf her and a blitzed Oasis over the following years. And many of the stories would carry my byline, as the 90s' twists and gurns dominated a voracious media.

Crazy it certainly was. As a working journalist, I cannot recall any awards ceremony that produced as many news angles as the 1996 Brits. At one point, Noel eyeballed the crowd and stated: 'I'm extremely rich, and you lot aren't.' Then, INXS frontman Michael Hutchence, who was presenting the best video gong to the band for 'Wonderwall', was mocked by Noel, who sneered: 'Has-beens shouldn't present fucking awards to gonna-bes.'

There had been previous beef between the Gallaghers and Hutchence, whose partner Paula Yates was bouncing around backstage. Paula, herself appointed as a *Sun* columnist in April of that year, had cheated on husband Geldof and their divorce was made official the following month, just weeks before the birth of Paula's daughter with Hutchence, Tiger Lily. Geldof himself was in the house, to present Michael Jackson with an award that seemed to have been made up especially for him.

To add to the fun that night, when picking up their British Album of the Year award, the brothers celebrated by bursting into an impromptu version of Blur's 'Parklife' retitled 'Shite-Life'. That was just before Liam called awards host Chris Evans 'ginger bollocks' and pretended to shove the statuette up his own backside. Story after story – I'd never seen anything like it. This was the lunacy and rebellion of the 90s condensed into one awards ceremony. A tabloid journalist's dream.

Blur may have been victorious the previous year in the 'Country House' vs 'Roll with It' singles battle soap opera,

WHAT'S THE STORY?

but it was somewhat pyrrhic. The accompanying album *The Great Escape* was declared triple platinum in the UK, eventually selling 900,000 copies, while Oasis's behemoth *(What's the Story) Morning Glory?* was certified seventeen times platinum, shifting 5.4 million copies in the UK alone. And there were to be no Brit awards for Blur that night and they skipped the ceremony, with bassist Alex James telling me they were suddenly out of the country, perhaps conveniently so.

The Blair–Oasis love-in would, of course, have made the headlines if it weren't for the actions of one skinny man that heady night, which crystallised the drama, humour and provocative nature of Britpop. Jarvis Cocker formed Pulp in 1978 and the band had had little success until their explosion in 1995, with what many consider the ultimate Britpop anthem, ahead of anything outputted by Blur or Oasis – 'Common People'.

Michael Jackson was 37 and making his first live UK TV appearance for twenty years. Brits organisers had dreamed up a special Artist of a Generation award as a lure, so that he would agree to play his recent Christmas number one, 'Earth Song'. Dressed in Christ-like white, and with arms biblically outstretched, he was permitted to perform the song surrounded by clusters of pre-pubescent girls and boys. Only two years previously, Jacko had settled out of court on a sexual abuse case brought against him by the father of 13-year-old Jordan Chandler. The food at the Brits can be hit and miss at the best of times, but this performance was even harder to swallow. In a moment of mad genius, Jarvis decided to moon the moonwalker after Jackson's 'extremely distasteful and crap' performance.

Then, later, as Jarvis was trying to leave Earls Court, he was invited by a police officer and the Brits organisers to discuss the incident in his dressing room, whereupon he was arrested on suspicion of an on-stage assault of the underage Jacko-worshippers. He was even accompanied to the toilet by police in case he made a run for it and was then whisked off to nearby Kensington Police Station for official questioning.

The exasperated singer was joined by comedian Bob Mortimer, in the audience at the evening's shenanigans, who offered his services in law, having worked as a solicitor in a previous life. Bob recalled entering the room where Jarvis was being held, asking what had happened and receiving the reply, 'I showed my bottom to Michael.'

Bob repeatedly questioned the illegality of 'upsetting Michael Jackson', explaining it had yet to be enshrined in Britain's statutory law books. Jarvis was eventually bailed and released after 3am, being handed a court date to answer any charges. Shattered, he had to perform in Brighton that evening for the opening night of Pulp's biggest tour to date.

'Jacko's Pulp Friction,' gasped the *Daily Express*. 'He's Off His Cocker,' *The Sun* screamed. *Melody Maker* went with 'Give Him a Knighthood!'.

An unrepentant Jarvis released his own version of events in a statement too: 'My actions were a form of protest at the way Michael Jackson sees himself as some Christ-like figure with the power of healing. The music industry allows him to indulge his fantasies because of his wealth and power. I just ran on the stage and showed off.'

David Bowie had hired his own personal film crew to document his appearance at Earls Court and meeting Blair that night; fortunately, they had captured the clearest footage of the Jarvis stage invasion yet, proving beyond doubt that the Pulp man had not assaulted anyone. After the film was released publicly, the case was swiftly dropped and Jarvis exonerated, with the Pulp singer thanking his hero Bowie for helping to set him free.

But the incident was to have long-term repercussions for the singer, who confessed he became anxious with his new level of celebrity and infamy. That didn't, however, stop him from attending so many celebrity parties that he topped *The Sun*'s silly Ligger's League, which we had dreamed up for the Bizarre column's pages, to mark our subjects' love of a showbiz freebie. I would commonly blag my way into the V-V-VIP area of celebrity events across the capital and Jarvis would oft be leaning elegantly at the bar sipping a complimentary glass of champagne. If I'm honest, I guess I would probably have been joint top of the aforementioned league myself but, under the strict league regulations, staff were exempt.

The Brits spectacle that night was edgy and refreshing, its stars half a world away from the sterile dullards in US boy bands like New Kids on the Block, Backstreet Boys and NSYNC, who had been dominating the charts – and the tabloid media. 1996 felt fun and anarchic, the music we were hearing untouchable. Suddenly, I was writing about super-talented people of my own age, who went to the same kind of schools, in the same parts of Britain as me and my friends. The early 90s had been monopolised by coverage of Take That and US music from Michael Jackson and his imitators, alongside boring, old, distant American stars like Sylvester Stallone and Arnold Schwarzenegger, whose lives seemed faraway and unattainable. And I certainly would never have been seen dead in a Planet Hollywood leather jacket, unlike some of my voguish predecessors, I might add.

What we didn't quite know then was that the 1996 Brit Awards was an assemblage of Cool Britannia A-listers, gathered for the first and only time, with nods to the towering greats who paved the way for this generation of creators – Bowie, Townshend, Brian Eno. We were dispensing with American heritage acts like Jacko and ushering in lads and ladettes from Colchester, Sheffield and Manchester. You'd regularly bump into them in pubs in Camden, unguarded and without a phalanx of security, managers and publicists. Perhaps it had been like this with punk twenty years before, but I was too young for all that; this felt like we were breaking not only new ground but also a steady stream of stories about these precocious popsters. Down to earth and approachable, these were cool British girls and geezers, unafraid to speak their minds and definitely not media-trained, thank the lord. A dream for a dedicated follower and coming-of-age chronicler like myself, clutching close that backstage pass to Britain's wildest year and decade, the copy pouring out of their lubricated mouths into print, then into the homes and offices of many millions across Britain, where an information-hungry, pre-social media tribe lapped up the flourishing coverage of this cultural quake.

Of course, most of the characters who graced the anarchic stage on that demented evening would go on to play some part in my life and career as it developed through the 90s. It was my job to be a paid-up eyewitness to the dawn of these momentous times, gaining access to the main players and their inner circles, with many of whom I still have enduring relationships, and who were prepared to share their analyses of 1996 and what followed, in exclusive interviews for this new historical assessment and reflection.

My journalism during that mystic year and the age that followed would help propel me from 90s showbiz reporter to editor of the Bizarre column, and then up through the ranks of the newspaper's hierarchy, where I would go on to hold a series of executive roles. And, ultimately, this would lead in 2009 to the most celebrated and controversial job in tabloid journalism, as the following decade came to a close. For it is then that I was appointed as the Editor of *The Sun*.

I would go on to meet and interview world leaders like Blair and his US counterpart Bill Clinton, Queen Elizabeth and King Charles. And to travel all around the world to interrogate musical heroes Sir Paul McCartney, David Bowie, Oasis, The Who, U2, Coldplay, Sir Elton John, Blur, Led Zeppelin, Sir Rod Stewart, and prominent figures such as Robbie Williams, the Spice Girls, Madonna, Beyoncé, Yoko Ono, Gordon Ramsay, Thierry Henry and the Beckhams, not to mention divas Celine Dion, Mariah Carey, Tina Turner, Pink, J-Lo and Cher.

1996

Musical genres were colliding and the tribal walls of popular culture were breaking down. I was the populist journalist in the right place at the right time, documenting this seismic and thrilling societal shift. Millions of Britons, then without the luxury of access to our new internet promised land, were flocking to newsagents en masse to read about these new cultural revolutionaries, with New Labour and our rock star PM-in-waiting masterfully inserting themselves into the narrative. *The Sun* was the nation's social media in this pre-tech time, itself peaking in circulation in 1996 as it captured this unforgettable moment in time.

The 90s was a wild age of incendiary and provocative creativity, stupidity, genius, hedonism, drunkenness and laddism, where art, fashion, music, the media, food, football and politics in some way detonated collectively and then became enmeshed. My journalistic career had begun at the dawn of that extraordinary decade, the year of the Italian World Cup and as acid house engulfed Britain.

1996, and that year's Brit Awards, became a figurative moment in British pop culture history – and in my vocation – illustrating an explosive shift of power taking place on our shores that year, both artistically and politically. The country was in the throes of rejecting the tired, old, grey conservatism, embodied by PM John Major, in favour of a more rock 'n' roll land led by an exuberant and youthful Blair, alongside his cohort of emerging female politicians and a football- and music-loving cabinet.

That thunderous night, the King of Pop was overthrown and excommunicated by a homegrown revolutionary

WHAT'S THE STORY?

guard of fresh-faced Britpop royalty, whose ascension to the golden throne of popular culture had been many years in the making.

Through my own archive, diaries and research, memories and experiences, along with a comprehensive series of fresh, in-depth interviews with the movers and shakers of 1996 and beyond, I will surgically explore, analyse and celebrate that envied epoch, dissecting its genesis, explosion and aftermath. I will explain why and how politics, the media and the arts conflated in such a powerful and globe-shattering way and discuss whether such seismic movements can ever happen again in a world now dominated by social media, technological innovation and cultural division.

I will study a number of prime ministers' legacies, take a biblical trip to Maine Road and then Knebworth via Blur, Bristol and Euro 96's Wembley Stadium, witness the emergence of both Robbie Williams and the Spice Girls, while assessing the revival of elder statesmen Paul McCartney, The Who, David Bowie and Elton John at that fashionable moment in history, where we all jostled for a slice of the Britpop pie.

So strap yourselves in and prepare for – in classic tabloid speak, if you'll forgive me – a no-holds-barred, anything-goes and everything-bared voyage to the fast-beating creative heart of 1996 and that 90s decade – where I witnessed Britain morph into the coolest place on planet earth.

My Ten Big Moments in My Personal and Professional Life

- Landed my first agency job in journalism after the Italia 90 World Cup and moved to London (1990).
- Met the love of my life and future wife, quickly moving in together (1991).
- Began freelance shifts on national newspapers including *The People*, *The Sun* and *Sunday Mirror* (1991/1992).
- Witnessed emerging Britpop bands live for the first time: Blur (1993), Pulp (1994), Oasis (1994).
- Wrote Kurt Cobain's obituary, then broke the story of Phil Collins' marriage split as *Sunday Mirror* staff reporter and was immediately poached by News International (1994).
- Landed my dream showbiz job at *The Sun*, covering Oasis at Maine Road, Knebworth and Euro 96, plus launches of the Spice Girls and Robbie Williams (1995/1996).
- Legendary concerts around the world with U2 and Oasis live in California, Blur in London, The Verve in Glasgow (1997).
- Promoted to *The Sun*'s Bizarre Editor alongside Victoria Newton and met new PM Tony Blair and his Cabinet at Blackpool Labour Conference and at Number Ten (1998).
- Married Michelle at Lake Tahoe, California, while covering the Spice Girls' US tour. Memorably

WHAT'S THE STORY?

interviewed Sir Paul McCartney for the first of many times (1998).
- Baby number one born weeks before we welcomed the New Millennium – the first bouquet of flowers arriving at our newly purchased inaugural home were from Posh and Becks (1999). Or was it their agent?

CHAPTER 1

Thatcher

The Conservative Prime Minister
who created Cool Britannia

To understand the genesis of the 90s and its 1996 zenith, we must head back to a darker time. A moment, in 1983, when the unemployment rate was touching 12 per cent under Conservative Prime Minister Margaret Thatcher.

Britain was a divided and discontented place. We were in the midst of civil unrest and rioting across the country's cities, on the cusp of the miners' strike, with The Flying Pickets at number one and English football hooligans regularly on the rampage.

The country felt like a crucible of hate, pain and bitterness — a little like the fractured Britain of today — with a struggling economy and uncertainty of direction.

And bands like The Smiths, New Order, Depeche Mode and The Cure were soundtracking those grim days, reflecting the anger and misery of the times, and heavily influencing a generation of songwriters whose turn would come next. Perhaps this will soon be repeated as we too navigate a difficult period in our nation and planet's history although I'm not sure certain conditions will allow it, with a splintered media, technological and cultural landscape.

1996

New Labour and Tony Blair basked in the morning glory of Cool Britannia, hailing its protagonists in Downing Street in 1997 and riding the wave of a creative tsunami which saw the arts, journalism, politics and football memorably coalesce – and explode like a champagne supernova in the sky.

Yet, rather ironically, if it had not been for Thatcher, the Madchester, Britpop, Young British Artists and Cool Britannia movements might not have emerged. It's not just me saying that, this is according to many of that era's most important characters.

Thatcher and the Gallagher brothers may seem implausible bedfellows and Lady T may have exited her stage in 2013, but, without one of her government's 1980s policies in particular, Britpop may have never birthed.

Leading figures from that era insist the seeds of creativity had been sown back in 1983, when Thatcher launched the Enterprise Allowance Scheme. The brainchild of her chancellor Geoffrey Howe, its aim was to stimulate entrepreneurship and employment and to restore a go-getter mentality to the country, with emphasis on the individual doing something for themselves. This was the attitude instilled in me around that time by my entrepreneurial father, who broke from a major organisation to set up on his own, rising at 6am each morning and building a successful business.

Recipients were provided with £40 a week for up to a year and claimants needed to prove they had £1,000 in savings, and to have been unemployed for at least eight weeks. The scheme supported 103,000 people annually at its peak, but received criticism from those who felt it was simply shielding true jobless figures. It is, however, credited with helping 325,000 people to become self-employed.

An unanticipated side effect of the policy, however, was its stimulation of the creative sector, with many key Cool Britannia figures taking advantage of it, encouraging a creative shift in the music and art worlds. Admittedly, Thatcher took money away from organisations like the Arts Council, but she emboldened a generation of trailblazers in music, art and fashion too.

One man the PM helped was somebody firmly on the other side of the political divide – Creation Records' Alan McGee, the man who discovered Oasis in 1993. He revealed that, were it not for the scheme's funding, an embryonic Creation may not have flourished, and said he felt that many would not want to admit Thatcher's crucial role – before adding for clarity that he still hoped she rotted in hell.

Similarly, Young British Artist Tracey Emin, synonymous with Cool Britannia and, today with an estimated fortune of £15 million, thinks Thatcher should be credited for her role in the creative industries – and the artist's own career. Tracey said she had immense gratitude for the financial help she received and that it saved her from the dole.

Other Thatcher beneficiaries include Pulp's Jarvis Cocker (back at number one in the album charts in 2025), Portishead, Chris Donald, the founder of *Viz* magazine, Julian Dunkerton of fashion label Superdry, and Turner Prize-winning artists Jeremy Deller and Rachel Whiteread, its first-ever female recipient. Another was Keith Jeffrey, who used the funds to establish Newcastle's legendary venue The Riverside and where Kurt Cobain's Nirvana played their first ever non-US gig in October 1989. So Thatcher brought grunge to Britain, too.

And Happy Monday Shaun Ryder wasn't afraid to admit that Britpop and the Madchester scene may not have happened if it weren't for the grocer's daughter from Grantham.

I've known Shaun for many years and first saw his band Happy Mondays live in my hometown Bristol in November 1989. Shaun was so out of it he delivered his vocals seated on the drum riser stage. Happily, when I spoke to him from his home in Madchester – sorry Manchester – he was a little more coherent but admitted he takes more drugs today than he did in the 90s – albeit most now available on prescription, swapping heroin and crack cocaine for thyroxine, among others, to treat his dodgy thyroid. He told me: 'When I was young, it didn't matter who was in fucking power, it didn't change anything for me. I couldn't see any changes. My mam and dad didn't get a load more money. I mean, the only thing really that I will say is Margaret Thatcher – she set up all the fucking bands from us to Blur. There was loads of us on the Enterprise Allowance Scheme that Thatcher set up. Pulp started off, we started off on it, you know, in the 80s.'

So, I asked, Madchester and Britpop may not have existed without Margaret Thatcher? 'Exactly,' he cackled.

Tory stalwart Lord David Willetts later said he believed Thatcher would have been proud of her creative legacy and that she appreciated anything that stimulated individual entrepreneurialism and get-up-and-go, noting that any scheme which kept Britons off benefits would be attractive to her. And Thatcher's prime ministerial successor, John Major, concurred, explaining that success in the arts is as good for the country's economy as any other sector.

Fellow Mancunian Morrissey of The Smiths, a major Britpop influence, once sang about his dream of seeing Thatcher on a guillotine. But, alas, the controversial leader helped fashion a 90s musical and artistic legacy that will live for ever and continues to stimulate the UK economy.

Many of us had spent our childhoods being lectured and educated about the 1960s by condescending quasi-hippie parents, who wouldn't stop banging on about that bloody decade of mop-tops and free love. Beatlemania, swinging London, minis and Mary Quant, Twiggy and The Stones, the Summer of Love and Sergeant Pepper, Dylan going electric and The Who – they never stopped dribbling on about it, insisting that those magical days were never to be witnessed again – and it really felt that way.

But their record collections were something to behold and gave bored countryside kids like me a mighty fine musical education. Before I hit double figures, I knew Beatles, Who, Bowie, Kinks and Dylan records inside out and a fair dose of prog too. Those intriguing vinyl curiosities were a precious training ground for the unfledged ears of youthful wannabe music journalists – and the trainee musicians about whom we would end up writing.

The dark, brooding 1980s had been sworn in by Pink Floyd's sprawling opus *The Wall*, which was terrifyingly intriguing to 10-year-old me. Then, the haunting assassination of John Lennon, a moment when our family home went into a period of mourning, and the horror of which has never really departed from our scarred brains, probably like JFK's murder for previous generations. The planet felt like a dour and miserable place, spooked by the spectre of nuclear war, AIDS, football hooligans, famine and unemployment, and captured on singles like The Specials' 'Ghost Town', UB40's 'One in Ten' and then Band Aid's 'Do They Know It's Christmas?' in 1984. There was an air of paranoia and depression about the place, with the inescapable Thatcher in the middle of it all. If you had told me then that I would be invited to attend the Iron Lady's funeral three decades later at St Paul's Cathedral as Editor of *The Sun*, I would have laughed in your face. That would have been absolutely unthinkable.

As the 80s dragged on, different slices of sound were emerging: a freshly polished New Order, *Hounds of Love*-era Kate Bush, The Cure, The Smiths, world music embraced by Peter Gabriel and Paul Simon, and, of course, Band Aid and the Live Aid concerts that followed, which had a profound effect on me as a socially conscious 15-year-old. I was mesmerised by the power of that movement and the force that music, celebrity and the media could exert on governments and the world. That's never left me and became something of a hallmark of my later career as a campaigning journalist and editor.

Back then, there didn't seem to be much in the way of prospects or inspiration for teenagers like me, growing up in a rural Somerset and then Cambridgeshire. But, by the age of 14, I knew exactly what I wanted to be. I was going to become a journalist, no question. Maybe I could somehow marry my writing ability with my love of music and humour in some way? I thought, as I listened to John Peel and Annie Nightingale's BBC radio shows and began to devour daily newspapers, the music press weeklies and then magazines like *Q* and *Smash Hits*, rather precociously noting their headlines, tone and writing styles.

In the pre-internet and smartphone era, the UK had three brilliant weekly music papers – the *NME*, *Melody Maker* and *Sounds*, which were all delivered to my teenage home and pored over forensically. So many inspirational writers were born within those explosive, yellowing pages – authors Tony Parsons and Julie Burchill, both of whom I would later court and lure to write for *The Sun*, *Loaded* founder James Brown, Stuart Maconie, Steve Lamacq and Mary Ann Hobbs (now BBC Radio 6 Music hosts), Steven Wells, John Robb, Jons Savage and Ronson, David Quantick, Nick Kent, Charles Shaar Murray, Paul Morley and Danny Baker. There was oodles of music journalism about, more important to me than any of my school textbooks and giving me an early education in wordsmithery.

The Tube, with Jools Holland and Paula Yates, was essential viewing to spot new bands, while *The Old Grey Whistle Test* had been revived by the BBC, hosted by Mark Ellen and David Hepworth, who, in 1986, launched *Q* magazine. I worshipped the mag's style, tone and language and would myself later employ some of its linguistic trickery and pizazz, clever use of expressions like Phew!, Er and Um for comic effect, and phrases such as rock and, dare I say, roll, or Chez Les Rozzers if someone had a run-in with the police. I nicked a few of these over the years. The pages shimmered and came alive. Journalists like the late Tom Hibbert were must-reads. This stuff was magic to my eyes and I stored it all somewhere in my overactive brain.

Mopping up the punk and new wave era, *NME* hit a circulation figure of 230,000 in 1980 and took a strong anti-Thatcher stance with Labour leader Neil Kinnock gracing its cover ahead of the 1987 election. It remained the bestselling music mag throughout the 80s, despite shedding sales, but enjoyed a revival to over 100,000 copies each week under legendary editors Alan Lewis and then Danny Kelly in the late 80s and early 90s. But in 1991, its rival *Sounds* was the first to go, followed by *Melody Maker*, which met its maker in 2000 as circulation dropped to 32,000. *NME* clung on, going free and poppy in 2015, but eventually, and sadly, giving up print in 2018, after sixty-six years. But its towering influence must not be forgotten. Memorable agenda-setting covers included 1989's 'Never Mind the Pollocks' classic with Kevin Cummins' momentous paint-spattered Stone Roses image, the best for me. And who can forget 1995's 'British Heavyweight Championship Blur vs Oasis' front page, which captured a national mood? (We'll come to all that devilment later.)

In an interview with *The Guardian* in 2015, former *NME* editor Conor McNicholas seemed to blame *The Sun* and me for the demise of his music paper because, as we filled columns and upped coverage of Britpop, it squeezed the music papers out of the conversation. As British music detonated in the mid-90s, *The Sun* would begin to run a daily double-page music and celebrity spread, which was devoured by 12 million people on a daily basis. That's not to mention the Oasis, Blur and Pulp stories on the front page and elsewhere – many with my name on them. And then, as the internet took hold, these sonic print bibles were rendered redundant – as is sadly becoming the case with many conventional news brands today, certainly those who have pulled a hamstring in the digital race.

As the 1980s edged forward, I began writing for some local newspapers and, ever the opportunist, managed to wangle some broadcasting on BBC Radio Cambridgeshire, thanks to broadcast legend Trevor Dann, the man who himself expertly produced the *Live Aid* TV coverage which had mesmerised me just a few years earlier. I began to enjoy the feel of this media lark; it seemed fun, and those inhabiting my brave new worlds seemed sociable, intelligent, entertaining, erudite, full of life, humour, spirit, knowledge and swagger. They knew stuff I wanted to know about and inspired me to want to be like them. I was determined to insert myself into these orbits, and this philosophy would guide many of my educational and career decisions.

Southampton University was the destination of choice for an English Literature degree, partly because it had a very lively, tabloid student newspaper called *Wessex News*. My first call was to its newsroom, where I – perhaps, in hindsight, rather pompously – announced my arrival and intention to become a journalist. Still only 18, I managed to wangle my way into becoming one of the multiple editors quite soon into my first term, working with David Charter, now assistant editor (US) of *The Times*, Dominic

Smith, who went on to edit lads mags, and Gary Thompson, later of the *Sunday Sport* and the *News of the World*, where I would also spend some time.

A slew of pretty decent bands would be booked to play in the Student Union hall and other venues in the city, including The Joiners Arms, where I first saw The Charlatans in February 1990, and The West Indian Club, which played host to My Bloody Valentine and The Blue Aeroplanes. The first big-name interview I conducted was with Led Zeppelin frontman Robert Plant, ahead of a uni gig, who made his entrance while thumping a huge baseball bat against the palm of his hand as he brooded and growled answers, like an Untouchable Al Capone.

I would land interviews with bands like James, The Wedding Present, The Primitives, The House of Love, The Wonder Stuff and Deacon Blue when they performed locally. I played a bit of piano but was never good enough for a group, not that there were any where I had grown up, but I had developed a taste for, and joy in, combining my love of journalism and music, all laced with that sense of mischief. My degree might suffer, but this would help chart the path towards my lofty ambitions, I gambled. At that time, my desire and enthusiasm for this newly learned craft was a precursor for my work later in my career, where I would go on to interview a catalogue of names much bigger than Plant, writing and editing columns and papers for decades to come, alongside some broadcasting too.

If we stumbled upon a good university story, we would sell it to the local or national newspapers. An exclusive about a mature student's extensive family being housed in a hall of residence, to the annoyance of their neighbours, made the front page of the *Daily Mail* and I received by first ever contributor fee of £40, no less. The journalist who stitched me up on the payment would later work under me at *The Sun*, and I would often remind him of it. It taught me early on to try and be nice to people on the way up. 'Cops Swoop on Wet Sex Romp' was a memorable headline we conjured up about police being called to a boisterous bit of bath-time action by a couple of noisy student lovers. Rather immaturely, we wore T-shirts emblazoned with the headline to the somewhat stuffy, *Guardian*-sponsored Student Media Awards in London. An unsavoury brawl broke out in the bar after a beery broadsheet vs tabloid argument with some snobs from Oxbridge and in front of an appalled Peter Preston, that liberal publication's esteemed editor. We tipped off their rival papers about that one too. Many fellow wannabe journalists in the room that day went on to big careers, including food critic Jay Rayner and Andrew Harrison, later editor of my beloved *Q*.

I was starting to build up a quite comprehensive cuttings file, as they called it back then, which helped me land a holiday job, in the summer of 1989, for a geeky record collectors' magazine called *Spiral Scratch*, named after the Buzzcocks record. Soon after joining the monthly, I was quick to arrange an interview with one of my then-favourite bands, the much-hyped Mancs Inspiral Carpets, at London's Dingwalls club in Camden. After the soundcheck, we decamped to The Hawley Arms opposite and were joined by a razor-witted and relentlessly ridiculing mop-topped member of the group's road crew. He made me buy him Guinness and left more of an impression on me than the band themselves. It was only 1989, but this was to be the first of my many encounters with Noel Gallagher.

Football, fashion, club culture and music were becoming fast entwined, stimulating and emboldening a generation of working-class lads and ladettes. In fact, the Carpets' Cool as Fuck T-shirts were the thing to be seen in, so Noel gave me ten to give away in a competition, which came in handy when I got the last train from London to Cambridge and couldn't get home, so ended up sleeping rough on a bench, wearing layers of all the T-shirts to keep me warm. It was cold as fuck.

All this wasn't long after DJ Paul Oakenfold had experienced his first life-changing encounter with the drug ecstasy, during his legendary trip to Ibiza, the famed Balearic island, with a group of friends, including DJs Nicky Holloway and Danny Rampling, then a humble painter and decorator. Oakenfold had been working in the music industry and had recently accompanied man mountain singer Divine to Ibiza for a live performance, who took to the stage on the back of a baby elephant.

There was a buzz about a club on the isle called Amnesia and its resident DJ Alfredo, an Argentinian refugee who had ended up in Spain and became famed for his eclectic, and ecstatic, sets.

Oakenfold talked to me over lunch at the Karma Sanctum Hotel in London's Soho, which he now part owns, and explained: 'Alfredo played Kool Moe Dee next to Bob Marley, next to Cindy Lauper, next to The Woodentops, and that is hip hop, reggae, pop and rock. And he would play U2, and then he played underground house music. So that's why we coined it Balearic Beat because there was no name for it. It was completely different and mind-blowing because, at the time, we were all listening to rare groove. We had flares on and floppy hats, I was listening to James Brown and music like that.

'This really was when the barriers felt like they'd broken down and anything kind of goes for a DJ. This was a moment where change came upon us and I think, because we had a little club of hundreds of people in Streatham in South London, we were in a position to start playing this music. There was an infrastructure of English workers and kids in our clubs from Sheffield, Manchester, Brighton, who'd all spent the summer in Ibiza, so we would reach out to them and say that every Friday, you're going to hear the Balearic Beat sound.'

The club's popularity facilitated a move to Richard Branson's Heaven, in the bowels of Charing Cross station in the heart of London's West End, which attracted party-goers from across the country, including the Manchester music scene. This included the visionary band New Order, who had themselves decamped to Ibiza and then, somewhat contrastingly, to Peter Gabriel's Real World Studios in the Wiltshire countryside, which I would also visit on assignment for *Spiral Scratch*. The band would regularly travel to London club nights like Oakenfold's Spectrum and then travel back to the West Country in the early hours to continue recording, with the electronica – among other things – still surging through their brains.

Their 1989 album *Technique* is a highly significant record that brilliantly fused the band's dance-rock sensibilities with Balearic beats and acid house synth genius. The Mancunians showed great prescience, capturing a moment in time, a zeitgeist where musical walls were being smashed down as fiercely as Berlin's later that year.

It was their fifth studio album and would reach number one in the UK album charts. The music was slick with sunshine-laden sounds, becoming a soundtrack to that summer, culminating in an imperious Friday night headline set at Reading Festival. Bassist Peter Hook attempted to set fire to his bass guitar on stage; when I later reminded him of this, he admitted: 'It was a nightmare. The wind was blowing and I just couldn't set it alight. It wasn't quite Hendrix.'

Oakenfold, who would go on to support New Order on tour, told me: 'The Happy Mondays would come down to London. Ecstasy was rippling through the country. It was popping its head up in Sheffield, Manchester, Liverpool, Brighton. So our club was revolving around music and ecstasy. I was playing The Cure next to INXS, all kinds of Stone Roses, all kinds of indie music. And, suddenly, record company people were coming down and digging this scene and hearing these records. So they started to ask me to remix them because, on indie records, the drums were pretty loose and to mix these records, you need a very rhythmic movement. So, suddenly I got asked to do a remix of the Happy Mondays track called 'Wrote for Luck' and it became a big hit in the clubs but not necessarily commercially. I changed the drums, made it more regimental in some respects, but it made it a real record. And that blew up.'

Svengali Tony Wilson, a TV host and founder of Happy Mondays' and New Order's label Factory Records, personally contacted Oakenfold soon after and asked him to produce a mix of Mondays track 'Hallelujah', followed by their new album, *Pills 'n' Thrills and Bellyaches*, one which Wilson would later describe as 'one of the great British albums of the age'. Oakenfold admitted: 'I was like, I don't know if I want to do that, because they were all on smack and partying. But it kind of became logical. I started getting offered a lot from record companies. I did The Cure's 'Close to Me'. I then started work on Cabaret Voltaire. I was doing all these alternative bands.'

The Mondays and 'Fools Gold'-era Stone Roses, who Oakenfold also remixed, would both perform on a legendary episode of *Top of the Pops* in November 1989; this was my moment of realisation that the revolution had come – Madchester exploded. It was the twilight of Thatcherism, old regimes across Europe were falling, with Baltic states collapsing and Germany embracing reunification. This felt like our moment in time, as we paid homage around the crummy telly in our shabby student house, with its hole in the lounge ceiling, and believed our generation had conquered the world, laying the depressing 80s to rest.

It was the same month we would make a pilgrimage to London's Alexandra Palace to witness The Stone Roses' mythical performance there. It felt like something of a tribal gathering – we had read voraciously of these type of events in the 60s and 70s, but now we had one for ourselves. As the crowd chanted 'Manchester, la la la', simian-strolling frontman Ian Brown would famously fire back: 'It ain't where you're from, mate, it's where you're at.'

Such momentous events were setting a tone for the emerging decade and wannabe musicians, artists and writers were taking note. Something was rumbling and forming.

But the band's supposed crowning glory was meant to be back in their beloved north, on 27 May 1990 at Spike Island in Widnes, Cheshire. Oakenfold would support them as fresh-faced future members of Oasis, Pulp and Mancunian dance society gathered to pay their respects in a shabby field surrounded by industrial chimneys. Oakenfold doesn't remember that day entirely fondly; during our interview he told me: 'Back in the day, I was lucky enough to open up for The Stone Roses at one of the iconic shows that they done at Spike Island. What was funny and difficult was I had to climb up a tower opposite the stage, with two boxes of vinyl.'

The sound was terrible and Ian Brown's vocals swirled in the biting wind. In 2025, Pulp would offer a nod to the gig once again on their song 'Spike Island', as they had on 1995's 'Sorted for E's & Wizz', written about fans constantly being offered ecstasy and amphetamines by drug dealers at the show.

Events like Spike Island were essentially covered by the music and fashion media and didn't cross over into the tabloid mainstream conversation, as those later in the 90s would. The national newspapers were out of touch and many journalists simply weren't living the scene and weren't tuned in to popular culture at that point, more likely to be seen besuited in Planet Hollywood or Stringfellows (where I admit I went a few times, purely for work purposes, you'll understand), rather than in a urine-soaked field in Cheshire or a riotous Ally Pally.

The newspapers had certainly been stung by the acid house scene. Just as the safety pin had become a symbol of rebellion in the late 70s, the smiley face had come to mean the same in late 80s Britain. But forget the high-profile, publicity-seeking figures like Rotten and Vicious, they had been replaced by an anonymous breed of pseudonyms like Bomb the Bass and M|A|R|R|S. Never Mind The Sex Pistols, This Was Acid.

Initially, newspapers like *The Sun* embraced the movement, running an 'Acid House Fashion Guide' and a 'Hit List for Acid Boppers'. Acid Boppers!!! Acidic remixes were swiftly prepared for artists like Yazz, Bros and even *The Sun*'s Page Three girl turned singer Samantha Fox.

The tabloid had recognised the influence of the music and the fashion, employing this to boost credibility among its four and a half million purchasers. They had, however, seemingly overlooked the drug association. It wasn't long before *The Sun* was no longer smiling – soon, the fashion guides and hit lists morphed into headlines like 'Shoot These Evil Acid Barons' and 'Acid Party Army of Baseball Bat Brutes'. The 'latest trend' had now become an 'evil menace', because of public and government hysteria over the eruption of illegal raves and the hallucinogens that accompanied them. As a reaction to this and to stamp out such gatherings, the government drew up the draconian Criminal Justice Bill, which would become law in 1994, sparking many protests. The legislation proscribed in law a specific genre of music, namely rave, 'wholly or predominantly categorised by the emission of a succession of repetitive beats'. This clampdown stimulated the rise of superclubs like London's Ministry of Sound and Cream in Liverpool, where Oakenfold would later have a residency.

One of those early ravers was Pulp's Jarvis Cocker, who attended his first party at Sunrise, illegally staged at White Waltham Airport, Berkshire, in 1989. The singer recalled the revelatory experience of taking ecstasy at the rave and dancing dreamily for hours. Alas, he was also blissfully unaware that his penis had accidentally slipped out of his underwear-free trousers and was swinging in time to the aforementioned repetitive beats.

The Sun would carry pictures of wild-eyed ravers at Sunrise, under the headline 'Ecstasy Airport'. A young Noel Gallagher would also embrace rave culture, attending life-changing gatherings in northern fields and then the Factory Records and New Order-owned Hacienda in Manchester. Noel admitted that the unity and communal spirit of acid house and rave tunes inspired his own songwriting, in which he emphasised inclusivity and togetherness.

But not his younger brother, Liam, who told *The Face* in 1995 that he shunned ecstasy in favour of pot, although admitting he took heroin one New Year's Eve, aged 15. He refused to engage with that drug and was therefore shunned by a friend who ended up in jail. Liam recalled that, on the day the lad was released, he himself was performing on *Top of the Pops*, proving the right decision had been made.

Ecstasy was formulated in 1914 as a sleep suppressant and used on soldiers in the First World War. In 1977, the UK government made it a Class A drug under the Misuse of Drugs Act but, in the 1980s, it was still available as medication from psychiatrists around the world, who talked of the drug's abilities to break down inhibitions. As club goers began to take ecstasy, molly, XTC or 3,4-Methylenedioxymethamphetamine – whatever you want to call it, or to use the parlance of the times, to 'get on one, matey', venues developed a friendlier atmosphere. In 1988, it became the UK's third most common illegal drug.

In between my scribblings for *Spiral Scratch*, during a university holiday in 1990, I landed another job at Cambridgeshire County Council's rather glamorous-sounding Waste Management Department. We had to monitor rubbish dumps across the county. One day, out of nowhere, my boss asked me what I planned to do as a career; I replied journalism, as opposed to waste management, although some may point to similarities between the professions. He then revealed that his best friend and fellow local cricketer was *The Sun*'s East Anglian correspondent, Kieron Saunders, a byline with which I was familiar. He immediately arranged for me to go out on work experience with him. Talk about right place, right time. I remember bombing around East Anglia in his passenger seat, as we lurched from one news story to another, and recall being very impressed by his brick-like car phone. I loved every minute – it was intoxicating, fun and we even stopped for a pint. Again, it reinforced my belief that media folk were riotous to be around, with a sense of mischief, chutzpah, intelligence and sparkle. It also proved that if you go out and do stuff – summer jobs, gigs, writing – then things can happen for you. Connections and contacts can be made which will serve you for the rest of your career. As a result of two summer jobs in succession, I had already interviewed Inspiral Carpets, Peter Gabriel and many others, met a young Noel Gallagher and a *Sun* journalist who would help inspire my career. That doesn't happen if you're at home in your bedroom, playing computer games.

When I asked Kieron for his advice to a would-be journalist, and whether I should apply to local newspapers or gain an NCTJ journalism qualification, he baulked and told me I should work for a news agency. I'd heard of the Press Association and Reuters, but at that time – and unbeknownst to me – most provincial cities in the UK were home to one or more press agencies, packed with hungry, lowly paid young journalists in-a-hurry, who would hoover up stories to be sold, sometimes for exorbitant amounts in that money-laden era, to the voracious national newspapers. Cut your teeth on one of those, he proffered, then land some news shifts on the nationals as a result, sharpen your skills and then you could earn yourself a staff job on a daily or Sunday title. There would be no better training. It's exactly what I did.

When I returned to Southampton, I immediately visited the university library to seek out the Yellow Pages. The

THATCHER

Yellow Pages were thick, er, yellow-coloured reference books containing business listings and telephone numbers, enabling one to contact companies in our pre-Google age. I nabbed the London volume and looked up press agencies; there were a load of them listed. I wrote letters to every one, attached some of my now extensive press clippings and, following a brief interview, was offered a junior role at Fleet Street News Agency, whose alumni packed the national newspapers' newsrooms.

The country was still buzzing from the Italia 90 World Cup shenanigans. England's lions, featuring Paul Gascoigne, Gary Lineker, Stuart Pearce and Chris Waddle, were knocked out in the semi-finals by West Germany on 4 July. I graduated a few days afterwards, Gazza's tears still staining the Turin grass, immediately moved to London and started my first job as a news journalist for the agency, earning £520 a month. There, I would go on to work alongside Gerard Greaves, who later became Deputy Editor of the *Daily Mail* and Editor of MailOnline, David Dillon, editor of the *Mail on Sunday*, and Damian Lazarus, once a journalist but who would rise again as a superstar DJ and electronic music pioneer. When I began working there, I had just turned 21, was single and couldn't really afford anywhere to live, so lodged with my cousin in scruffy Lewisham, paying him £50 a month in rent. The house was walkable to The Venue in New Cross, a former cinema that became home to up-and-coming indie bands such as Suede, Blur and Pulp in the early 90s. We'd go and see groups like Heavenly Records' Flowered Up, who graced the cover of *Melody Maker* before they had even released a record, under the headline 'Southern Scallies Fight Back!'. They were being hyped as London's answer to Happy Mondays and featured a dancing, modern-day Bez-meets-Peter Gabriel called Barry Mooncult, who would bounce up and down on stage dressed as a giant flower.

The band dressed baggy and were fronted by heavy-eye-browed, Irish-blooded working-class brothers Liam and Joe Maher, who sported retro haircuts and a snarling attitude, with rasping cockney vocals and shimmering guitars. Looking back at the band, it feels like a prototype Oasis, but the group would implode and end in tragedy with both brothers dying young, Liam from a heroin overdose in 2009, after a term in jail, and his brother three years later from health complications following years of drug abuse. What might have been.

One particularly memorable gig was at East London's Shoreditch Town Hall in August 1990. I'd never witnessed anything quite like it; it felt as if something was emerging from the newly fused London club and alternative, indie rock scene – if this was what London life had in store then I was 'avin it. News journalist by day, gig-devouring musicologist by night and weekend football fan, the sport becoming ubiquitous in Britons' lives and the media after its transformative moment in Italy.

Nowadays the prospect of getting your hands on tickets for the opening game of the new football season, featuring two of England's biggest names from a life-changing and culture-shifting World Cup only weeks earlier, would be remote, to put it mildly. But a couple of us easily got in to watch Tottenham Hotspur play Manchester City at North London's White Hart Lane on 25 August 1990. The game would showcase the skills of Italian sunshine-tinted Gary Lineker and Paul Gascoigne, in front of a worshipping crowd, including 1966 England captain Bobby Moore. Spurs were managed then by future England gaffer and part-time crooner Terry Venables, a bon viveur whose company I would later cherish, signing El Tel up for *The Sun*'s 2010 South Africa World Cup ad, in which he memorably belted out Elvis Presley's 'If I Can Dream'. A sadly missed larger-than-life itself visionary character who himself helped transform modern football further as England manager at Euro 96.

The match day programme cost £1.30 and, as the teams ran on to the pitch, the stadium announcer asked fans to show their respect for the players who had lit up the international stage that summer. Fans of both home and away erupted in unison and cheered in admiration. Cue goosebumps. Lineker scored the first of his brace after just two minutes, and Gascoigne, the very man I was now writing about by day, slotted home the third in a 3–1 victory, wide-eyed and sliding on his knees towards us in celebration. It was like a domestic coronation for our Italian heroes, who were box office names in the newspapers I loved – and now served. I could not quite believe I was seeing them up close and within touching distance, so soon after the World Cup. I could get used to this here London.

In November 1990, I stumbled upon an interview with Gazza in my favourite magazine, *Q*, in which he attacked George Best and I wrote it up; it made the front and back pages of the tabloids, the contributor fees easily covering several months of my agency salary. Nobody else had spotted it. Nowadays, the magazine's publisher would have an in-house media team, who would release the story ahead of publication, with a copy of the cover and logo, insisting on their use.

Then, when I discovered a grim criminal case at Middlesex Guildhall crown court in Westminster, which involved one of Gascoigne's childhood friends and ex-teammate, the agency sold it to the *Sunday People* as a front-page exclusive for more than they paid me annually. What a business model.

I was skint yet making good money for the agency, but the work was fine-tuning my skills and instincts as a journalist. I couldn't afford a car and would hop on and off Routemaster buses and the tube, building up an intimate knowledge of London, covering crime stories in areas like Brixton, Clapton, Hackney, Tottenham, Islington and beyond. When I was dispatched to Streatham in South London to cover a particularly harrowing story involving rape, attempted murder and arson, I knocked on the door of the suspect's address at a top-floor council block flat, leather briefcase in hand, baby-faced and clad in a gleaming, double-breasted chequered suit from Next. A bloodshot-eyed monster of a man in a torn vest burst out of the newly installed and unpainted front door, presumably a replacement for the one kicked in by armed police some time earlier that week. The clearly intoxicated thug grabbed my neck and pinned me over a balcony, insisting he was going to throw me off it and into the car park, 120 feet below. A couple of deranged-looking young women wearing very little clothing (who would now, no doubt, be referred to as crack whores) then emerged and pulled him from me, but not before he had delivered a powerful head-butt. It was clearly a drug den and that was probably one of my closest brushes with death to date. As I legged it down the shabby concrete stairs to find Streatham train station, I noticed the graffiti scrawled on a grubby wall of the communal hallway: 'Clean up this mess, you filthy n***ers'. My work was certainly giving me a glimpse into a seedier side of the capital city that I now called home.

But, like most competitive young journalists desperate to make it, I was always driven by the desire to nail a story and grab the byline. In January 1991, I landed the front-page splash in the *Daily Mirror* and *Today* the day before the Gulf War broke out after identifying Britain's youngest soldier and tracking down the fresh-faced teenager's family in East London. 'Your Country Needs Him' was the headline in Rupert Murdoch-owned and now-defunct mid-market daily newspaper *Today*, where future Blair aide Alastair Campbell had been political editor and his partner, Fiona Millar, was news editor. The daily paper pioneered full-colour printing, sometimes with eye-squinting three-dimensional results, but was closed controversially by Murdoch in 1995. My capacity to crack these stories was signalling an ability to persuade subjects to open up to me. I enjoyed – and seemed to be reasonably competent at – interviewing interesting people from all walks of life.

At that time, the only way of communicating with the office was via public telephone. With a pocketful of ten

1996

pence pieces, I would have to ring my copy in and dictate it to someone in the office, often one of the agency's news editors. I remember queues forming behind me many times and being scowled at in fury as I hogged the phone. Our cheap suited-pockets were bulging with pads, pens, gadgets and coins in those pre-smartphone days. If I needed to record an interview, I would have to use an annoying Dictaphone with its spooled, mini-cassette tape that would often jam and appalling sound quality, then spend hours transcribing it by hand. Now, I can record on my phone and AI gives me an instant transcription. Calling in stories had its hazards too. At News International, the copy takers were, invariably, elderly women stationed somewhere in the north and, not necessarily familiar with the nuances of modern alternative music, their howlers sometimes made their way into print. I remember cringing when seeing one of my published pieces, which inadvertently named Supergrass as Supertramp (them again) and another that referred to The Stone Roses' Spike Island as Strike Island. Mortifying and, boy, did I get some stick.

At this time, The Stone Roses themselves were struggling to follow up their forceful, eponymous debut record. Creation Records' Primal Scream had built on the Madchester trend and cleverly fused club culture and rock with the Mercury Music Prize-winning *Screamadelica*, peerlessly produced (in parts at least) by DJ Andrew Weatherall, an Oakenfold contemporary.

But the Americans were coming for a disaffected British youth, filling a post-Madchester gap with grunge. Nirvana's towering *Nevermind* blew us all away. I remember buying

THATCHER

it on CD at Manchester's HMV store and was gobsmacked. The album would go on to shift more than 30 million copies. 'Smells Like Teen Spirit' was clearly era-defying and rock music had altered for ever, but some of it wasn't melodic, uplifting or – I suppose – British or positive enough. A group of Mancunian young men, brothers with Irish blood and spirit like me, were probably only a few miles away from where I was standing that day in HMV; maybe they were feeling the same thing as they honed their lighter and more optimistic sounds and words from England and Ireland, but with no concept of how those melodies would drench the nation, and in such a short space of time.

Back in London, Pearl Jam supported Neil Young and Booker T. & the M.G.s at Finsbury Park for a memorable show, the artists uniting for a head-spinning encore of 'Rockin' in the Free World'. We were all moshing at the front and it felt euphoric – but it was all very American.

Meanwhile, Blur had money troubles at that point, stumbling after their hit single 'There's No Other Way', but their label was determined to take them to the US. Bassist Alex James admitted to me: 'Our first manager wasn't a great businessman and we had a VAT bill we couldn't pay – we were really in the shit financially. But Jesus Jones, the only other band on Food Records, were fucking number one in America, so the record company managed to leverage loads of tour support. They stuck hundreds of thousands of dollars into this thirteen-week epic tour of America to promote our album *Leisure*. We literally got there the day that *Nevermind* came out. They'd had this

Manchester invasion of America – the Inspirals, Stone Roses, Charlatans, Happy Mondays, and then suddenly this disaffected white American youth had a record, had a star, had a look and we were really superfluous to requirements. But the gigs were great and they were packed. Many thought we were from Manchester and we managed to get a T-shirt deal to pay the VAT man. But when we got back it was all grunge on the cover of *NME* and *Melody Maker* and all the music magazines.'

But not long after grunge's domination engulfed Britain and the world, its flag-bearer Kurt Cobain took a shotgun to his head, killing himself – and the movement. By then, I'd graduated to the *Sunday Mirror* and, surrounded by more senior journalists, I was tasked with writing up Cobain's obituary, largely because nobody else there really knew much about Nirvana, a glimpse of what would follow for me. I actually had tickets to see the band's aborted gig at London's Brixton Academy dated the day of what would be Kurt's death. I sent one back for a refund of £13.50 but still have the other. It's worth a few quid now.

Back to Alex James: 'I was doing an interview with BBC Radio Bristol just after Kurt Cobain died and the journalist was like "listen to this" – it was recorded just before and Kurt was asked "What are you listening to?" And he was like: "Oh, nothing much, there's this one song by one British band" and he fucking sings 'There's No Other Way'. God it was so sweet. He didn't do many interviews at all. There was a period of time when every music magazine either had a picture of Damon or Kurt Cobain's face on it. And then one was dead and that was a little bit scary.'

THATCHER

Just as Cobain's suicide had opened up a new opportunity for British music, so another shock death one month later would do the same in politics. Modernist Labour Party leader John Smith suffered a fatal heart attack at his Barbican flat – *The Sun*'s coverage the following day read: 'Britain's next Prime Minister died yesterday'.

It was one of those rare occasions when a stunned and frozen newsroom falls into a disbelieving silence for just a moment, before igniting into a frenzy of phone calls, keyboard-bashing and bellowing, when everyone stiffens and just does their job. It is astonishing to witness – the most soul-searching being when the 9/11 attacks hit New York and then the 7/7 terrorist assault on London, the latter just a few hundred metres from the News International offices in 2005. There's an uneasy mixture of adrenaline and fear – a professional desire to capture the correct mood and tone on the front page, while terrified and aching inside but unable and unwilling to leave one's station.

John Smith's death would spark the ascendancy of a 41-year-old Tony Blair, who himself loved football and Bowie. Like the music we were obsessing over, his New Labour project filled us all with hope and optimism for the future. You'll be hearing more about him later, but things were already changing around here, our generation was rising and you could feel it – we'd all had enough of squares like John Major and his sleazy Tory government.

The British media were beginning to take notice of a generation of creators (yes, funded by Thatcher's Enterprise Allowance Scheme) whose work was beginning to percolate across all artistic spheres. And, at the same time, newspaper's editorial budgets were bursting; the British read more newspapers than any other nation in Europe – except Sweden. With 16 million copies being shifted on the Sabbath and 14 million each day during the week, advertising revenues were booming. Editors were splashing big money and packing their pages with royal exclusives alongside more and more celebrity and football stories, for which I had an eye and which would usually boost circulation. I'd timed my run as well as one of Lineker's.

At the same time, in the slipstream of Italia 90, football had become fashionable again, with a shiny new image and a wealth of new TV coverage. Worshipping the beautiful game went hand in hand with wearing top clobber and walking to the sound of our favourite tunes. New Order's 'World in Motion' had encapsulated this holy trinity of modern 90s life immaculately.

Figures like Lineker, Pearce, Waddle and Gascoigne, whom Thatcher entertained at Downing Street after the World Cup, and rock star baller Ryan Giggs, who made his Manchester United debut on 2 March 1991, emerged as fresh heroes now dominating our screens and the wider media.

The Premier League was launched, transforming the sport for ever and emboldening a modern generation of working-class kids, turning them into TV celebrities and kicking off a Fleet Street feeding frenzy. So, by 1996, the new kids really were on the block: in music, football, fashion, in Westminster – and in journalism. Once again, I'd landed in the perfect spot, watching the media narrative shift, ever ready to document that enthralling transposition of power from old to young.

Soon, Britain's spanking new wave of guitar bands would be performing to thronging and adoring crowds in the very same cavernous stadia inhabited by their footballing heroes, at Manchester City's Maine Road and Wembley Stadium, with many such players in the audience. A mesmerising mutual appreciation society.

1996 was year that bore witness to the dethroning of music's old guard. Phil Collins and his prog rock dinosaurs Genesis were the last act to headline at Knebworth Park in Hertfordshire in 1992. Exactly four years on, two biblical brothers and their youthful apostles would be the revelation, crushing the memory of their ageing predecessors and writing themselves into history – as Stuart Pearce and his teammates looked on.

What I didn't quite foretell was the heady war of words, violence, feuding and vitriol which would walk hand in hand with my career in journalism from then on – but it certainly made great copy.

And I don't think any of us would have anticipated that Phil Collins himself would end up in a vicious feud with Noel Gallagher – and then clash with me in a truly bizarre encounter, which I have written about for the first time in the next chapter.

1996

My Top Ten British Albums of the 90s

1. *Definitely Maybe* – **Oasis (1994):** It can't really be anything else, can it? 'Slide Away' is perhaps Noel's most stirring of anthems, 'Rock 'n' Roll Star' and 'Supersonic' lay out the band's manifesto. All thriller and killer, no filler. Its sounds will, indeed, live for ever.
2. *(What's the Story?) Morning Glory* – **Oasis (1995):** Two classic albums in just two years, Noel's songwriting was golden and unstoppable at this moment. Eight of the record's tracks featured on the Live '25 setlist. Astonishing.
3. *Urban Hymns* – **The Verve (1997):** Many thought the 90s were slipping away and then this gem whacked us around the chops. Belter after belter. Come on!
4. *Parklife* – **Blur (1994):** Love the artwork, the production, the sentiment. Bright, bold and joyous in the main but I adore its more sensitive moments like 'To the End' and 'This Is a Low'. 'End of a Century' is a highlight too.
5. *Different Class* – **Pulp (1995):** Who needs Americana when you have Jarvis singing about poverty, wood chip and damp British weather? Perfect northern pop tomfoolery.
6. *OK Computer* – **Radiohead (1997):** A rather more intense take on the 90s from the band named after a Talking Heads song. 'Lucky', 'Let Down', 'No Surprises' and 'Karma Police' provide a stream of

classics while 'Paranoid Android' is a powerful and unique alchemy of beauty and violence.

7. *Dummy* – **Portishead (1994):** The Mercury Music Prize-winning collection of haunting electronica and Bristolian trip hop, with irresistible nuggets like 'Glory Box', 'Sour Times' and 'Numb'. Beth Gibbons is chillingly glorious, soaring above an odd array of curious squeaks and sounds. A one-off.

8. *The Masterplan* – **Oasis (1998):** Sorry, them again. How can an album of B-sides and misfits sit so supreme? The majority probably should have made up the band's third album with many tracks superior to the A-sides they supported. 'Acquiesce', 'Talk Tonight', 'Half the World Away' and the title track are mind-blowers.

9. *Screamadelica* – **Primal Scream (1991):** Inaugural Mercury winner, a triumphant collision of blissed out rock, neo-psychedelia and baggy Madchester sounds. Truly groundbreaking, the drugs ooze out of the speakers, with Andrew Weatherall's glorious wizardry.

10. *Blue Lines* – **Massive Attack (1991):** The first trip hop album marries dub, reggae, soul and electronica, and is unique. The mighty 'Unfinished Sympathy' is its glistening diamond.

CHAPTER 2

Maine Road

And the night, against all odds, when Phil Collins tried to headbutt me

I'd only recently joined *The Sun* as a humble showbiz reporter – and was dispatched to cover a 1996 homecoming concert by balding balladeer Phil Collins at the prestigious Royal Albert Hall in Kensington, perhaps the finest venue in the country.

Following the performance, I was handed a VIP pass and whisked to the lavish afterparty. It was one of the most extravagant gatherings I had ever attended, a grand and regal room at the Albert, packed to its golden rafters with besuited somebodies, very much wealthier than me, who were being force-fed champagne and seafood. That was dinner sorted.

After much guffawing and enthusing about how wonderful the performance was, this glittering room hushed and the moneyed guests turned their heads as a rather sweaty, diminutive chap was jubilantly ushered in. It was the star of the show and he was lapping up the sycophancy. Phil's excitable American publicist breathlessly told me that she was going to grant me an audience with the great man.

What she didn't know was that a couple of years previously I had broken an exclusive story, which reverberated around the world and kick-started my journalistic rise proper. I had interviewed Phil's then soon-to-be-ex-wife Jill extensively about their crumbling marriage for the *Sunday Mirror*. I kept schtum, assuming the meeting wouldn't happen or that Phil might fail to make the link. But then, there he was, Philip David Charles Collins. Former child actor, Genesis legend and one of the most divisive male solo stars on the planet, right in front of me and quite a bit shorter, a man on whom I had built my embryonic career in the profession he detested, arm in arm with a publicist who hadn't done her homework – and for whom I was starting to feel a little sorry.

'Hey, Phil, I want to introduce you to Dominic Mohan, a writer for *The Sun* newspaper,' she drawled.

'Dominic who?' he shot back inquisitively, his eyes narrowing.

'Mohan,' she repeated.

'Dominic Mohan? I know that name … Weren't you the guy who did those interviews with Jill?' he snarled with a stare of menace.

'That was a long time ago, Phil. But yes. That was me …' I stuttered. 'Anyway, great to see you, amazing show [blah blah blah, etcetera].'

He then muttered under his breath, before leaning back and beginning to spring towards my forehead as if to nut me. Fortunately, he seemed to have second thoughts and pulled back, failing to make any connection, before turning on his heels and storming out of his own sumptuous party.

He'd only been in there for a couple of minutes. The room hushed again. I made a swift exit, almost as quick as his. Hello, I must be going, indeed.

The, um, genesis of this shocking encounter came back in July 1994, when I learned that Phil may have been experiencing some difficulties of a marital nature with Jill, mother of future *Emily in Paris* actress Lily, who would have been five at the time.

Loved by millions and detested by more because of his ubiquitous balladeering and conservative views, Phil was one of the biggest names on the planet at this point and a rather large media deal, after following up his Genesis success with a bunch of solo albums such as *Face Value*, *Hello, I Must Be Going!*, *No Jacket Required* and ... *But Seriously*. He has flogged over 150 million records worldwide and is one of only three artists, alongside Michael Jackson and Paul McCartney, to have shifted over 100 million records both as a solo artist and as a member of a band. But he had a reputation for being prickly and confrontational, with little love for the journalistic profession I had not long entered, sometimes even bothering to personally telephone local newspaper journalists in order to berate them about negative record reviews.

His radio and television omnipresence and success led to him becoming something of a bête noire for the emerging wave of 90s British talent. Before the Oasis debut *Definitely Maybe* was even released in August 1994, coincidentally just after my *Sunday Mirror* story had been published, Noel Gallagher was filmed declaring: 'We're gonna get rid of Phil Collins and Sting – junk food music, McDonald's music – we've got to get in the charts and stamp them out. I want the severed head of Phil Collins in my fridge by the end of this decade. And if I haven't, I'll be a failure.' He also berated Collins for his support for the Tories and life as later a Swiss tax exile. However, it is worth noting that Noel did later admit he was a fan of Peter Gabriel-era Genesis, after he became friendly with the prog giants' original vocalist at their kids' school gates.

Anyhow, I knew Phil was away on his *Both Sides* tour so I took a drive down to a beautiful and quintessentially English village in lush West Sussex, to visit the family estate on the off chance that Jill might be home. I walked through the manicured gardens and banged on the front door, spotting stacks of pop memorabilia in the front window – including a large and rather spooky-looking doll, depicting the actress Shirley Temple, sitting on a chair and clad in a sweater emblazoned with the words 'Welcome The Rolling Stones'. I thought I recognised it from somewhere and then realised the collectors' item featured prominently on the Peter Blake-designed cover of *Sgt. Pepper's Lonely Hearts Club Band*. Of course. And the original. Bit of an invitation to burgle though, I thought.

I waited patiently and, eventually, a rather ashen-faced woman answered the door. She appeared to have been doing a lot of crying – it was Jill, and she was in the mood to talk. Endlessly. She let rip about her soon-to-be-ex-husband, tearfully telling me: 'Phil's going through that 40-something thing. It's hard on everybody at the moment. I feel like a single mum. But I'm letting him have his space. Lily keeps bursting into tears and weeping, "I want my

Daddy." She hasn't seen her father for two months. Phil sends her faxes with little pictures, but I know she would rather hear the sound of her Daddy's voice. He doesn't telephone very often because he has to save his voice for the next show. She misses her Dad. She wants to give him a cuddle. It's not fair. I'd hate to see us separate, but I'm a person too. Sometimes I wish we had more quality time together. I'm his second priority. If he did have a one-night stand with another woman I think I would probably understand. He's going through that stage when he may think he needs to try something else. But if he became involved with someone else I don't think I could. I don't want to ask him about it – he'll tell me if he wants to. But with AIDS around you need to get medical certificates off people before you sleep with them.'

Wow. It was a sensational interview and, as soon as she uttered these powerful words about one of Britain's most popular rock stars, it was obvious it would make the *Sunday Mirror*'s the front page. And so it did. On Sunday, 10 July 1994, and inside on a double-page spread with the headline: 'Phil's like a jealous kid, always expecting us to be there. But he can't expect us to just sit around waiting for him to call.'

It was early in my career but, even by then, I had learned that if editors had a world exclusive in their hands such as this, they would choose to, what the industry calls, 'spoof' the first edition. That means to print initial copies of the newspaper with an alternative front page, to protect the exclusive and to prevent rival newspapers from plundering the words for their later editions. It makes commercial sense and ensures ownership of the exclusive, more important now than ever. But not in this case, which was something of an oversight. I was learning young and from other people's mistakes.

A furious Piers Morgan was angered because the rival paper he edited, the *News of the World*, had failed to land the exclusive, particularly a celebrity one, which was meant to be his area of speciality. They piled in and copied the story almost word for word, even having the audacity to label it a 'World Exclusive'. Imitation is the sincerest form of flattery and all that.

Fast-forward: Phil then dumped Jill, allegedly via fax (although Phil Collins always denied this). The following year he moved to Switzerland and set up home with the glamorous translator Orianne, who was working on his tour. They had two sons, one of whom, Nic, would himself become a talented drummer, and who performed on the final Genesis tour, in the place of his physically incapacitated father.

The Tuesday after the story ran, I had a call from Piers' deputy editor Phil Hall, for whom I had previously worked shifts for on *The People*, also part of The Mirror Group. He invited me to a hastily arranged lunch at a five-star restaurant, one that the *Sunday Mirror* would never have shelled out for. He asked me why I was playing for Sheffield Wednesday when I could be a star at Manchester United, offering me a decent pay rise. Piers even turned up to join us in his chauffeur-driven Jag, which then dropped me back at Mirror HQ. Flashy touch. Aged 25, I had been officially love-bombed and poached and it was Phil Collins' infidelity that would bring me to the Murdoch empire, home of *The Times*, the *Sunday Times*, *The Sun* and the *News of the Screws*. Once inside the Murdoch stable, sister paper *The Sun* came for me, not long after I broke a few news and celebrity stories and I moved next door, which I enjoyed much more.

The older Gallaghers' war with Collins would later flare up in person, 4,000 miles away from London on the Caribbean island of Mustique, in 1996 itself. Noel was working on demos for the third Oasis album, *Be Here Now*. Phil also happened to be holidaying with Orianne and was setting up with some local musicians in a small bar called The Firefly when he noticed actor Johnny Depp, his squeeze Kate Moss and a Labour MP, with Noel and his wife Meg, in a corner. Phil sidled up and introduced himself before Meg insulted him, followed by Noel dismissing the invitation. Embarrassed Phil retired to the bar before Kate Moss approached and apologised for the encounter. Noel et al. stood up and left as Phil's trio played on regardless.

Just as younger politicians were coming to the fore and Britain was modernising and becoming more hip, my generation of journalists was breaking into the mainstream and the country wanted a fresh soundtrack for our new lives. A break from the Live Aid generation, from Phil Collins and Sting, prog bands like Genesis, Dire Straits and America's grunge.

So, with characteristic aplomb, a brighter and more optimistic brand of quintessentially British music began to explode out of the music press and into the mainstream media. As I have already outlined, Manchester had, of course, been relentless in its production of supersonic bands – The Smiths, Joy Division, New Order, Happy Mondays, Inspiral Carpets and, perhaps most importantly, The Stone Roses. The Roses looked like they'd stepped off the terraces of Old Trafford and took the spirit of late 80s acid house culture and welded it with supreme guitar lines and a strut that heavily influenced the style, look, attitude and sound of what would become Oasis. Liam Gallagher declared the Roses as the greatest band he had seen live, transforming the way he would walk, dress and live, for ever. But the Roses never quite hit the mass media in the way Oasis would. Why? The Gallaghers were better looking, had punch-ups on ferries, gave outrageous interviews, and wrote euphoric and relatable anthems – and more of them, as showcased on one of Britain's greatest albums, *Definitely Maybe*.

This was just over a year after Alan McGee had signed the band after seeing them in Glasgow. Johnny Hopkins, Oasis press officer from 1993 until 2000, recalled that night: 'Around midnight on 31st May/1st June 1993 I'm in bed when the phone rings. Pre-mobiles. Just an old phone fixed into the wall. Initially I wasn't going to pick it up – perhaps it was a wrong number – but then changed my mind as the phone kept ringing. Perhaps it was an emergency or someone had died. Neither. It was Alan McGee, wanting to talk about this unknown, unsigned band he'd just seen fourth on the bill at a small Glasgow venue, King Tut's Wah Wah Hut. The band was Oasis. He was raving about them and said he wanted me to be their PR. "Great. Looking forward to hearing them. Let's talk in the morning," I said and went back to bed. About half an hour later he called again. Even more enthusiastic, divulging a few details. I was intrigued, said, "Bye. Speak tomorrow." I went back to bed. Anyway, he called me every half an hour throughout that night. Each call was more intense than the one before, the story more elaborate. Across those [early hours] calls he stated that they had amazing songs and were the best new band he'd seen; described the singer who was dressed all in white and looked like a total star; and how the band had threatened to trash the venue if they weren't allowed to play. They were not originally on the bill. Alan is a natural salesman and I was totally sold on them without hearing any of the music! According to the band, he poured a bottle of Jack Daniel's over his head at the gig as he was so blown away by them.

'Creation was a brilliant place to work for most of the 90s. A bit eccentric, but it worked. One big happy dysfunctional family. Us against the world. McGee employed Meg Mathews when she was already going out with Noel. Meg brought a new positive energy to Creation and she sure knew how to organise a party. It was good to have her around. Yes, I believed Oasis could be that big. They had all the key elements, but we had to get the strategy right – press, marketing, live plot, etc. Everyone worked hard to make it happen. They faced intense press scrutiny, particularly Liam and Noel. But they dealt with it really well considering. They had that strength. When you start PR-ing an act, you think about which publications they should be seen in and when. This strategy is, in part, based on what media the band themselves read. So the tabloids were always going to be in there at some point, specially when they became successful. Of course, the tabloids were interested in them because they were big personalities, involved in all sorts of incidents and gave attention-grabbing quotes. Appearing in the tabloids connected them to new areas of their audience. Around this point the tabloids expanded their coverage of music.'

Johnny's words are powerful and give great insight into the absolute adrenaline rush felt by McGee as he heard Oasis's embryonic wall of sound for the first time, something to which most members of their early audiences will attest. You were also struck by both men's unassailable belief that the band were going to be successful and dominate the mainstream media.

A voracious tabloid reader at that time and a man a few years younger than me, who was moulding himself on the Gallaghers in their native north-west, was Oasis-tousled TV and radio host Vernon Kay. I wanted to talk to Vernon because he was the perfect age to witness the emergence of acid house, Madchester and Britpop close up – as a fan, before he became famous. He invited me to catch up at London's rather salubrious Lanesborough Hotel. We shared a couple of Peronis each with the bill coming to more than £50. That certainly isn't 90s prices. Vernon reckoned the band's relentless aggression in interviews is what set them apart, alongside the tunes, naturally. He explained: 'I think it's the attitude that both brothers had and that they were always on the front foot. They were never defending, were they? They were attacking, attacking, attacking. They had to. We're the best. We're the ones. You, we're the one that you should be looking out for. And no one else ever said, everyone else is shite, forget everyone, they're crap. I remember someone asking Liam, "What do you think of the Rolling Stones?" He said, "The only thing the Rolling Stones are good for is, Keith Richards lay on the floor, put a golf tee in his mouth and I'd smash a golf club over his face." I was like "What?" So then, whether you like them or not, your ears prick up.'

Post-*Leisure*, The Kinks-tinged Blur were also emerging fast and I witnessed an early explosive show at London's Kentish Town Forum. The band performed breathtaking songs from their retro-sounding masterpiece *Modern Life Is Rubbish* album and when asked if Blur were an anti-grunge band, Damon replied: 'Well, that's good. If punk was about getting rid of hippies, then I'm getting rid of grunge.' They then followed up with *Parklife* in April 1994, an instant epic with music hall sensibilities, wit, sparkle and Quadrophenian cheeky chappie Phil Daniels, plus 90s anthem 'Girls and Boys', which tackled sexual fluidity and Club 18–30 holidays. It was as if the 60s baton was being handed on to my g-g-generation and both Oasis and Blur were rising together, their sounds very different but appealing to similar audiences. I've always been puzzled by the Oasis vs Blur division because it's absolutely fine to enjoy both bands' music, as I do. They are, by no means, mutually exclusive. (I blame the media …)

Alex James admitted that Blur's new direction was a very conscious decision to move away from Americana and to make a statement about British culture and beauty, telling me: '*Modern Life Is Rubbish* was very much a deliberate step away – we are doing our own thing now. Until you start travelling, you don't really realise where you're from. It was very much Damon's initiative of tapping into that great tradition of British songwriting – Ray Davies and Pete Townshend and The Beatles. The record company came down and demanded to hear something and they were like "Fucking British pop. British pop? You are fucking mad." They wanted to get us to re-record everything with (Nirvana producer) Butch Vig. They were like – OK, we will back you, but this is absolutely your last fucking chance. But we were so irrelevant in many people's minds.

'The record company had faith and we felt we were starting to get the hang of it but, if it was today, we would absolutely have been dropped by then. A British movement was percolating. There was a whole kind of infrastructure, little venues up and down the country that we used to play that were becoming places for all the cool people in every provincial city in the UK. Every town had a music scene and local radio and local press, as well as a national media machine. It was a gallivanting, good time, it felt a really safe, warm and colourful and creative environment. Yes, there was a lot drinking and stuff, but it was people really just dreaming their dreams and enjoying themselves.'

Alex said his first encounter with the Gallaghers came in 1994 when their tours crossed in California. 'Face to face, we always got on. I always found Liam particularly impossible to dislike and Noel makes me fucking laugh. I saw them play that night and they did 'I Am the Walrus' and I thought yes, he's really got a fucking good voice. And then the first time I heard 'Wonderwall', I was like, OK, that is actually really good. It was boozy, argy-bargy. Looking back now, it was just two fucking great bands. It was Blur and Oasis leading the charge, but there were loads of other great bands – Pulp, Supergrass, Radiohead, Prodigy, so many genres, so much brilliant music happening, all at the same time.'

My first live experience of Blur's adversaries-to-be Oasis came on Tuesday 16 August 1994, a night that would change everything. Yes, we'd seen The Charlatans and The Roses five years previously, admired Suede and watched Blur tear it up – but this was something on a higher plane.

A friend had tipped me off, presumably by letter or landline phone call at that time, about the band's visceral live presence, describing them as a cross between The Sex Pistols and The Beatles. The Sex Beatles as some might say. I don't remember it being sold out, nor far from home, so that night we made the first of what would be many, many pilgrimages to see a curious band by the name of Oasis at London's Kentish Town Forum, as an intrigued music obsessive rather than in a journalistic capacity.

Definitely Maybe was on the cusp of release but we had yet to hear 'Live Forever' or 'Slide Away' but singles 'Supersonic' and 'Shakermaker' had teased our ears and roused considerable curiosity.

That evening, Oasis were incendiary. Intimidating. Aggressive. With that ear-perforatingly loud wall of sound that blew your brains out and ignited something within – they were truly unforgettable. Forget eleven, these amps were turned up to twelve.

The band prowled the stage like a coked-up gang of football hoolies who had stepped straight off the terraces, were staring you out and wanted to smash your face in. They were brooding and surly – tough-talking and stalking Mancunians wanting to prove a point to us Southerners. The missus admitted it was the first time she had ever been afraid at a concert. It felt as if intoxicated violence could kick off at any moment – and the band acted as if they wanted it. Too young for punk, I'd never witnessed anything like this. Sod fey young men in blouses, this was how I wanted my rock 'n' roll served.

The classic line-up of the brothers with Paul Arthurs aka Bonehead on guitar, Paul McGuigan on bass and drummer Tony McCarroll assaulted us with head-crippling renditions of 'Columbia', 'Fade Away', 'Digsy's Dinner', 'Shakermaker', 'Live Forever', 'Bring It on Down', 'Up in the Sky', 'Slide Away', 'Cigarettes & Alcohol', 'Supersonic' and 'I Am the Walrus' – a setlist more established acts would still be homicidal for today.

This was the most menacing and powerful music I had ever heard live. These were 90s hymns that put a spring in your stride, sent your blood rushing, made you feel glad to be alive. It was as if they injected you with an instant swagger – you could put your troubles to one side, erase the 80s, stick two fingers up to the world and live in the moment. Oasis were going to become the country's biggest and greatest band, it was obvious to me from that very moment, an on-stage riot and onslaught that captured a moment in time, made you want to drink too much, put your arms around one another and sing. And I was sensing an urge to write about them. Why did they connect with me instantaneously? Perhaps I liked the sense of optimism in their songs, the cool Britishness and eardrum-bleeding power, the self-assuredness – it chimed with the growing confidence and contentedness in my own life and career. It felt like being on the football terraces – a shared, communal joy. I had a feeling straight away they would connect with millions of others – as they had with me.

These were paeans that would soon echo relentlessly from pub jukeboxes and be chanted in the streets at closing time across the land for many years. Of course, I didn't know then what a powerful and pivotal role these young men would play in my world and career. It was the start of a symbiotic relationship and the embryonic moments of what would explode into Cool Britannia over the following years, a movement I would witness and chronicle close-up and one on which I would further build my reputation in journalism.

1994 felt like the underground version of 1996, the practice lap if you like. Modern English football culture had begun to rise alongside captivating new strands of British music. The man who would later become my boss, Rupert Murdoch, was looking for some action – new sports rights in an attempt to stimulate his BSkyB satellite TV business. Apparently, NFL and golf rights were too pricey even for him, so he plumped for newly fashionable football's Premier League broadcast rights with a £304 million bid for a five-year deal.

The effects of Sky Sports Football on British culture cannot be understated. It elevated players like Ryan Giggs into sex symbols and rock stars like never before; thereafter he was featured in the emerging lads' mags, gossip columns and the front half of mostly tabloid papers – not just the back. Gazza had set the scene in 1990 – but without the looks, the representation or business acumen. Giggs began dating celebrities, including TV's Dani Behr, who hosted Channel 4's *The Word*, where Oasis and Nirvana had made their live UK TV debuts, the booker a certain Jo Whiley before she went on to become a critically acclaimed DJ and broadcaster. A prototype Posh and Becks had been born. Football was the new showbiz and this dizzying cocktail of sport, music, entertainment and glamour was to stimulate newspaper sales and dominate bar-room conservations over the years the followed.

Laddish football shows like the BBC's *Fantasy Football League*, hosted by comedians David Baddiel and Frank Skinner, and Sky's *Soccer AM*, both launched in 1994, in a bid to capture the zeitgeist. *Soccer AM*, most famously fronted by Tim Lovejoy and Helen Chamberlain, also featured musical guests, with Noel Gallagher regularly appearing, as would I later in the decade, shamefully missing a penalty kick live on air. It still rankles today.

At precisely the same moment, as Mancs were partying in the Hacienda while others were hanging with the Junglist Massive and ravers, in the basement of an unassuming pub on the corner of Great Portland Street and Euston Road was one of the best London club nights of 1994.

The Albany was nestled opposite the entrance to Regent's Park and the Portland Hospital, where celebrity – and bona fide – royalty would choose to welcome their nepo-babies. During that balmy summer, it became home to The Heavenly Sunday Social and, for just thirteen weeks, it was an unforgettable – actually, on occasion, forgettable – night out, with resident DJs The Dust Brothers, who later had to change their name to The Chemical Brothers after a dispute with the American producers going under the same moniker. The club night was the brainchild of the tastemakers at the Heavenly Recordings label, who had released some memorable records by acts like the aforementioned Flowered Up, Andrew Weatherall and Saint Etienne.

It was an intense, sticky, smoky, dark basement with decks on rickety old pub tables and an official capacity of about 160, but there were many more than that crammed in, loads of whom were pretty flippin' famous. On a night, you'd commonly see Paul Weller, Tricky and Primal Scream there, with Beth Orton dancing on the bar. I recall walking in to see a surly-looking chap in a Brother-sponsored Manchester City shirt leaning at the bar staring people out. It was just before *Definitely Maybe* came out and not too many people knew who he was. It's mind-boggling to think that, within two years, The Chemical Brothers would be supporting the younger Gallaghers' Oasis at Knebworth, with both performing in front of 250,000 fans, including me. At that moment, we were all assembled in a grubby cellar, united in a dingy dress rehearsal for a shiny, mass Cool Britannia communion that wasn't too far off in the future. None of us would have believed it then. And just a few years afterwards, Liam and I, by then editor of *The Sun*'s Bizarre column, would be in a pub, just a few steps away, toasting the birth of his baby son Lennon with serial rock-star conqueror and pouting actress Patsy Kensit in bed at the hospital right opposite.

MAINE ROAD

The Chemical Brothers would play block rockin' sets at The Sunday Social, mixing acid house, techno, hip hop and psychedelic rock, dropping records like 'Tomorrow Never Knows' by The Beatles, 'Live Forever', The Mondays' 'Wrote for Luck', Flowered Up's 'Weekender', 'Pump Up the Volume' by M|A|R|R|S and their own emerging studio tracks like the head-banging 'Chemical Beats'. The records would often skip as gurning punters banged into the tables. It was electrifying – having arrived a little late to acid house and Oakenfold's eclectic wizardry, I'd never been to a club night before when any genre of music was, literally, on the table. To hear The Beatles in that context, next to banging techno and 'Open Up' by Leftfield was, well, how can I put it, heavenly. Oh, and it was three quid to get in.

But Ed Simons, one half of The Chemicals, had mixed emotions when remembering those heady nights and admitted that playing there was 'a pain in the arse', with drunken club goers falling on to the decks and records jumping. I don't *think* that was me.

You'd wake up the next day with the Heavenly logo stamp still on the back of your hand, clothes stinking of smoke as this was, of course, pre-smoking ban, not good for the asthma. The ban in England later made it illegal to light up in all enclosed workplaces in England, including clubs and bars, and was brought into force in July 2007 as a consequence of the Health Act 2006. This ban was one of Tony Blair's government's finest achievements and will have extended many lives, including mine, probably.

Meanwhile, in the smoke-filled Hacienda two hundred miles to the north-west, baggy-clothed teenager Vernon

Kay was living and breathing Madchester, mingling with Mancunian royalty, while kneeling at the altar of acid house culture. 'I remember walking in to The Hacienda and thinking, 'This is like church,' he explained. 'Everyone was just worshipping this shadow. They were in a booth which was tucked to the rear and you knew they were playing but you never saw them. It was like we are worshipping this person in this box who is faceless. The Inspiral Carpets were always about, if they weren't on tour. They felt like the face of the movement. New Order's Bernard Sumner was always in The Hacienda, saw him and Hooky a lot. The odd Man United player. Noel loved it, the music and that collective element. That was our sanctuary. You had the Scousers in one corner, the rich kids from Cheshire in another and it just brought everyone together. What I'm trying to say is it was a big cooking pot for everyone. It was young people expressing themselves. I think that's the spark that literally exploded Britpop. Madchester was the dress rehearsal. Because of all the great music that was coming out of there, everyone within the surrounding area, Greater Manchester, felt like it was theirs.

'Movements have an identity, and when you look at Britpop, it was the fact that the youth had had enough of the dirge of what happened before. It went from everyone being like Bowie in make-up then, all of a sudden: 'Oh, I'm a lad.' Hooliganism fading and then you put the music layer on top of that and then the evolution of the summer of love in 1989. It's just an amazing blend, a timeline of, right, we're building up to a huge something. And that something became Britpop.'

MAINE ROAD

Blur had assembled the ultimate Britpop line-up for their mesmeric Alexandra Palace show in October 1994 – supported by Pulp, Supergrass and Corduroy, and then stormed Mile End Stadium in East London the following June. This was too where singer Damon would clash with Liam at a Soccer Six tournament. Jarvis Cocker also played in this bizarre, all-star Britpop kickabout. Jane Savidge, of Pulp's PR company Savidge & Best, remembered: 'We went to Mile End for the first ever Soccer Six tournament, with Liam playing, Damon playing, Jarvis playing. There were all these girls there, like they'd escaped from somewhere, who ran on the pitch from behind some rope. The bouncers were pulling them back and the TV were there and the girls were being asked which one they like best. "I like Liam. I like Damon." It was ridiculous, I'd never seen anything like that before.'

Blur won 1994 in many ways and their ascension that year was crowned at the 1995 Brit Awards in Alexandra Palace. The band would be the first to go home (actually they probably didn't go home that night) with four Brits, the first act ever to do so.

Alex James admitted that was the moment their careers went to a level above: 'The 1995 Brits was when it detonated. Winning four Brits had never been done before. I mean, everyone wins four Brits now, but we went from indie outsiders to a household name. Things are more frightening for singers and guitar players, while bass players are happy to just get on with it. I didn't feel the weight of it. I was just having the time of my life.'

In the media room that night, I was intrigued to meet a wackily dressed, supposed BBC TV journalist for the first of many times, who peppered some of the night's grandest names with cutting questions. He went by the name of Dennis Pennis and wasn't quite yet on the radar. The character, played by actor Paul Kaye, would go on to land his own one-off BBC 2 show in September 1995 called *Anyone for Pennis?*, followed by *Very Important Pennis* in 1996. We would end up on the *Top of the Pops* stage together in 1998 as part of the Fat Les collective for a performance of footie anthem 'Vindaloo', but I shall come back to that. His trademark was to harass celebrities and catch them out with ridiculous questioning. My kind of humour.

When a triumphant Blur stepped on to the stage for their obligatory post-victory media appearance, chain-smoking and swigging Moet champagne straight from the bottle, Pennis grabbed the mic and announced: 'Can I ask a question for the drummer?' Guitarist Graham Coxon chipped in: 'Hey, drummer question, everyone,' before Pennis asked: 'What's your name?' Dave Rowntree, the man in question, who had his name painted on to his right cheek as a dig at Prince's similar 'Slave' etching that night, looked embarrassed before replying, 'Brian'.

But Damon did go on to say: 'This year, British music has started to re-establish itself. It's not us, on our own. Maybe we were the first people to start shouting about it. We've paid our dues a bit. But, I think, bands like Oasis, who – as far as I'm concerned it should have been a joint thing – best band.'

Then, when Madonna was brought backstage for her turn to meet the British media, Pennis asked a stunned-looking Queen of Pop: 'You've had most of your anatomy photographed. I wonder if you maybe had thought about bringing out a book and letting us see some internal organs, possibly your kidneys, er, fallopian tubes?' Followed by: 'Madonna, you've had your navel pierced, do you think you'll get your brain pierced so you can have a stud in your head 24 hours-a-day?' MC Bernard Doherty, who expertly ran the Brits media operation, looked disgusted as he escorted a bewildered Madge off stage.

Increasingly, Blur were being pitched against Oasis in the music press, and then the tabloids, with both refusing to rest on their Fred Perry laurels; in August 1995, they went mop-top to mop-top in the battle for number one with 'Country House' and 'Roll with It', Blur ultimately claiming victory. It was even on the BBC News.

Blur producer Stephen Street remembered going out for some al fresco drinks with the band in London's Covent Garden, between the releases of *Parklife* and *The Great Escape*, just after 'Some Might Say' by Oasis had hit number one. Suddenly, out of nowhere, they were approached by a surly Liam. 'I was with Damon and Alex and Liam walks up to Damon, he's swaggering. Quite aggressive. He is right in his face. Damon was standing his ground and wasn't going to rise to it. And Liam's like "Number One," right in his face. And he was really giving it large to Damon and then went off. Damon kind of sniggered and was laughing, So that might have led to the people behind Blur and Oasis knowing they had something cooking here with this rivalry, and the thing about putting out the single to kind of block the other one. A lot of this was the record company. But I think it was like, because of that episode with Liam, I think when it was first mentioned, they said, "Let's fucking take him on."'

And, after the disappointment of only reaching number two with 'Roll with It', Liam admitted he wanted to beat up Damon but thought he would take him to court, branding the singer a 'fucking idiot, like a little student trying to be a lad'. He said Blur's songs were joke music and the feud was 100 per cent genuine – and escalating.

Alex heard the news of their triumph on the way back from Devon and told me: 'I was driving back from Damien Hirst's house in the West Country, with Keith and Lily Allen, who was like eight or nine, a little kid. I didn't know who was number one. No one had a mobile, we were literally listening to the Top 40 countdown on the radio. That's bonkers. We thought we had it but didn't know for sure. We were away for most of that year. We were looking at it from afar, it felt like an explosion going off in the distance. Then we would come home and it would be more and more crazy.'

The band would celebrate their victory at a swiftly arranged record label party at Soho House – but it was a little downcast. Stephen Street elaborated: 'One of the worst singles they'd ever put out. I've never loved it, and it was put up against one of the worst singles by Oasis. There's an irony in that, isn't there? Food Records put on a celebration at Soho House, the original one. I remember Graham being in a very agitated mood. Graham doesn't like playing the game at all. He could get quite morose and he wasn't happy about it at all. And I remember it being quite subdued. I felt more like celebrating the success we had with 'Girls & Boys' getting in the top five rather than being number one with 'Country House'. I guess it was to do with the hype because there was so much going on in the media. Alex was loving it, getting champagne down his neck, but I guess Alex is a lovely, kind of affable chap. Such different personalities in the band.'

Around this time, in an interview with the *Observer* newspaper, Noel would declare that he hated Alex and Damon and hoped that they would catch AIDS and die. He immediately retracted the comment and apologised, but the damage was done and the feud was further escalated, exploding into the tabloids.

Oasis press man Johnny Hopkins told me the rivalry between the groups began to fester in a pub in Camden, North London, and spilled into the media, when the bands would exchange barbs. 'It happened early on at The Good Mixer,' he explained. 'While Oasis liked some Blur songs, there were inevitably personality clashes. It was unheard of back then for an indie band to be media-trained. But I did discuss stories and my campaigns with Noel. He was media-savvy and had even done media interviews on behalf of the Inspiral Carpets when he was a roadie for them. As it was clear that incidents continually happened around them I started writing down all the stories in notebooks and told Noel to call me anytime anything happened. He called at least once a day. The stories were always hilarious.'

Between Blur's *Parklife* and *The Great Escape*, which featured hit singles 'The Universal' and 'Charmless Man', Oasis recorded two albums and close to twenty other new songs, including some classic B-sides. But the productivity – and quality – of both bands' golden songwriting was unprecedented at that time.

Three weeks after the release of *The Great Escape*, in September 1995, *(What's the Story) Morning Glory?* came out – I couldn't believe what I was hearing. Driving back from Liverpool one Sunday evening, Steve Lamacq was premiering the Oasis album on his Radio 1 show before its release. As we heard 'Wonderwall' for the first of many hundreds, no probably thousands, of times in our lives and Liam's transcendent vocals came in, we all felt collective goosebumps and turned to one another, jaws dropped. It was instantaneous. This was the 90s Beatles – an anthem for us, for our times – and we hadn't even heard 'Don't Look Back in Anger' yet.

'Wonderwall', fabled to be about Noel's lover Meg – but later denied – was properly born in May 1995 at Rockfield Studios in Wales, where Oasis spent a fortnight recording. Noel initially came up with the title 'Wishing Stone' before altering it after taking inspiration from George Harrison's 1968 solo album *Wonderwall Music*. To date, it has been streamed more than 2.6 billion times via Spotify. Noel said none of the band rated the track initially, with his brother branding it reggae. We've all heard it on so many occasions, but do you remember the first time you heard such a mesmeric sonic legacy? The brothers re-evaluated this national anthem for Live '25, rightly restoring this spiritual canticle to the climax of an already epic set.

Pulp's Mercury Music Prize-winning *Different Class*, meanwhile, spawned the unforgettable 'Common People' and reached number two in the charts, which were filling with Britpop bands like Suede, Elastica, Supergrass, Echobelly, Skunk Anansie and the Manic Street Preachers.

Suede's lithe frontman had, in many ways, been the early poster boy for what would be christened Britpop, Brett Anderson gracing the cover of *Select* magazine back in 1993, with the headline 'Yanks go home!' and a Union Jack backdrop. But he had reservations about the movement, finding it distasteful, laddish and jingoistic. Gaz Coombes from Supergrass, an Alright singer, had similar reservations and Skin from Skunk Anansie grew tired of its ubiquity.

Drummer Nick Banks thought it ridiculous that his band, Pulp, who had been going for more than fifteen years, were being described as a trailblazing Britpop group and found their inclusion in the movement 'comical'.

I'd been an enthusiastic follower of Pulp after first seeing them perform live at the launch party for Quentin Tarantino's *Pulp Fiction* at London's Ministry of Sound in October 1994, where they performed a memorable version of 'Girl, You'll Be a Woman Soon', from the film's soundtrack; I would try to pepper *The Sun* with stories about Sheffield's finest as often as possible. I remember a classic picture of Jarvis with his precious, ancient Hillman Imp car, which neatly summed him up, and would compile features like: 'Ten things on the Cocker of the North', illustrative of how popular Jarvis, in particular, and the band had become, following his Jacko stunt at the Brits. (You know you've made it when *The Sun* writes a 'Ten Things' about you.)

Then, just over one year after seeing them at the humble Forum, Oasis were headlining sold-out shows at the cavernous 20,000 capacity Earls Court, in November 1995, supported by The Bootleg Beatles who joined them on stage in shiny Sgt. Pepper uniforms for a storming and surreal encore of 'I Am the Walrus'. It was the ticket to have and you should have seen the queue for the toilets. Madonna, Pet Shop Boys, The Specials and George Michael stood with us in the audience for the biggest celebration of Britpop so far. It was all happening so fast – surely it couldn't get any bigger?

The Sun seemed to be capturing something of the spirit of the times. There was a steady stream of Oasis stories, on an almost daily basis, alongside regular tales of Chris Evans, Blur and Pulp, The National Lottery, TV shows *EastEnders* and *Gladiators*, Gazza, Robbie Williams and Princess Diana, as she prepared for divorce. Page Three was still there, alongside heavy celebrity glamour content featuring figures such as Ulrika Jonsson and Pamela Anderson. There were also numerous stories about Mad Cow Disease after British beef was banned in twenty countries, with fears that four million animals would be culled. Headlines included: 'Sad Cow Disease', 'MAD Council Disease', 'Mad Bull Disease' and 'Will Mad Cow Disease Wipe Out the Tories?'. There were also many articles bubbling about a possible referendum on membership of the EU and the virtues of a possible exit, but enough of that frivolity.

Labour leader Tony Blair was certainly starting to contribute regular articles for the newspaper, indicating a political shift to the centre left. In fact, tellingly, on 1

January 1996, both he and PM John Major were given equal billing for their New Year messages. Blair (or most likely Alastair Campbell) wrote: 'The New Year is beginning just as 1995 began 12 months ago. The government is in chaos. The divisions are irreparable. Incompetence is the Tories' trademark. The Tories didn't win four elections. We lost them. And we lost them because we lost touch with the people. In 1996, we will show that it is Labour, not the Tories, that understands the modern world and the issues of concern to the people. It is Labour that can deliver prosperity through a dynamic economy. It is Labour that can rebuild Britain as One Nation. It is Labour that can tackle crime, improve schools and hospitals, provide a transport system that works. It is Labour that is best able to lead Britain into a new century.' The front page that day was 'Paula's Preggers – Hutch Is Dad of Baby No4' about soon-to-be *Sun* columnist herself Paula Yates's impending child with the INXS frontman. Tragically, both Paula and Hutchence would be dead within five years.

Early in 96, on 10 January, a small – but ultimately significant – story said: 'Liam Gallagher is the latest star to bring out the mothering instinct in Patsy Kensit. Patsy, who married Jim Kerr of Simple Minds four years ago, enjoyed a lively night out in Manchester with Liam, 23. She and the Oasis wildman went to a club opening then back to an all-night knees-up at the Victoria and Albert Hotel, where they were both staying. A pal said, "They had a wild time. I'm sure they'll be seeing more of each other." Others to receive the Patsy treatment include Michael Hutchence and soccer stars Ryan Giggs and Ian Walker.'

1996

But Britpop wasn't quite permeating every echelon of British society. High Court judge Mr Justice Harman, an Old Etonian, confessed he had never heard of Oasis, telling the court: 'I certainly haven't heard of the band. I don't listen to bands.' He was also mocked after he once asked, 'Who Is Gazza?' When told that Gascoigne was actually incredibly well known in football, Harman responded, 'Is he a rugby or association footballer?' before adding: 'Isn't there an operetta called *La Gazza Ladra*?' Who dares claim our legal profession is out of touch?

But Oasis had fans of all sexual orientation. Gay mag *Attitude* made Liam its Pin-Up of the Month, with the caption warning him to keep his 'back up against the Wonderwall'. Times were certainly very different then, in all corners of the media.

In the weeks before the band's Maine Road gigs, *The Sun* was hitting new heights with that all-time top daily full-price circulation of 4,783,359 on 30 March. The place was buzzing. And so was I. The Bizarre column had also increased in size and Saturday Bizarre was launched to satisfy the insatiable hunger for Britpop twists and related shenanigans. But it wasn't all joyful and positive. There was other big news at this time – the aftermath of the Dunblane horror and the collapse of the trial in the Stephen Lawrence murder, which repulsed us all.

The Dunblane massacre dominated the news agenda throughout and I found it impossible to even look at the photographs of the young victims. We all felt helpless. But then we were approached for help by Scottish musician Ted Christopher, who had conceived the idea of a protest

MAINE ROAD

song against Britain's liberal gun laws. With full backing of the Dunblane parents, he recorded at Abbey Road Studios with children from the town and a band of local musicians. The lead song was a version of Bob Dylan's 'Knockin' on Heaven's Door'. Ted adapted the words – this was the first (and only) time Dylan had allowed anyone to alter his lyrics. Simon Cowell was then just a humble (actually, not so humble) executive at BMG Records and a mate – and the label agreed to release the track. Dire Straits frontman Mark Knopfler, who had himself produced Dylan records, joined us at the famous Beatles' studios to play guitar in the unique way only he can. I will never forget sitting one metre from Knopfler within those hallowed walls, watching his magic fingers as he embroidered the song with his distinctive sound. It was the first of several number one charity singles I would be involved with during my career. Released on 9 December 1996, it sold 673,000 copies, raising money for charities and helping to put pressure on the government to toughen up gun control.

So, here's a thing, just five months on from Earls Court and two after Oasis's triumph at the Brit Awards, there was the small matter of two mega-gigs in their hometown and a pilgrimage to the pre-Etihad home of the brothers' heroes Manchester City, just a Stone Roses' throw from where they grew up in the Burnage council house that is still home to their mother Peggy. Noel has been going to see City there since 1971, from the age of just four.

I was dispatched to the north west to cover the band's biggest shows to date, starting on 27 April 1996. Their relentless rise was unstoppable. Stepping off the train at

1996

Piccadilly, there was something in the air – and I'm not only talking about the overwhelming whiff of weed that hung over the city's streets. Mancunian cries of 'Get yer Oasis T-shirts', 'Madferit bucket hats for £3' and 'Anyone want any tickets?' greeted us – the city completely engulfed in the excitement of these two crowning concerts.

Manchester is so different to London, my home for thirty-five years. When there's a massive football match or outdoor mega-gig, the whole city comes alive and is swept away with the fervour. In the capital, there might be ten different music and sporting events staged simultaneously. What I love about Manchester is the enthusiasm and support it gives to its hometown football clubs and bands. It was the same feeling when The Stone Roses re-formed and played at the Etihad in June 2016. The whole city seemed to be behind them and it was rocking.

Two days before Maine Road, I had tracked down Noel's ex, Louise Jones, who worked for the promoters SJM, and who was described as the 'Beauty Who Broke Oasis Noel's Heart'. They had been together for years as he began his songwriting career and she told me: 'I'm still like a daughter to Noel's mum Peggy. I'm part of the family. I don't want to belittle our relationship because it was very special. The five years we lived together were great times. It's very personal but that chapter is over for us.'

It's hard to believe that Liam was just 23 years young at that time, and so distinctive that it was tricky for him in Manchester. If he mooched into a pub and bought everyone a drink, he would be branded flash and showy. If he didn't, then he was a tightwad who'd moved to London and forgotten his roots. In fact, I discovered that security had to be stepped up at the Manchester concerts because of kidnap threats to Liam in letters and phone calls from local gangsters. He would later address this from the stage. Someone close to the brothers told me: 'The band are all a bit paranoid and it's not being taken lightly. They are never out of the security staff's sight and nobody's taking any chances.'

Londoner Alan White would be wielding the sticks at Maine Road, in place of jettisoned local drummer Tony McCarroll, and before what seemed like the entire population of Manchester – including the brothers' mum Peggy and extended family, England's 1990 hero Stuart Pearce, United players Giggs and Lee Sharpe, who were pelted with pies and beer. On arrival at the decaying stadium, we queued for our guest passes and spotted goggly-eyed Happy Monday Bez and his mates snaffling tickets from the box office with a bent coat hanger from the Portakabin roof, while the staff had their backs turned. Welcome to Madchester.

Ocean Colour Scene and the Manic Street Preachers supported admirably with tickets at a modest £17.50, but we were only here to see one act at their highest watermark. Liam ambled on to the stage and screamed, 'Manchester. Maine Road. Madferit' and they were off. The brothers duetted on 'Acquiesce' with its chorus of 'Because we need each other. We believe in one another.' Epic.

The gig was a giant mosh pit, a stadium levitated, its worshippers gasping at a storming, boisterous, swaggering return to home, with the brothers visibly basking in the adulation and Noel spanking his Union Jack guitar. The goosebump moment was when Liam turned his back to the crowd during 'Live Forever' and Noel's fabled guitar solo pierced the stadium as giant monochrome images of Bob Marley, Sid Vicious, Elvis and finally John Lennon flashed up on the screen.

Referring to the threats, Liam defiantly told the crowd: 'Those guys who want to kidnap me had better hurry up and do a good job because we'll all be waiting for them.'

Looking back, it is probably one of the band's last great pre-reunion setlists, eclipsing those from Knebworth, which included some substandard tracks which would appear on *Be Here Now*. Beginning with a euphoric 'The Swamp Song' and segueing into 'Acquiesce', then 'Supersonic', 'Hello', 'Some Might Say', 'Roll with It', 'Morning Glory', 'Round Are Way', 'Up in the Sky', 'Cigarettes & Alcohol', a sprawling 'Champagne Supernova', 'Whatever', 'Cast No Shadow', 'Wonderwall', 'The Masterplan', 'Don't Look Back in Anger', 'Live Forever', 'I Am the Walrus' and Slade's 'Cum On Feel the Noize'. Not too shabby.

Liam's first encounter with future wife Patsy had been at the city's V&A Hotel, which is where I had been billeted that night after the triumphant and earth-shattering show. It was a strange-looking place, with some rooms named after TV shows like *This Morning*. But I was in 227, a number which has been seared on my brain ever since – and here's why. The bar area was absolutely heaving – and appeared to be mutating into a monstrous, raucous unofficial aftershow gathering of locals, hangers-on, drug dealers, gangsters and musicians. The band had wisely done a runner to a country hotel outside the city to escape the madness of Mancunia.

Regrettably, some of the group's entourage discovered my hotel room number and allocated more than £750 worth of drinks to it long after I'd staggered into bed – triple Glenfiddich whiskies at 7.20am, I recall. On bleary-eyed inspection of the titanic total and learning of such fraudulent skullduggery, I had to plead at checkout and told them I was in bed by four. The kindly receptionist agreed to reduce it and I scarpered, exhausted and filing copy on the train home.

I caught sight of Martin Rossiter, lead singer of Smithsesque indie darlings Gene in my carriage and approached. 'What a gig last night, incredible wasn't it? Oasis were astonishing,' I said, assuming he had been present for that transcendental evening. He looked me up and down as if inspecting a small piece of detritus attached to the bottom of his finely stitched shoe and sneered, with Morrissey-like condescension, 'They're really not my cup of tea, to be honest. I wasn't there. Goodbye.' At least he hadn't tried to headbutt me.

But these live performances we had the privilege to witness were monumental, life-changing in many ways. 1994 and 1995 were the warm-up laps but 1996 was the moment this movement went full throttle, exploding into the consciousness of the wider public, hitting the mass media, the tabloids' influential front pages, penetrating all corners of an overexcited nation and its most cavernous venues.

That Live Aid lot were being wiped out, the status quo being shaken up. Nemesis Phil, Dire Straits, Sting and Duran Duran seemed ageing and irrelevant. Freddie was dead and Queen dethroned.

In 1996, the musical revolution was firmly on our shores and its creators were exuding a new-found confidence, arrogance even, as was our nation and its cocky young politicians, a strutting media and a generation of footballers with the world at their twinkling feet. The country had a palpable buoyancy and impudence, a risk-free artistic licence to push barriers and embrace daring creativity and art but alongside a sense of hedonistic fun and irreverence, which chimed with my attitude as both human being and journalist. With the new millennium approaching, there was a sense of optimism and drive, a feeling that it was our time and we could achieve anything we wanted.

This anarchic rebellion would punctuate the decade to come and, as I will next explore, combine to concoct some of the 90s most memorable moments in all forms of artistic, sporting and literary expression.

My Top Ten British Films of the 90s

1. *Trainspotting* **(1996):** Danny Boyle's masterpiece marked the true arrival of Ewan McGregor after actor and director worked together on excellent precursor *Shallow Grave* in 1994. A hilarious yet hideous portrayal of a gang of Scottish smackheads and their

run-ins. Glorious soundtrack. The best of the decade and a film of which we had seen nothing of the like.
2. **Lock, Stock & Two Smoking Barrels (1998):** Guy Ritchie's directorial debut is a comedic crime caper set in gangland London with bungling heists and career explosions for footballer Vinnie Jones and ex-diver Jason Statham among others. Brilliantly shot and edited in a very 90s way. Superb soundtrack too.
3. **Fever Pitch (1997):** Adapted by Nick Hornby from his best-selling book, this stars Colin Firth as a troubled teacher and long-suffering Arsenal fan, whose football obsessiveness impacts on his love life. Laugh-out-loud moments galore with some worryingly accurate insights and a wonderful climax.
4. **The Full Monty (1997):** Jobless steelworkers form strip troupe with side-splitting results. £2.8 million budget and £156 million box-office takings. There were similar very British, parochial film concepts in the 90s but this was the best. Robert Carlyle a stand-out performer again, but isn't he always?
5. **Secrets and Lies (1996):** Winner of the Cannes Palme d'Or, this is director Mike Leigh's triumph. A young adopted black woman's hunt for her biological mother is gripping and uncovers hidden truths and uncomfortable realities, Brenda Blethyn and Timothy Spall give stirring performances. An absolute gem and just so British.
6. **Shakespeare in Love (1998):** Seven-time Oscar-winner, the cast is astonishing with Joseph Fiennes, Gwyneth Paltrow, Colin Firth (him again), Ben Affleck

and Judi Dench. An extremely smart and cleverly assembled film, depicting a fictional Shakespeare love affair. Breathtaking final scenes shot on the beautiful Holkham Beach in Norfolk, my favourite in Britain.

7. ***Notting Hill*** **(1999):** Richard Curtis's amusing follow-up to *Four Weddings* and I prefer it, not least because of Rhys Ifans's brilliant role as scruffy Spike, Hugh Grant's housemate, and Julia Roberts of course. The hotel press junket scenes with journalists hurried into interviews is spot-on, believe me I've been there. Roberts caused a media stir at the London premiere – sporting hairy armpits!

8. ***Brassed Off*** **(1996):** Ten years after the miners' strike ripped apart communities, Pete Postlethwaite and Ewan McGregor light up this comedy drama which focuses on a brass colliery band's travails with tears and laughter. Beautifully soundtracked. *Billy Elliot*'s precursor in many ways.

9. ***The Crying Game*** **(1992):** Mesmerising crime thriller from Neil Jordan focusing on an IRA member played by Stephen Rea with themes of love, deception, gender and that most memorable twist. Absorbing.

10. ***The Commitments*** **(1991):** One of my favourite directors – Alan Parker – with his musical comedy based on Roddy Doyle's novel is an audio powerhouse, showcasing the talent of Andrew Strong, also starring The Corrs. Life-affirming.

CHAPTER 3

Blur

Alex James, Damien Hirst and Keith Allen in women's lingerie at the footie

Blur had spent much of the first half of 1996 touring across Europe and North America promoting their fourth studio album *The Great Escape*, indeed a great escape from the madness in many ways.

As rivals Oasis tuned up for City's Maine Road, Blur had been haring around France and, just hours after the Gallaghers ended their Manchester stint, Damon's band released their fourth and final single from the collection, 'Charmless Man'. Its B-side highlighted a much darker and rawer side of the group, which signified the shift in sound evident on the eponymous album which was to follow. The single was the group's farewell to Britpop and a sign they were burning the Union flag, burying their cheeky mockney personas and bailing out of Britannia.

But it was at another football stadium – my boyhood team Bristol City's in fact – where bassist Alex James would stumble on a dramatic change of direction for his own musical career.

Terrible trio Alex, artist Damien Hirst and actor Keith Allen had each slipped on matching sets of women's lingerie, piled into a hen-night-style white stretch limo, loaded up the booze and whatever else, and headed off to watch Fulham away. It was hellraiser Keith's birthday and he wanted to celebrate in cross-dressing style, with three gurning slebs shivering on the terraces of my beloved Ashton Gate in Bristol.

It is a silly scene which sums up the 90s in many ways. A trio of grown millionaire men behaving badly and acting like sniggering schoolboys. But it also ignited a creative spark, the moment when Keith – who had of course co-written New Order's 1990 World Cup theme 'World in Motion' – heard the hypnotic beat of a supporter's drum that would inspire him to co-write another football anthem – 'Vindaloo'.

The bonkers video for the song, the unofficial England national football anthem, featured Paul Kaye – that man Dennis Pennis again – actor Rowland Rivron, a young Matt Lucas and David Walliams, in their early guise of Mash and Peas, alongside appearances by Allen's young children Lily and Alfie. Its mesmerising drumbeat is accompanied by nonsensical lyrics such as: 'May I introduce you please to a lump of Cheddar cheese?' with the refrain: 'We're gonna score one more than you.' I don't think any other nation on earth could have produced such an example of senseless gibberish and bizarre song structure, but remember, this is the same corner that brought the planet Lewis Carroll, Spike Milligan, Shakespeare, Peter Sellers, Monty Python, Vic and Bob, *Little Britain* and the Bonzo Dog Doo-Dah Band ...

This is art and creativity through drunken stupidity, a process that sparked many of the nuttiest of decade's greatest and most enduring moments. It typified much of the artistic and sporting genius of the decade – hedonistic and irresponsible behaviour resulting in moments of brilliance and joy, whether in music, art, football or otherwise. Boozed-up Gazza in the dentist's chair followed by his greatest goal and the accompanying celebration at Euro 96. Chris Evans's irresponsible all-nighters and his compelling radio shows just hours later. Noel Gallagher's imperious booze- and drug-soaked songwriting. Tracey Emin drunk on TV discussing the Turner Prize.

Alex spoke to me as he was about to debut his Britpop Classical project at the Big Feastival event he hosts, a musical celebration of the 90s where he would perform classics from his own band, The Charlatans, Ocean Colour Scene, Pulp, The Stone Roses and, yes, Oasis. He recalled: 'I remember Keith got a kind of hen party stretch limo. He liked wearing women's underwear and standing on the terraces singing, taking cross-dressing to the masses. Ahead of his time really, quite provocative. So, me and him and Damien dressed up in some nice lingerie.

'We're all absolutely bladdered wearing women's underwear, freezing in the cold and there was a drummer just doing that beat that really invites chanting over it. The verse stuff that was the sort of thing you might start singing along to if you're on the terrace, "Where on earth are you from?" – a question and answer thing. Keith was like, "Let's do a football record!" and he wouldn't shut up about it.

'We literally did it in 15 minutes. Damien was saying he really liked it. I think maybe there was a sense that Blur were kind of moving in a different direction from wearing women's underwear and getting drunk at Fulham games – I can understand it now, looking back. I was having fun. Sometimes, in an accounting period, it out-earns the entire Blur catalogue if England have a good tournament. Every two years, so it's half as good as a Christmas song.'

I arranged to sink a few pints in Crouch End, North London, with someone who many call the ultimate Britpop PR. Publicist Jane Savidge worked with Pulp, The Verve, Elastica, Alex, Damien Hirst and the Vindaloonies and Fat Les. She told me: 'That's what they do – women's knickers – they wave them to Louis Saha and all that. It's Keith – Keith's fairly insane. He's thinks it's absurd. He also used to walk down the street naked because I don't think he thinks anything matters. They were at Bristol City and they heard a chant, which was just the makings of "Vindaloo".'

And so, Alex's spin-off band, Fat Les, was born and I became a member, sort of. My relationship with Alex over the years is a curious one. From first seeing Blur in 1993, to then writing about them throughout the 90s, seeing them triumph at the 1995 Brit Awards but miss out in 96, I would perform (actually just jump around a bit) on stage with the Fat Les collective in 1998 and, at the beginning of the following century, hire Alex as *The Sun*'s food columnist, as he started to move from music into cheese production and wine-making.

These extra-curricular activities, alongside his wild and hedonistic nature, have made Alex the most compelling member of Blur in many ways. Sure, Damon is the creative genius who never stops working, but Alex has a multi-faceted portfolio of interests and passions, all of which seem to be driven by a sense of fun and mischief. It's why I hired him.

Readers would often ask me how I decided what to put in my column – and later the paper. My response is always that if I find something or someone interesting, then I'm sure millions of others will – whether related to music, football, cheese, the welfare state, a glamorous woman or army kit shortages. It just has to be compelling in some way, revealing facts or opinions that would prompt one human being to want to communicate to another. It applies online as equally as in print. It used to be called the 'Fuck me, have you seen this, Doris?' theory. It's the same principle now – the publication of content worth sharing. It's amazing how many papers back then were stuffed full of material I found distinctly uninteresting. In the 1880s, Arthur McEwen, journalist and editor for William Randolph Hearst, declared: 'News is anything that makes the reader say, "Gee whiz!"' There was a sign emblazoned with those words in *The Sun*'s newsroom when I first joined, alongside another which read: 'Walk tall, you're now entering *Sun* country.'

I asked Alex about his odd, curious, career path and he told me: 'It is bonkers, but I love it. There might not be as much work in music, but there are other options than being in a band now you know, the kids do aspire to being chefs. It's weird having one foot in the music industry where people are losing their jobs, and one foot in the food industry where everyone is opening restaurants. I think you just have to fucking work really fucking hard and good things happen. You just wanted to go out and do stuff, meet people and see what happens. I don't think it's like that any more. It's all about appearance fees and it's commercialised. It was innocent then – it was a party that never stopped and people would dip in and out. There were interesting people coming along all the time.'

The catchy yobbery of 'Vindaloo' and the message the song carried was perfect for my 90s audience. I travelled up to the BBC *Top of the Pops* studio, just outside London, Three Lions on my shirt. We headed to the bar – there was some entourage there – maybe around thirty of us. We filmed a pre-performance march around the *EastEnders* set and Albert Square before waiting in a corridor. There were a couple of giant sumo blokes in nappies with us, hired from the Ugly Models Agency, and it must have been quite a sight. Out of nowhere, the Spice Girls appeared, still then a five-piece and just hours before Geri would quit the group. They looked confused when they saw me and they chirped, almost in unison as was their way back then: 'What are you doing here?'

'I'm here with Vindaloo,' I replied. 'What the hell is Vindaloo?' they responded, again in harmony. I tried to explain before Keith turned and snarled, 'Let's show them what Vindaloo is,' before clapping his hands together and beginning to chant: 'Where the fuck are you from? We are from In-ger-land …' and we all joined in for a raucous version of the anthem – just for them. The girls were serenaded by an intimidating, baying gang of thuggery – comedians, fat blokes, musicians, lairy children, wrestlers and a journalist in an England top. They looked absolutely petrified. Alex remembered: 'I feel a bit bad about that actually. They did look terrified. It was a big mob. I still watch that when I get drunk occasionally.'

Keith was an accomplished actor and I first saw him in the memorable Comic Strip collective, which brought alternative comedy to Channel 4 and helped launch and enhance the careers of Adrian Edmondson, Dawn French, Rik Mayall, Nigel Planer, Peter Richardson, Jennifer Saunders, Robbie Coltrane and Alexei Sayle. It spawned groundbreaking sitcom *The Young Ones*, which I used to be able to quote pretty much verbatim; we all knew that the world records for stuffing marshmallows up one single nostril and for the world's stickiest bogey were both held by Toxteth O'Grady, USA. Keith was also a master of stand-up comedy and would often appear live naked and threw darts at hecklers. One evening he walked to the front of the stage brandishing a mug of instant coffee granules, peed into it, and then necked the lot.

Keith reckoned the success of the surrealist 'Vindaloo' is down to its quintessential Englishness and humour, the same wit and zaniness embraced by writers, poets, comedians and songwriters from dear old Blighty over the centuries.

Alex, Keith and Damien became something of a hedonistic unholy trinity in the 90s, spending much of that period at the Groucho Club in London's Soho, and a considerable slice of their royalties on cocaine and champagne.

But Alex insisted such debauchery was actually the perfect research for his new life as a food and drink guru and that it was all money well spent: 'It was mostly champagne. The Colombian president did write me a letter and

I've made amends for that, that's all in the past. But the champagne part of it – I thought I was just wasting all that money – these may not be the golden days of British music, but these are the golden years of English wine-making. There was no English wine commercially available whatsoever in 1990, but now Britain is making some of the finest sparkling wines in the world. Turns out it was research and a good investment. That's the thing, if you just go out and do stuff and enjoy yourself, get involved, stuff happens.' It's the same point I made earlier about creating your own luck, inserting yourself into the right place at the right time and altering the course of your life.

The Blur guitarist and the painter and sculptor – now Britain's wealthiest living artist with a fortune of more than £600 million – initially met at Goldsmiths College in south-east London.

Alex recalled: 'I lived in a squat at first when I was at college. Central London wasn't all fucking billionaires. I think university education was still good and still free in those days. I started at Goldsmiths in 89 and Graham Coxon was the very first person I saw when I got out of my parents' car. He was getting out of his parents' car. I went there by accident because I fucked up my A-levels. That was my first really big fuck-up. Graham had the room next to me, and he was doing art. I didn't even know Goldsmiths had an art department. But he said, "I've got this crazy guy next to me who just paints spots all day. His name's Damien. He's mad."'

To be seen out and about in the West End, not least in pubs, was an integral part of British youth culture at that time. Bands, models, PRs, agents and journalists were all being signed in pubs – I certainly was, as a journalist and not a model, I might add for the record. I haven't had a CV for decades – nearly all my jobs have been offered to me over a chat, a handshake and a beer in some London hostelry. This is why I love dear old Blighty and could never stomach a move to Dubai or the US. I love being in a pub where I know Charles Dickens or George Orwell once sat, wrote or drank and there are few better places than the British boozer, particularly in wintertime. Our intemperate climate has also played a key role in the nation's disproportionate artistic output; our creatives forced to stay inside and write stories and songs, produce art and fashion, stimulating imaginations and dreams, away from the elements, rather than playing beach volleyball in a pair of budgie smugglers and barbecuing.

Alex added: 'Before I got to the Groucho, it was all happening in pubs. The gigs were in the pub, the meetings were in pubs, and then we were hanging out in pubs with journalists from *Smash Hits* and stuff, playing darts in The Crown on Brewer Street. Football is hand in hand with all this. The Premier League was just starting to kick in because it had been dark days in football with hooliganism and rioting, and obviously music was swinging and fashion was amazing. You had Alexander McQueen, Stella McCartney, fucking supermodels. Yes, the music was fucking brilliant, but that had kind of happened before with The Beatles. I think the big cultural shift of all in the 90s was British art going from something that was just tabloid-shocking and appalled people occasionally – with people like Damien and Tracey and the YBA crowd – to a global phenomenon. And Banksy. Music kept on getting better, but it was art that went supersonic. And the following decade has been about Britain discovering its food and drink credentials. Post-war, for decades, Britain was the land without food. Because of the empire, our eating and drinking habits did really shape the eating and drinking habits of the entire globe. 95 was the year that Damien won the Turner Prize and took British art global and you forget the food was fucking kicking as well. 95 was the year Marco Pierre White became the youngest chef ever to win three Michelin stars and the first British one; and the fucking Ivy and Caprice in London were literally the best restaurants in the world. And how good was fucking the Groucho?'

I thought he might mention the Groucho. They didn't always let journalists like me in, probably because of the nefarious activities that went on inside in those days. But, one Saturday, I went to see Chelsea with Madonna's PR Barbara Charone, now on the club's board, and we bumped into Suggs from Madness. BC went home, but Suggs asked me if I'd like to accompany him into Soho. Who wouldn't want to be given a tour of Britain's, perhaps the world's, most hedonistic square mile by Mr Soho himself?

Complete Madness was the first album I owned and I loved their irresistible anarchic slices of poppy ska, insane videos and sense of buffoonery; perhaps they were a colourful London precursor to the Britpop of Blur and Supergrass in many ways. First stop was The Colony Room Club in Dean Street, a bohemian drinking spot born in

1948 and favoured by bon viveurs like artists Francis Bacon and Lucian Freud, writer Jeffrey Bernard, jazz musician George Melly, David Bowie and, later, the Young British Artists like Damien Hirst and Tracey Emin. We had a couple in there before Suggs slurred: 'We are going to the Groucho.' I began to stumble down the creaky stairs, but Suggs pulled me back, before opening a window, which appeared to lead to a precarious rooftop. We clambered across the tiles and then, one step beyond, was the Groucho's famous second-floor snooker room, its window agape. Quite what the members made of seeing the somewhat refreshed lead singer of Madness and a columnist from *The Sun* leaping into their periphery, I'm not entirely sure, but this was the 90s.

Suggs was one of the big-name guests at Barbara's 50th birthday party not long after. BC is one of the world's leading music PRs, a former Warners director of press and music journalist, and a fierce media gatekeeper for R.E.M., Pet Shop Boys, Rod Stewart and Keith Richards for many decades, along with Madge. We did oodles of memorable work together and she facilitated my exclusive interviews with King of the Lads, Rod, and Queen of Pop, Madonna, on numerous occasions. So I made the cut for one of the hottest industry tickets of the year.

BC, always formidable and, on occasion, brash, had chosen London's Home House for a lavish celebration with fifty hand-plucked guests – including Pet Shop Boys Neil Tennant and Chris Lowe, Peter Buck and Michael Stipe of R.E.M., Chrissie Hynde of The Pretenders, the late, great Andy Fletcher from Depeche Mode – and me.

1996

For such gatherings, it was often customary to organise a spoof *Sun* front page to be made up as a gift for a friend of the paper's special occasion. I produced a unique and bespoke Page One with the headline '50 BC' as a secret pressie and headed to the party, which was being hosted by Barbara's long-time pal Paul Conroy, former head of Virgin, Chrysalis and Stiff Records, where he had himself worked with Madness. I granted him a sneak preview of the offering and he chuckled while scanning the moderately amusing copy which read: 'The world last night celebrated the 50th anniversary of the birth of celebrity public relations. The globe's No1 PR executive notched up her half-century at a glittering West End bash attended by the cream of show business.'

Somewhat ironically, it described Barbara as 'the softly spoken American' and there was a strapline that read: 'Party Special: Pages 2, 3, 4, 5, 6, 7, 8, 9, 10. Bin Laden Found: Page 11.'

Me and the celeb-filled enclave all took a rather deep dive into the complimentary rosé and scran before Paul stood up and delivered a well-observed speech. He then announced to the room that there was a very special gift for Barbara … and asked its provider to come up to present.

Blimey. That was unexpected. I quickly pulled myself together and handed over the framed front page and was then tasked with reading out the words I'd written – to occasional drunken hilarity and the odd mild ripple of celebrity applause – apart from Chrissie who, of course, has always hated *The Sun*. Barbara adored it and the keepsake still adorns her office wall, decades later.

A few minutes after I reclaimed my seat, relieved, I was approached by Michael Stipe, one of the world's leading songwriters and dynamic frontman for what was the greatest band on the planet at one point, R.E.M., a group I had discovered through the sacred pages of *Melody Maker* many years before.

'Hey, Dom, can I just say one thing to you, that was absolute genius,' he offered, shaking my clammy hand and keyboard-gnarled knuckles. 'You had the room in stitches. Hysterical. I just don't know how you write that stuff.'

I looked at him puzzlingly and replied: 'Thank you, Michael. That means a lot coming from someone like you. But it's not exactly "Losing My Religion" is it, mate?'

Barbara's client Madonna had always been a tabloid staple throughout her career, but her British stock rose to arguably its highest point in the 90s when she produced two of her most enduring records with eccentric dance wizard William Orbit – *Ray of Light* and *Music*. When I was first introduced to William, I casually asked how he was and his response was: 'Not too good actually. I've only just been released after being sectioned.' Some opening gambit that.

Madonna soon began dating *Lock, Stock and Two Smoking Barrels* director Guy Ritchie and set up home in London, where the Queen of Pop became an honorary member of the Cool Britannia set. They wed in a Scottish Castle in 2000, which I covered – there had been an information lockdown and details were scant. I recall undertaking twenty-two different television interviews with crews from around the world, shivering outside

Skibo's icy, ancient walls, the broadcasters desperate to fill their bulletins with any old waffle. The couple split eight years later.

In days when record companies had money to torch on lavish press campaigns, Barbara and I flew business class to Los Angeles and slummed it at the Four Seasons Hotel in Beverly Hills to attend a glittering launch party for Madonna's album *Music*. Yes, an album launch party. In LA. Barbara was never one to penny-pinch, especially when Warners were reimbursing, but such an opulent trip just wouldn't happen today as the labels would refuse to sign off such profligacy. They would more likely bung a few dollars to a couple of local influencers to plonk some cringe-worthy pictures on Insta and that would be it and quickly forgotten. How boring.

And the media is poorer for it. Ultimately, that night I managed to land an interview with Madonna and Guy at the party, she resplendent in a torn and plunging T-shirt promoting Guy's new epic, with the rather saucy slogan 'Coming Soon – Snatch'. It was the couple's first night out since Madge – her novel tabloid nickname – had given birth to their son Rocco. As we chatted, she pushed her cleavage up towards my face and declared: 'I'm still breast-feeding, can't you tell?' That was the front-page headline and picture in the bag then.

She was gushing and very emotional about her newborn boy, who had been delivered the previous month, and told me: 'It's just wonderful to fit into my trousers again, although this shirt is a little tight. It's like I'm celebrating two releases tonight – Rocco and my new album. It's a very odd feeling being out on the town again while he's at home sleeping. I need to cuddle him.' My eldest son ended up going to college with him many years later.

Other guests at the party included testicle-squeezing footballer-turned-actor Vinnie Jones, Hollywood's Vince Vaughn and Stephen Dorff, songstresses Sheryl Crow and Macy Gray, plus model Kelly Brook, who was on the front pages regularly at that time.

With prescient foresight, obsessive footie fan Barbara had organised a baby-sized Chelsea shirt with Rocco emblazoned on its back as a gift. When I saw this, I kicked myself, wishing I'd dreamed up such a wheeze but then quickly asked her: 'Can I give that kit to them? This will make a great picture and story.' And so this immaculate conception came to pass. And some memorable front-page pictures were captured that night. Madonna was delighted – she had shown a softer side talking about motherhood and one of her best albums to date was being discussed in Britain's bestselling paper. Barbara's client was on the front page, so she was happy too. Guy Ritchie was delighted his film was being promoted to a populist audience, which would go on to devour it. I was living it up, Hollywood-style, with a world exclusive interview in my lap – and Warners had their money's worth. That's how the entertainment and media ecosystem functioned back then. Simples.

The previous March, in a significant, landmark moment for *The Sun*, I had broken the exclusive that Madonna was pregnant with her second child. I received a nod about the news on a Monday morning and was advised that a formal announcement was going to be made later that day, when America woke up, meaning that by the time the next day's paper had been printed the world would already know and the exclusive would be dead. So, with agreement from Madonna's camp, I broke the revelation on *The Sun*'s fledgling website, a strategy the company had never employed up until that point. The story dropped at 2.40pm and, within minutes, was followed up around the world on TV and radio stations and other websites, with *The Sun* credited. These days, of course, this is commonplace and it sounds archaically old-fashioned to say so, but this was an historic media moment and provided a glimpse of, and insight into, the growing power, speed and global influence of digital publishing. There had actually been pushback from senior figures on the newspaper about this tactic, with some claiming it would be madness to allow an exclusive to be published on a free website, cannibalising the print product's sales. In retrospect, and in light of current newspaper circulation figures, perhaps they had a point, but it was brave and innovative and, at 5.11pm, an announcement came from Warners confirming *The Sun*'s inaugural global digital exclusive.

In the 1970s and 80s one of the jobs to have in journalism was royal correspondent. Expenses-paid trips around the world as part of the regal press pack and front pages on a weekly basis, minimum. But, as the 90s dawned, the celebrity gossip columnist role had become highly coveted as the public's appetite for news from the business of show became insatiable. *The Sun*'s Bizarre column first launched on 17 May 1982, fronted by John Blake, who would go on to edit the *Sunday People* and run his own publishing empire. Journalists who followed him included LBC's Nick Ferrari, Martin Dunn, who would edit the *New York Post*, future *Mirror* Editor Piers Morgan, *News of the World*'s Andy Coulson, *Sun* columnists Jane Moore of *Loose Women* fame and Garry Bushell plus, on the *The Mirror*, Rick Sky and Matthew Wright. They were quasi-celebrities themselves, their bylines starting to feature more and more frequently in the red tops.

Increasingly, it was becoming evident that splashing certain celebrities on the front page would be circulation Viagra, with paranoid, stressed and job-security-conscious editors developing a hard-on for such content. From Gazza to Kylie, Take That, Madonna, Liam and Noel, then the Spice Girls, Robbie, Britney and, of course, Posh and Becks – the moment when football and entertainment fused at a higher level. Generally, these were individuals for whom just a first name or nickname would suffice. This was a pre-internet era, without any access to the wealth of data and analytics of how certain stories would perform and interest the public. But when the print circulation figures came through the day after publication, they would usually indicate that tales about celebrities and sports stars, particularly footballers, their transfers and dalliances, prompted sales uplifts for the paper, so the daily beast would have to be fed.

The Beckhams were a journalist's dream later that decade, as their coupling was greater than the sum of its parts, sparking a hunger for information and ticking the football and celebrity boxes in one swoop, creating a curiosity in their relationship and sex life that is still prevalent today.

In their bygone print editions, *Daily Mail* columnists like Nigel Dempster would haughtily inform one that Lady Smythe-Montague had regretfully passed away in Kensington, aged 97, when most of us never even knew she had been alive.

As the 90s wore on, the *Mail* and, in turn, the broadsheet titles, appeared to cotton on, making room for growing celebrity column inches, albeit focusing more on names like Joanna Lumley, Mick Jagger, Kate Winslet, Gwyneth Paltrow and the like. But as the internet took hold and with instant data at publishers' fingertips, the secret was out – showbiz content did the numbers and still does. The *Mail* continues to flood its online version with celebrity frivolity and their sidebar of shame is something of a supposed guilty pleasure for millions around the world every day. It is a digitalised red-top tabloid under a mid-market moniker.

This, in turn, has prompted huge growth in the UK celebrity public relations industry, a personal publicist the must-have accessory for any rising star. In the 90s and beyond, many global mega-names didn't have specific PR representation in Britain and that became a dangerous game to play. But many Hollywood agents viewed the British media with disdain; some refused to even engage or communicate with journalists like me.

But as online UK media juggernauts like the *Mail* and *The Sun* exploded, building some of the most-read digital news platforms on the planet, many A-listers were caught cold, their representatives having naively failed to develop relationships with journalists here. The last time I looked, *The Sun* had 55.4 million monthly digital visitors, with the *Mail* managing an astonishing 238.8 million. First in the global rankings of English-language news websites is nytimes.com with 657.3 million, followed by, at time of writing, the licence fee-funded BBC, pulling in 550.6 million each month.

A number of Hollywood über-names have seen their reputations tarnished globally within minutes online, courtesy of the UK media, illustrating the enduring power and influence of the British press. As an advisor, I have worked with a number of US-based A-listers, who now realise they need media expertise and some degree of control here, to help protect their brands around the world.

On some days in the mid-90s, *The Sun* was shifting almost five million copies, which is why politicians, the music and entertainment business, and their publicists, were somewhat keen to tap into that colossal audience, which equated to around 12 million readers, with copies being shared around homes, offices, vans and building sites.

In many ways, the music industry has cyclically returned to the days of big, bankable A-list stars, the Hollywood model, with less emphasis on bands. It certainly reduces risk, focusing on a smaller number of sure-fire big-hitters like Taylor Swift, Ariana Grande, Dua Lipa and Harry Styles, the starlets of their generation. It's more expensive and time-consuming to take a chance on a load of hirsute-bottomed blokes with a phalanx of valuable guitars and even more expensive drug habits. In fact, in the UK, the only rock band to have a number one single this decade are The Beatles with 'Now and Then'.

Blur's Alex James reflected on the death of the group at the expense of a new wave of Doris Days and Marilyn Monroes: 'Big works, medium doesn't work and small, as sure as shit, doesn't work. It feels like it's more corporately controlled. You could get away with being quite badly behaved and you couldn't get away with being rude like that any more and being drunk; you've got to work too hard. There's a brilliant clip of Noel Gallagher on the radio where he's going, "Briefly in the 90s, it was Blur, Pulp, Oasis, Primal Scream, all pissed on a fucking Tuesday, out of control." And the music industry doesn't like it when everyone's pissed on a Tuesday. They want to tell Harry Styles what dress to wear, what songs to sing and when to go home.'

These hedonistic moments in the 90s music industry were mirrored in other creative industries; the birth of the Young British Art movement can be traced back to 1988, when its notorious leader Damien Hirst organised the exhibition Freeze. He was still a student at Goldsmiths College of Art, where he had, of course, met half of what would become Blur. Freeze included the work of fellow Goldsmiths students, who also became celebrated Brit artists, such as Sarah Lucas, Angus Fairhurst and Michael Landy. Many works were snapped up by Charles Saatchi, one of the UK's most prolific art collectors, who had spotted a new domestic trend, which he sensed could go global.

Saatchi would also go on to buy the controversial 1995 painting *Myra* by Marcus Harvey, a reproduction of Moors murderer Myra Hindley's police mugshot made with casts of a child's hand. It caused huge consternation in the, particularly tabloid, media and brought Young British Art to the red-top news pages; controversy sells art as much as it sells records and newspapers. It is now owned by Hirst. A voracious media and the movements of the 90s frenziedly fed off one another, like one of Hirst's hungry sharks.

There is little that links the artists in style, but they are united by rebellion and nonconformity, whether that be the preservation of animal corpses in the case of Hirst, the use of old medical objects with Christine Borland, Cornelia Parker's steamroller-crushed objects or Tracey Emin showcasing her messy bed as art.

The acronym YBA itself was coined in 1996 by *Art Monthly* magazine; it became compelling branding for an entrepreneurial, worldwide movement and sent art prices rocketing.

Hirst was, of course, awarded the Turner Prize for his infamous sculpture *Mother and Child (Divided)* – a floor-based installation containing a bisected cow and calf preserved in formaldehyde within four glass-walled tanks, showcasing the animals' internal structures. Conservative Cabinet Minister and then-*Sun* columnist Norman Tebbit would write: 'Have they gone stark raving mad? The works of the "artist" are lumps of dead animals. There are thousands of young artists who didn't get a look in, presumably because their work was too attractive to sane people. Modern art experts never learn.' Of course, his rant would have been much improved if he had said 'shark-raving mad' instead.

1996

Bowie and U2 producer Brian Eno presented Hirst with a cheque for £20,000, which he was unable to locate the following day. The artist had forgotten that he had, in fact, put the money behind the bar at the Groucho and blew the lot in one mighty sesh with The Clash's Joe Strummer and Alex James. Again, the genius and stupidity of the 90s summed up in one incident.

Alex recalled: 'No one batted an eyelid: after all, we were the guys who paid the pianist £500 just to play "Wichita Lineman" for an hour while we attempted to ride bicycles up and down the club's main staircase.'

On accepting the award, Hirst had told the audience: 'It's amazing what you can do with an E in A-level art, a twisted imagination and a chainsaw.'

During the Turner Prize exhibition at London's Tate Gallery, many visitors were outraged. One letter complained: 'How anyone can consider a stuffed cow as art must lie even beyond the most illiterate mind. I fear you have smeared the great name of Turner with this waste of space,' while another wrote: 'My sixteen-year-old daughter was at the Tate two weeks ago, as part of her A-level Art course, and, having seen this particular exhibit, has suffered nightmares, poor sleeping and cannot eat beef as it makes her feel sick.'

One critic, Julian Spalding, penned a particularly vitriolic review in *The Independent* and pronounced the work as worthless and with no artistic content. I'll bet that really rankled with Hirst as he went to Coutts to bank his latest £10 million cheque.

But this radical art movement was attracting media attention in places that didn't usually write about such highfalutin subjects, in the same way that the controversies around Oasis saw them jettisoned from the inner pages of the *NME* to the front of the tabloids. Like the Gallaghers, Hirst shared a bedroom with his brother in a violent area of a northern city, in his case Leeds, and fell into a life of burglary, sniffing glue and bingeing on cider aged 12. Similarly, Noel was expelled from school for throwing flour on a teacher and received six months' probation for robbing a corner shop, aged 14. It was during that probationary period that he taught himself to play guitar. And Liam has admitted to stealing clothes, mountain bikes and lawnmowers from Mancunian gardens and selling them to buy drugs.

Hirst would later talk about the importance of sculpture and how it can become embedded in ordinary people's lives, as meeting places outside football stadia or in town centres. But when he first sold his shark in formaldehyde for £50,000 it was considered preposterous. I recall *The Sun*'s memorable headline was: '£50,000 for fish without chips'.

The Physical Impossibility of Death in the Mind of Someone Living features a preserved tiger shark submerged in formalin in a glass-panelled case. Saatchi (him again) sold it in 2004 to collector Steven A. Cohen for an undisclosed amount believed to be around £10 million. Author Don Thompson would go on to write a book entitled *The $12 Million Stuffed Shark: The Curious Economics of Contemporary Art*.

Like Tebbit, many of the elder statesmen and women in *The Sun*'s newsroom were unable to fathom the power of this punk art movement. But witnessing that shark close-up in the flesh was mind-blowingly unforgettable. I remember arguing with ageing executives and editors over the outrage, with many falling into clichéd headlines such as, 'But is it art?' The country's musicians, fashion designers, filmmakers, writers and artists were kicking over establishment tables and forging new ground, with many of our elders finding that troubling.

Drugs and alcohol have always been front and centre in many artists' lives. Vincent van Gogh penned a letter to his brother in March 1889, addressing concerns about his lifestyle and that 'instead of eating enough and at regular times, I kept myself going on coffee and alcohol,' claiming it was necessary for his work. 'I admit all that, but all the same it is true that to attain the high yellow note that I attained last summer, I really had to be pretty well keyed up.'

Hirst owns five originals by his hero Francis Bacon, an artist who would later proclaim that he had been 'drunk since the age of 15'. Bacon died in 1992 and would binge in Soho establishments every afternoon. He became a founder member of the infamous and aforementioned Colony Room Club in 1948, where a blitzed Freud and Frank Auerbach could often be located.

Hirst's signature butterflies would feature in his thought-provoking exhibition *In and Out of Love*. Perhaps as a metaphor for his own drunkenness at that time, rotting fruits placed on a table render the majestic winged creatures inebriated, trapped and unable to fly. The artist said of the piece: 'A butterfly gives us hope because it looks so alive even when it is dead.'

Talking of his idol, Hirst admitted he initially tried to emulate Bacon's affinity for alcohol and would sometimes turn up at openings steaming drunk, his suit covered in dirt from falling over in the street. Hirst had a monstrous reputation but gave up booze and drugs in 2006. I met him backstage at the Royal Albert Hall before a Kasabian Teenage Cancer Trust gig I was at with my young son, who had developed something of an obsession with Hirst's spot paintings. Hirst was charming and gracious, grabbing a nearby poster and drawing a shark on it along with his signature; we chatted until the band were about to come on. He insisted I provide him with our home address as he was interested in my son's knowledge of art and wanted to send him something. I told him not to worry as the show was about to begin. But in the same room afterwards, Hirst made a beeline for us and demanded our details once more, which I scribbled on the back of a crumpled receipt, thinking no more of it. Several weeks later, an Addison Lee courier van turned up at home with a huge package that contained a signed and shark-scribbled framed lithograph of his diamond-encrusted *For the Love of God* artwork and half a dozen Tate Modern T-shirts.

I had reminded him we'd met previously at the World Cup in France. 'I must have been with Keith if it was football,' he chuckled.

That French tournament in 1998 was emblematic and proof of the cultural evolution and revolution that was now upon us, one that had permeated the mainstream like never before. With Keith Allen, Alex James and Damien

Hirst's 'Vindaloo' echoing around the boozers of In-ger-land, Radio 1 chose to broadcast live ahead of the domestic teams' games with DJs Zoe Ball, Kevin Greening and Simon Mayo all there. And they took me along for the ride. What a beano that was. Again, file under 'wouldn't happen today due to budgetary carnage'. Zoe had halted a decline in listening figures following Chris Evans's sacking the previous year. The BBC had initially replaced Evans with northern duo Mark and Lard, but they only lasted seven months, with Mark Radcliffe revealing that the Radio 1 controller Andy Parfitt had admitted that the last thing people want to hear at 6.30am is two northern blokes shouting at each other.

Ahead of the opening England game against Tunisia in the searing Monday lunchtime heat of Marseille's gleaming Stade Vélodrome, trouble was afoot. And, almost inevitably, after that 2–0 victory, courtesy of Alan Shearer and Paul Scholes, we were ushered past an estate of high-rise tower blocks, whence hails of beer bottles were lobbed at those of us in red, white and blue. As we ran for our lives, I spotted two wide-eyed gentlemen beside us, one of whom was gesticulating and screaming 'Let's 'ave it' at some volume. On closer examination, I realised we were suddenly in the riotous company of Damien Hirst and Keith Allen, who invited me and the missus to join them at their hotel, where we celebrated an England victory in style, before getting the hell out of Marseille. At least thirty-two people were injured during three days of rioting and violence there. A similar scenario would unfold during my second visit to the city for the Euro 2016 game between

Russia and England when, once again, it all kicked off. I won't be heading back there en vitesse.

Before Scotland's opening game against Brazil in Paris, I joined the Radio 1 team at a café bar, close to the Stade de France where the morning shows were being broadcast live. Catatonia were at their creative highpoint and singer Cerys Matthews was with us to perform an acoustic session. Afterwards, we spent the morning sitting outside the boozer, where I watched Cerys expertly put away five pints of high-strength French lager before midday. Mon dieu! Zut alors! And Sacré bleu, indeed!

Cerys, Keith Allen and Damien Hirst's presence at the tournament, alongside BBC Radio 1's superstar DJs and an entertainment journalist like myself, was evidence of this growing intersection of British music, art, football and media. Prince Charles and a young Harry would also attend the England vs Columbia game in Lens and Mick Jagger was at the Argentina clash later, when a petulant David Beckham was sent off. After the incident, *The Mirror*'s front page would scream '10 Heroic Lions, One Stupid Boy', an example of the brutal treatment Becks received, and a reminder of the intensity of media scrutiny and public opinion that now engulfed our beautiful game and its contemporary poster boys.

The 1996 'Three Lions' anthem, written by indie band The Lightning Seeds and comedians David Baddiel and Frank Skinner, still echoes around England football stadia today was a fun take on England's failures. It was less absurd than 'Vindaloo' but still captured the spirit of the time.

1996

Good humour and silliness are such important facets of the British psyche and are key to some of the nation's most memorable moments in art, television, film, music literature and media, as I have just demonstrated. It is the ability to see hope and humour even at the most troubling times. I remember the warm spring day after a particularly punishing, tax-heavy budget, I went with the front-page headline 'At Least It's Sunny'. It is the same sentiment as 'Always Look on the Bright Side of Life' or 'Keep Calm and Carry On', a very British outlook, perhaps forged through the stoicism of living through two world wars. This is something which must not be lost, but I fear that vital quality and attitude is fading among a more serious and risk-averse younger generation, perhaps afraid of making risqué observations for fear of being cancelled online.

We see this in politics and sport too. Over-media-trained prominent figures undertake banal interviews and rarely say anything of interest, or with any panache and wit, unlike an unvarnished 90s Prescott or Gazza.

And yet, the emerging mid-90s success and glamour around the England football team, and its fusion with the arts and media, indicated the nation had taken a creative stride forward, a culture clash that would not have ensued at any previous World Cup tournament. Its seeds had been sown initially in 1990's Italy, then on home soil in 1996, when football *almost* came home, England agonisingly close to ending thirty years of hurt.

Thus, it is to the crumbling Twin Towers of Wemberlee we now head to give 90s football a thorough dissection, one of which Hirst himself would be bloodily proud.

My Top Ten Brilliant British TV Shows Born in the 90s

1. ***TFI Friday:*** Launched in 1996 on Channel 4, Chris Evans's must-watch controversial riot of music, chat and silliness ran until 2000. The series encapsulated the 90s, not least its theme tune from Ocean Colour Scene.
2. ***The Royle Family:*** The greatest sitcom of the 90s, launching in 1998, and confirming the late Caroline Aherne as one of Britain's comic greats. It was an expertly pitched BBC showcase of life on a Manchester council estate, with uber-slob Jim Royle masterfully played by Ricky Tomlinson. The Oasis theme was the icing on a perfect cake.
3. ***The Word:*** *TFI* precursor, running on C4 from 1990 until 1995, with hosts including Terry Christian, comedian Mark Lamarr, Dani Behr and Katie Puckrik, *The Word* lays claim to the first TV appearances from Nirvana and Oasis. Its production and camerawork were nuts and left behind in the 90s.
4. ***The Big Breakfast:*** Channel 4 and Chris Evans again, who presented the anarchic early morning essential alongside Gaby Roslin from 1992. Paula Yates conducted seductive interviews from a bed, most notably with squeeze Michael Hutchence. An invitation to rise early.
5. ***Soccer AM:*** Doesn't date well but this was the soundtrack of hungover Saturday mornings before

going to the match. Ran on Sky from 1994 until 2023 and glory day hosts were Tim Lovejoy and Helen Chamberlain. Wacky takes on modern football, fab music and guests, it served a daring weekend dollop of lairy laddishness.

6. **Father Ted:** Razor-sharp comedy writing at its finest, this side-splitting look at the life of calamitous co-habiting Irish priests launched the careers of Ardal O'Hanlon and Graham Norton. I once interviewed Cher and she quoted it verbatim. Feckin' genius.

7. **Later ... with Jools Holland:** This superlative BBC music television brilliance launched in 1992 with the lovable Squeeze keyboardist at the helm. R.E.M, The Verve, Oasis with strings, Radiohead, Johnny Cash, Pulp, Bowie and Faithless were among some of the many legendary performances.

8. **The Mrs Merton Show:** Spoof BBC talk show with Caroline Aherne that hit screens in 1993 and showcased the host's acid wit. Memorably asked Debbie McGee, wife of magician Paul Daniels: 'So, what first attracted you to the millionaire Paul Daniels?' and controversial comedian Bernard Manning: 'Who do you vote for now Hitler's dead?'

9. **I'm Alan Partridge:** Steve Coogan's nauseous alter-ego first featured on BBC Radio 4 in 1991, but the inept and tactless broadcaster moved to television in 1994 on *The Day Today*. Partridge led his own sitcom from 1997 and is eminently quotable; he's an enduring and odious character still on screens today, but not a patch on his 90s heyday.

BLUR

10. ***Men Behaving Badly:*** Launched on ITV in 1992 but moved to BBC in 1994 as laddism became the must-have media commodity. Martin Clunes and Neil Morrissey are bawdy, boozy, burping and boob-obsessed 90s lads. The series ran until 1998 but hasn't dated well either.

CHAPTER 4
Euro 96

Gazza's toothbrush, Robbie Fowler's bottom and the trifling matter of a domestic football tournament

The British media and public revel in a spot of drunken silliness and buffoonery from our rock stars, artists and writers – but not when it concerns our sportsmen.

The squad preparations for, and indeed behaviour around, England's Euro 96 Championships were, let's just say, far from perfect.

Herewith, the charge sheet.

An oblivious Paul Gascoigne brushing his Geordie gnashers after teammate Robbie Fowler had secretly inserted the Spurs star's toothbrush up his backside. Diminutive midfielder Dennis Wise safely stowed and asleep in an overhead aeroplane luggage locker and then Gazza punched in the face by an air steward after he patted his bum.

That's not to mention the infamous drink-soaked night out in the dentist's chair in Hong Kong, and an alleged £5,000-worth of smashed up televisions and damage aboard a Cathay Pacific flight back to In-ger-land after Liverpool stars Jamie Redknapp and Fowler apparently shaved off Gascoigne's eyebrows as he slept – all just weeks before the tournament was to begin on home soil.

EURO 96

Many had been against the idea of the England squad jetting to the Far East in May that year, but manager Terry Venables wanted to take the pressure off himself and his players out of the media glare, telling doubters: 'We need to get away.'

Maverick Gazza set the tone for the trip on the thirteen-hour journey out, touching a flight attendant's bottom to grab his attention – and another beer. The steward delivered a powerful right hook into the side of his stunned babyface.

Former BBC journalist-turned-Football Association Executive Director David Davies has something of a unique perspective on the evolution of English football during the 1990s – as both an insider and outsider. He was embedded with the England team at Italia 90, in his capacity as a BBC TV news reporter, and later served in a variety of senior roles at the FA, until his retirement in 2006. These included director of communications and public affairs, head of football affairs, director of international strategy and executive director. He worked extensively in the preparation of Euro 96 and had an extremely close relationship with Venables and accompanied him on the shameful (but lucrative) trip although against the idea. On the pitch, however, the team beat China 3–0 and then headed to Hong Kong where they scraped a 1–0 against a Select XI. Off it – and with many out of it – England took a pummelling. From the fans. The media. Politicians. And the suits at the FA.

When Venables permitted the team a night out after the victories and before the arduous flight back to Blighty the next day, Davies asked: 'Are you sure, Terry?' 'They've earned it,' he replied.

Many of the players – and Venables' number two Bryan Robson, himself partial to the odd bevvy – ended up in a notoriously wild nightspot called the China Jump, which housed an old dentist's chair, upon which thirsty revellers would be drenched with spirits straight from the bottle.

Needless to say, Gazza dived in and a barman captured the moment for posterity – and a few quid. The midfielder and Robbie Fowler threw drinks at one another with Gascoigne thinking little of it until his family called and asked him: 'Fucking hell, have you seen the papers?' Striker Alan Shearer said he was trying to keep a low profile in the club because he knew the team's presence there could be controversial and admitted he had an inkling there may be uproar as he watched Fowler, Steve McManaman and Gazza ripping each other's shirts off in public.

And, indeed, an uproar there was. The pictures of Gascoigne were sold to *The Sun*, which ran them under the damning headline 'DISGRACEFOOL' alongside a 'You the Jury' telephone vote line, which asked readers whether Gazza should be dropped from the squad.

The furious copy raged: 'This is the photo that shows shamed Paul Gascoigne "in training" for the biggest soccer tournament in England since 1966.

'Grinning drunkenly, his shirt torn to shreds and a beer bottle in his hand, Gazza looks more like a soccer yob than a £20,000-a-week superstar. The oaf knocked back cocktail after cocktail in a Hong Kong club after he led a huge binge with England teammates including Teddy Sheringham and Steve McManaman.'

It added: 'The only thing that we'll win is the Men Behaving Badly trophy for drunken also-rans.' Admittedly, this was the era of *Loaded* magazine and laddism, with some accused of misogyny – there were evidently ugly sides to the 90s, on television and radio and sometimes in the pages of magazines and the tabloids. To that end, *Men Behaving Badly* was the sitcom that averaged 13 million viewers, starring Martin Clunes and Neil Morrissey. (Increasingly, their real lives seemed to mirror those of their on-screen creations. They'd often bowl around town together, and I once saw the chortling cohort spilling out of a toilet cubicle together at some awards do at the Albert Hall.)

The squad's egregious behaviour would only get worse in the Cathay Pacific Marco Polo executive upper-deck section on flight CX251 back to London. Gascoigne fell asleep and a giggling Redknapp and Fowler shaved off his eyebrows.

But the players agree that the public and media reaction to the misbehaviour, and the way in which Venables handled the furore, galvanised the team and brought them close together. David Davies revealed that it was decided that the team would accept collective responsibility for the misdemeanours to try and move the story on and shift focus to the tournament itself. He told me: 'The dentist's chair incident was a low point and Cathay Pacific were furious at the damage to the plane on the journey home. Dennis Wise allegedly was discovered in an overhead locker. Politicians got involved. Gazza was on the phone to me in tears. He was so upset, asking what was going on, worried he would be out of the team. He loved playing for Terry Venables. We came up with a strategy of taking collective responsibility, but not all the players liked that because it made them all look guilty and some of them had nothing to do with it.'

The media calmed and the players kept their heads down, and then the tournament was upon us, another crucial ingredient in the wildest summer of our lives. I'd chronicled Oasis at Maine Road just weeks earlier and the Euros would occupy me for the month of June, before documenting Knebworth five weeks after that. It feels now as if every day of that glorious summer was sun-drenched, the frenzied country abuzz. I'd even managed to snaffle tickets for the quarter- and semi-final games. Life then was a continual haze of punishingly long office days, football, pubs and clubs in Soho, Islington, Primrose Hill, Hampstead and beyond, with mates who went under names like Tight T-Shirt Tim, Debbie Double D, Muscles, Army Mark, Goatee Jon, Mad Mark the Dentist, Billy the Barman and Wonderbra Mitch. My favourite nickname, though, was reserved for an employee saddled with a lower-than-average IQ and blissfully unaware she was secretly referred to as Albert. As in Einstein. Genius.

Every boozer seemed to have a jukebox back then and we would feed those music-filled machines with our hard-earned shrapnel, casting ourselves as the evening's tastemakers. It was a non-stop avalanche of 'Don't Look

Back in Anger', 'Born Slippy', 'Wonderwall', 'Girls & Boys', 'Firestarter', 'Champagne Supernova', 'Parklife', 'Some Might Say'. And, of course, 'Three Lions'. A certain euphoria was in the air. Frequent singalongs at closing time, embraces with strangers in the streets after watching matches on the big screen really were a thing. No mobile phones to stare at or be stolen from one's hand, zilch social media, didn't know anyone with ADHD. Sure, there was the brooding spectre of the IRA, but that would soon pass. London felt safe and secure and the world a better place. You could safely wild swim in rivers then too.

I'm no sports writer so don't plan to explore all the details and intricacies of England's tactics, set-piece routines and formations. They started the tournament off slowly against a stubborn Swiss – then exploded against Scotland. These two sides first faced each other in 1872 in the world's first international football fixture and it's always something of a rivalrous game of grudgery. Gazza achieved redemption with his career-best goal, after lobbing the ball over stumbling Scot Colin Hendry. The celebration couldn't have been scripted any better – Gascoigne slid on to his back, stretched out both arms, opened his mouth, with Shearer and Sheringham, alongside McManaman and Redknapp, squirting a water bottle into his foaming gob. A dentist's chair re-enactment. The famous Wembley roar. The team's elation and a national release of tension. Ballboys and photographers celebrating and the front rooms, pubs and sun-kissed streets of England's green and pleasant land exploding into an orgasm of jubilation, the flag of St George proudly draped

1996

everywhere you looked – and with nothing but a celebratory association.

Sorry, Scottish readers, but this was one of the most indelible moments in England's sporting history, football for the gods in front of 75,000 homeland supporters – and against the auld enemy. An editorial in the *Daily Mirror* later read: 'Mr Paul Gascoigne: An Apology'.

Just as the Brit Awards four months earlier had been the coronation for Cool Britannia and Britpop, themselves many years in the making, so Euro 96 became something of a crowning glory for sexy English football and the shiny new Premier League, formed four years earlier. The Turin grass stained with Gazza's streaming tears, the anger at failing to qualify for the World Cup in 1994, the new all-seater stadia installed across the nation and the plans for a new, gleaming Wembley had all led to this moment. Gazza's drunken stupidity in the run-up to the tournament was forgiven and his moment of genius is what is saluted and celebrated today. Artistry and flair born out of idiocy and absurdity – just like Vindaloonies Alex, Keith and Damien on the terraces dressed in women's lingerie.

Needless to say, the team's celebrations that evening would reach new levels of immaturity. As was his wont, Venables permitted Peronis to be polished off with the team back cocooned in their Burnham Beeches Hotel in the Buckinghamshire countryside. Gareth Southgate, Stuart Pearce, Teddy Sheringham and Tony Adams chose to relax and play Scrabble together. But Gascoigne, whom previous England boss Bobby Robson had branded 'daft as a brush', decided to hide in a darkened kitchen before Scouse striker Robbie Fowler entered; as he did so, he poured a huge, industrial-sized vat of tomato ketchup over him.

Fowler headed to bed. The next morning, as he brushed his teeth, Gazza was pondering and worried about his teammate's reaction over breakfast. He apologised and Fowler said it wasn't a problem before pulling out a, presumably Polaroid, photograph of Gascoigne's toothbrush up his own backside.

During and after his career Fowler, who made twenty-six appearances for England between 1996 and 2002, assembled a portfolio of more than a hundred properties in Britain's north-west, building up an estimated fortune of £38 million. *The Observer* called him the 'richest sportsman living in Britain'. Amazingly, in 1999, police investigated one of the striker's goal celebrations, when he pretended to snort the pitch's white line after converting a penalty in a 3–2 win over Everton. Paul Oakenfold said he would regularly see Fowler, McManaman, Jamie Carragher, Steven Gerrard and other Liverpool faces when he had a residency at the city's superclub, Cream, once again emphasising the blurring lines between football, music, dance culture and fashion.

Pranksters Fowler and Gazza's frivolities did not seem to hinder team spirit nor performance. The rapturous country's exhilaration would reach even more frenzied heights the following Tuesday, when England crushed the beautiful artistry of a fancied Holland team in a high-tempo 4–1 skirmish. Our SAS strike force – Shearer and Sheringham – nabbed two goals each and North London's hostelries and streets thronged with dizzy and disbelieving fans, with repeated, collective refrains of 'Football's coming home' and 'Sooooo, Sally can wait' booming around our high streets late into the night. These were magical moments and ones to savour – and then capture in the pages of Britain's newspapers, which had hot-wired themselves into the mood of their nation.

Shearer declared England's performance as the greatest of modern times, while BBC commentator Barry Davies hailed the pre-eminence of England that night: 'I repeated the exact words I had used after Diego Maradona's second goal against England in 86 – "you have to say that's magnificent" and it was true. It was magnificent.' One evening, years later, I was walking to an Arsenal game and was close to the looming stadium when a flustered man begged me for directions to the ground. I recognised the warmth of his familiar tones. It was Barry Davies, no less. You'd have thought he would have known the way by then; the structure was rather hard to miss.

England were in the quarter-finals against Spain on Saturday 22 June. After a Friday night of clubbing and pubbing, I traipsed, wearily I admit, to Wembley. The game was a 0–0 stalemate and is remembered for the penalty shoot-out, when Stuart Pearce prevailed, clenched fists, eyes bulging and face a shade of crimson, exorcising the six years of pain and tension that had wracked him since his miss at Italia 90. It was the first time I had heard 'Three Lions' sung in unison by that Wembley choir and it was truly something of goosebump gorgeousness. Afterwards, we celebrated a semi-final against the Germans alongside an inebriated Chris Evans, who leapt about with a bloke dressed up in a Carlsberg elephant costume.

Venables gave the players a day off and punk-obsessive Stuart Pearce approached his manager near the hotel's reception desk and enquired: 'Boss, mind if I pop into town this afternoon to see a concert? I'll be back by 9pm. Gareth wants to come too.' Venables looked troubled but wanted to reward Pearce and Southgate for their heroics the previous day. 'OK. One condition. I want someone from the FA to go with you to keep an eye on things.' And so the dynamic duo would be chaperoned by the FA's media relations chief Steve Double, with whom I had worked at the *Sunday Mirror* several years previously. The trio would join us and 30,000 others, including Liam, Patsy, Kate Moss and Johnny Depp, in London's Finsbury Park for a hotly anticipated Sex Pistols reunion show, supported by Iggy Pop and Skunk Anansie. It was Southgate's first ever concert.

Never Mind the Bollocks, Here's England's New Heroes. The pair were wildly applauded as they stepped on to the stage to introduce the band, Pearce in his official England Umbro polo shirt and Bambi-eyed Southgate looking flummoxed.

That balmy evening united the world of football, celebrity and music new and old, another hallmark of that summer, in many ways. Ageing punks, worshipped by the snarling voice of Britpop and his glamorous actress partner, alongside Hollywood and catwalk royalty, gathered together in reverence of England's unlikely footballing gods. And that weekend was illustrative of my career and life at that juncture. Late Friday nights in Soho and clubs like Velvet Underground, Hanover Grand, Ministry of Sound, Bagley's, Subterrania and The Cross after a punishing work week, football on a Saturday and gig on a Sunday. As Chris Evans's new pal the elephant might have declared: 'If Carlsberg did weekends …'

But, seventy-two hours later, Southgate would himself be performing in front of his own ecstatic Wembley crowd, nearly three times the size of the Pistols' audience – but, alas, it was us who would feel pretty vacant by the end of that gruelling night. And Britain's press would have a bit of a week too.

In the run-up to the England vs Germany Euro 96 semi-final clash, the *Daily Mirror*'s front-page splash read: 'Achtung Surrender – For You Fritz, ze Euro 96 Championship is Over'. *The Sun* was also criticised for its headline 'Let's Blitz Fritz' (nothing to do with me, I might add), while the *Daily Star* threw down the gauntlet with 'Herr We Go – Bring On the Krauts' and warned 'Watch Out Krauts: England Are Gonna Bomb You to Bits'. Don't mention the war and all that.

The Press Complaints Commission, which monitored accuracy in the press, received more than 300 complaints against the titles, which the commission said 'misjudged the public mood'. Complainants said the offending headlines were in poor taste, while others alleged they breached the code of conduct requiring newspapers to abstain from derogatory references to race, colour, religion and sex.

The Star insisted its jokey coverage was 'in the best tradition of the down-to-earth humour that has been a mainstay of our culture for centuries. They were never malicious.' And *The Sun* claimed its treatment was 'intended to bolster national pride, and was good-natured'. My boss Stuart Higgins was summoned by Channel 4 News, and he proclaimed: '*The Sun* has maintained a jingoistic approach, rather than a xenophobic one.' The *Daily Mirror* published a front-page apology with a photograph of a German player receiving a Harrods food basket from the newspaper, with the headline 'Peas in Our Time'.

It is absorbing, on occasion alarming, to look back at those copies now. Namely, they seem ancient, from a bygone era, which I suppose it was – treatment of such events just wouldn't happen in modern media. When Germany were knocked out of the World Cup in 2018, *The Sun* captured the moment on its splendid front page with the headline: 'Schadenfreude' alongside a dictionary definition of the word, which explained 'Noun (from the German): Pleasure derived from another person's misfortune'. *Wunderbar*.

It was a non-xenophobic but well-judged, witty, intelligent and outstanding headline, hatched from the frustrations of Italia 90 and Euro 96, where we saw England crushed at the Hans, sorry hands, of the Germans. I don't need to go into the details of that harrowing game as I have attempted to erase it from my mental hard drive, but the collective chorus of 'Three Lions' was something positive to behold and gloriously take away from it. Baddiel and Skinner were sitting not far from me and looked overcome. Of course, the Germans would ultimately chant those familiar Albion-penned words as a taunt back to England.

1996

One of German captain Jürgen Klinsmann's prized possessions is a photograph of him receiving the European Championship trophy from the Queen after Germany's 2–1 defeat of the Czech Republic in the final we couldn't stomach. Klinsmann, injured for the semi, watched from the stands and spoke of his awe at the atmosphere and the collective chorus of 'Football's coming home', admitting it gave him chills and that his team would also sing it, even belting it out on their Frankfurt victory parade. The single would end up selling 100,000 copies in Germany alone. Schadenfreude, indeed.

On 23 March 1996, I had penned a story that Ian Broudie from The Lightning Seeds – nominated as best band at the Brit Awards a month earlier but perhaps not the favourites, alongside the rather potent force of Oasis, Blur, Pulp and Radiohead – had been chosen to score the England Euro 96 football anthem with funnymen Baddiel and Skinner, hosts of the *Fantasy Football League* TV show, which was pulling in millions of viewers and some prominent guests. I thought it sounded like a terrible idea.

The comedians would be photographed for the pre-tournament edition of *Loaded* magazine, edited by James Brown, alongside a risqué photoshoot with pouting models in figure-hugging England shirts, which the lads were inevitably attempting to remove. In one shot, Baddiel was snapped pleading on his knees, at the feet of a blonde dressed as a referee, with the caption: 'Baddiel begs to be pulled off at half time.' Fnarr fnarr.

Loaded launched in 1994 with Gary Oldman as its first cover star; it ended up selling 350,000 copies each month.

Inside, its inaugural editorial declared that it was a new magazine dedicated to life, liberty and the pursuit of sex, drink, football and less serious matters. Its manifesto finished by admitting that the publication was for the man who believes he could do anything, if only he wasn't hungover.

It was a quasi-magazine version of Bizarre and *The Sun*, with chutzpah alongside the sparkling writing that is oft overlooked in both titles. I would later be offered editorship of the mag but rejected such overtures. Following Brown's departure, the pioneering publication mutated into a glamour mag with low-rent soap stars on the cover, its groundbreaking journalism fading, after attempting to ape the success of rival title *FHM* and then *Nuts* and *Zoo*. The print version was shuttered in March 2015 after a 21-year run. One edition, from May 1996, featured nightie-clad 22-year old *EastEnders* actress Danniella Westbrook as the cover girl, clutching a tub of Chupa Chups lollies, one between her lips with the headline: 'Suck this'. It was strong stuff.

In this country, when we find ourselves in times of trouble – or joy actually – that beautiful combination of singing and drinking will oft be prominent. At a funeral, we sing and then quaff, at a marriage or christening there are the hymns and then the toasts – it's the same with sport, whether rejoicing or consoling. 'Three Lions' embodies that spirit in many ways, speaking as it does of dreams, hopes and disappointment. It is a unique song with a peculiarly British construct and resonance and, like 'Vindaloo', I don't know that it could have been conceived anywhere else on the planet.

1996

The record roared to number one in June, eventually selling 1.6 million copies and becoming the first song in history to have four different stints at the top spot in UK history. Incidentally, Oasis had seven singles in the top 100 that week. Broadcaster Chris Evans sent his drinking pal Gazza a CD player and a copy of 'Three Lions' to the England hotel, the early-rising midfielder waking up his squad most mornings by blasting the song outside their bedroom doors. My boss Stuart Higgins begged the team to pose for photographs with three real lions he had located, but the stunt was thwarted on safety grounds.

Football songs had been pretty dire until New Order showed up in 1990. England had performed pretty well on the pitch at the previous tournament, with Gary Lineker winning the Golden Boot in Mexico 86, But their soundtrack then was the rather lacklustre 'We've Got the Whole World at Our Feet', which, at the end of the day, ticked all the football song cliché boxes, if you know what I mean, Barry.

David Bloomfield had been at the FA since 1982, beginning as an accounts clerk. He had graduated through to the press office in the run-up to Italy and remembered watching a late-night TV show featuring veterans George Best and Rodney Marsh showing film clips from great matches and their own personal anecdotes. He was drawn to its theme tune, which was credited as 'Music by New Order'. The following day, he telephoned New Order's Factory Records and then spoke with their guru Tony Wilson and offered the band the England football song. Footballers around this era were probably more likely listening to Phil Collins, Lionel Richie or Luther Vandross so it was a bold move.

The group agreed and, so, 'World in Motion' was born, featuring classic New Order synth riffs, said to be leftovers from the *Technique* sessions, a solo rap performed by England and Liverpool winger John Barnes, samples from the 1966 World Cup commentary and lyrics by that bloke again, actor Keith Allen. Football was cool and it even had its own theme tune, written by one of the hippest bands on the planet. It soundtracked the first summer of the new decade and would herald a sense of fun and mischief, a realigning of the rules of the game. An alternative band doing a football song? Unheard of, but a unique coming-together of counter and club culture mixed with footie, a highly significant moment in modern popular culture. All my loves brought together in four minutes and thirty seconds of pop perfection. Keith's working title for the song was something rather different: 'E for England'.

The entwining of musical entertainment and Britain's football industry was never really up there with the Super Bowl though. It's not quite Beyoncé, I know, but there was always a moving rendition of 'Abide with Me' before FA Cup Finals, a tradition that went back to 1927. Yet there has always been an intrinsic link between the two. Since the late 1800s, fans would regularly be treated to marching bands provided by the emergency services, particularly at big games at Wembley. Arsenal were one of the last big clubs to regularly call on the skills of the Metropolitan Police band, who were accompanied on vocals by singing policeman, constable Alex Morgan, for several decades.

They would lap the pitch, the band leader lobbing his baton into the air, with the baying crowd desperate for it to be dropped. Constable Morgan sang for the last game at the Highbury stadium in 2006, before the short skip to the Emirates. His son Patrick told local paper the *Islington Gazette* in 2017 that his father would receive serious abuse, especially as the band never performed music of the day, more likely opera.

My own encounter with the Met Police at Highbury had come a few years before the move. As Bizarre columnist, I had become embroiled in a written dispute with London listings mag *Time Out*, which I always devoured, after a right-on reader berated my young son on its letters page for daring to disturb their liberal luncheon for squawking in the achingly hip restaurant Banner's in Crouch End, North London, where you would often see members of Oasis, Travis and Feeder, or actors like Martin Freeman, Simon Pegg and Cathy Tyson. A blissfully ignorant and licence-conscious waitress once famously declined Bob Dylan's request for a beer there, because he refused to order food following a recording session at Eurythmic Dave Stewart's studio up the road.

When I wrote back to *Time Out* to ask for clarification on what zones of the capital I should avoid for future grub, the magazine was bombarded with responses such as 'Two areas. Inner and Outer London'. Bantz. While enjoying a half-time half at Highbury not long after, I saw a group of hi-vis-clad cops with batons eyeing me suspiciously and pointing over. As they approached, I feared the worst and wished I hadn't forgotten my toothbrush. 'It's Mr Mohan, isn't it?' one boomed in a rather menacing tone. A sheepish yes was followed by a rather large outstretched and gloved rozzer's hand. 'We just wanted to congratulate you on your letter to those idiots at *Time Out*. Well done for standing up against the haters. It made us laugh, we loved it.'

I guess the letters page spat was a taste of things to come, a slice of pre-social media proto-trolling, conducted in a rather more measured and civilised way, through the letters page of an urbane weekly mag. Fortunately, as a high-profile journalist at that time, I didn't have to endure online abuse, only the very occasional heated discussion on the street, terrace or at an event. Perhaps a nasty letter or, later, an email, here and there. Colleagues who succeeded me had it a lot worse. However, I was once threatened by an obsessive fan, weirdly, of *EastEnders* actress Martine McCutcheon, who wrote to me, and then stalked me near the office, claiming he had a gun. The police were alerted and I was given a special emergency number to call, but he backed off. Imagine the indignity of being assassinated by a crazed McCutcheon fan.

Later, I would witness the monumental change in digital discourse and online bullying – some claim it levelled the playing field somewhat, but much of it was violent, threatening and slanderous, overstepping a line and becoming unrecognisable when compared to regulated mainstream media content, which is subject to stringent libel laws and legal scrutiny.

Living in the leafy, leftish North London environs of Highbury Hill in the early 90s, neighbours included designer Katharine Hamnett, Sade, Pet Shop Boy Chris

1996

Lowe and an up-and-coming MP by the name of Anthony Charles Lynton Blair, who resided on the next street. (Let's talk about him in a bit.) Our pokey flat – you could lie in the hallway and stretch a limb into each of the rooms – was also a couple of minutes' walk from Arsenal's stadium and I had begun to secretly cheat on my beloved Bristol City with the Gunners. No membership cards required, we'd just pay £20 cash at the rusting turnstiles. One evening in 1992, and thanks to my boss-to-be Rupert Murdoch, Sky Sports launched their Monday Night Football concept for the newly formed Premier League and clearly felt the fans of Arsenal and Manchester City that night would be seduced by an Americanised experience. At half-time, scantily clad cheerleaders flooded the hallowed turf and a minuscule stage with two keyboards was hastily erected. Out stepped ravey electronic dance act The Shamen, who began to belt out two of their hits to a baffled, and soon-to-be booing, crowd. It was quite mind-boggling and the on-field strains of 'Move Any Mountain' – another Oakenfold production – and 'Ebeneezer Goode' didn't suit our game at all. We weren't in some yank Enormodome, we were sipping Bovril and chewing on a limp Cornish pasty in a very traditional, quintessentially English football ground. The duo were immediately pelted with coins and one of the group's founders Colin Angus described the night akin to performing at their own public execution.

I've always admired terrace wit and the spontaneous humour that spills from the football stands. It reminds me of smart tabloid headline trickery and effrontery at times.

EURO 96

When the Rangers and Scotland goalkeeper Andy Gorham returned to the field after being treated for schizophrenia, he was greeted with the chant: 'There's only two Andy Gorhams'. Immaculately dressed Chelsea boss José Mourinho, known for his fine collection of natty, tailored outfits, smirked as echoes of 'Your coat's from Matalan' emanated from the Stamford Bridge away end. 'He's big, he's red, his feet stick out the bed' was aimed at lofty Liverpool striker Peter Crouch, while buck-toothed Luis Suárez was taunted with 'Your teeth are offside'.

When life wasn't too good at my boyhood club Bristol City, disgruntled fans would point to manager Alan Dicks and chant 'Dicks out', a further example of British gallows humour in tricky times.

In the 90s, I would sometimes blag a press ticket for a Bristol City game and sit with the sports journalists in the press box. Afterwards, we would be ushered into Ashton Gate's bowels, but the stadium which I had once thought was a gleaming sporting cathedral was actually falling down. Embarrassingly, the seating hadn't been updated for decades, it seemed, with rotting wooden panels making an annoying clapping sound when everyone stood up at the same time.

We were served post-match drinks in the gymnasium area, which was shabby and dirty, foam bursting out of rusty equipment and torn mats. It wasn't quite how I had imagined things as a boy. One night, a greying man with a distinctive moustache shuffled towards me with a tray of drinks and offered me a Beck's. I looked him in the eye and thanked him. I knew I recognised that tache from somewhere – 'Are you Clive Whitehead?' I asked disbelievingly. 'I am,' he shot back with a mixture of pride – but also wearing a hint of embarrassment. The most-loved player of my childhood, a man I idolised and wanted to be, had absolutely not retired with a property portfolio, playing golf on the Algarve. He was serving me a warm bottle of beer in a dilapidated, dingy gym on a wet Tuesday night in Bristol.

The facade had crumbled. These lionhearts, whose mythical names had been emblazoned across my precious teenage football programmes, had been chewed up and spewed out before football's great financial revolution. City's most prolific goalscorer at that time, Tom Ritchie, was earning around £400 a week in the top division and ended up working as a postman in Portishead. These heroic men were in the right place at the wrong time. Ritchie's equivalent is now pocketing £60,000 a month in the second-tier Championship and will have few financial worries throughout his insulated life.

Football and its financial model had fulminated in the 90s, its celebrated contemporary superstars thrust from the back pages of the tabloids to those up-front, with *The Sun* leading the charge.

Yes. There was Gazza's krazy ketchup kalamities and Robbie Fowler's wretched revenge, but football was coming home, both on and off that fragrant, green, home-grown grass.

Those intoxicating weeks of the summers of 1990 and 1996 had propelled the country's twinkle-toed athletes to heightened levels of media fame, wealth and scrutiny like none before. This privileged crop certainly would not end up working as postmen and struggling for a living, like the generations before them, in many ways thanks to my boss Murdoch.

And there I was, blessed to be thrust into that chaotic moment to chronicle the unprecedented, accidental, organic, cultural collision with which the nation was obsessed.

In the Wembley stands alongside Liam Gallagher, Baddiel, Skinner and Robbie Williams, I'd stood witness to England's heroic failure, as a journalist and a fan. But I was immediately back on duty and heading for a mysterious midnight press conference with one of the country's most troubled singers, a man who would soon become Britain's biggest solo star.

A First XI of the Most Memorable Football Matches I Attended in the 1990s

1. **England 1 Germany 1 (England lost 6–5 on penalties) – Euro 96 semi-final, 26 June 1996:** Wembley Stadium, London – *Heartbreak but such absorbing drama with one of the greatest atmospheres. Gazza's near-miss still haunts me some nights.*
2. **England 0 Spain 0 (England won 4–2 on penalties) – Euro 96 quarter-final, 22 June 1996:** Wembley Stadium, London – *Hearing 'Three Lions' sung live for the first time in the stadium and witnessing Stuart Pearce's penalty redemption lives long in the memory.*
3. **Bristol City 3 Chelsea 1 – FA Cup Fourth Round, 27 January 1990:** Ashton Gate, Bristol – *The*

achievement of my hometown Bristol City team knocking a club like Chelsea out of the Cup should not be underestimated.

4. **England 2 Tunisia 0 – World Cup France 98 Group Stage, 15 June 1998:** Stade Vélodrome, Marseille – *Cannot believe this England team never won anything. My first ever England World Cup game as I didn't have the money for Italia 90. Blindingly hot and tense day in Marseille and a riot to follow. Scholes and Shearer won it before we were pelted with bottles. Memorable.*

5. **Bristol City 1 Liverpool 1 – FA Cup Third Round, 19 January 1994:** Ashton Gate, Bristol – *Compelling match abandoned due to mysterious floodlight failure. City won the replay at Anfield and manager Graeme Souness was sacked.*

6. **England 2 Colombia 0 – World Cup France 98 Group Stage, 26 June 1998:** Stade Félix-Bollaert, Lens – *Lens was a ghost town due to fears of hooliganism. Indelible free kick from Beckham sealed passage to last 16 after shock defeat to Romania. Argentina and a red card awaited.*

7. **Bristol City 1 Bristol Rovers 1 – Second Division, 15 December 1996:** Ashton Gate, Bristol – *You don't get many Bristol derbies these days but this was particularly volatile. Remembered mainly because of the pitch invasion and fighting at the game's climax. I treated my father – he was horrified.*

8. **Scotland 1 Brazil 2 – World Cup France 98 Group Stage, 10 June 1998:** Stade de France, Paris – *A privilege to be in the presence of Roberto Carlos,*

EURO 96

Cafu, Dunga, Rivaldo and Ronaldo on a balmy Parisian day for this sizzling World Cup opener. A long day after sinking pre-lunch pints with Cerys Matthews.

9. **Arsenal 1 Manchester City 0 – English Premier League, 28 September 1992:** Highbury Stadium, London – *A surreal evening as Sky Sports try to bring some razzmatazz to their Monday Night Football package for the newly formed Premier League. The Shamen perform at half-time with a dancing troupe. Ian Wright can certainly move any mountain – and won it for the Gunners.*

10. **Tottenham Hotspur 3 Manchester City 1 – Premier League, 25 August 1990:** White Hart Lane, London – *Gascoigne and Lineker each score as they are welcomed home after a glorious summer at Italia 90 as Bobby Moore and Terry Venables looked proudly on.*

11. **Everton 1 Manchester United 0 – FA Cup Final, 20 May 1995:** Wembley Stadium, London – *A triumph for the young underdogs. Somehow managed to bullshit my way into the players' lounge afterwards where I stood at the bar with a glum Sir Alex.*

CHAPTER 5

Robbie

The Take That star, heroin and the biggest night of his career

It was the most important moment in Robbie Williams' meteoric career to date.

At one minute past midnight on 27 June 1996, just after England had been dumped out of the Euro 96 championship by Germany – a game both he and I attended – the former Take That star was to announce the launch of his solo career to a lavish and packed ballroom, in it assembled the cream of the world's media at London's Royal Lancaster Hotel.

Four months on from his appearance at the Brits, where his band had won the best single award for 'Back for Good', Robbie had been at the match with a group of friends, including producer and DJ Andrew Weatherall. His new label EMI had hired one of Wembley's executive boxes for their prized asset, which – perhaps rather unwisely – was provisioned with a plentiful supply of free booze for which, at that time, Robbie had a certain fondness.

His record company had also flown in an array of executives and well-known journalists at considerable expense from across the planet to show off their acquisition – with a series of important one-to-one interviews scheduled after the press conference to proudly herald the deal.

But after the conference a wild-eyed Robbie went missing in action as journalists patiently awaited their interviewee. His panicked publicist Chris Poole went on the hunt and hurried to a hotel room in which he had been informed Robbie was relaxing. As Chris entered, a distinctive smell hung in the air and joints were being handed around. On the biggest night of his life so far, Robbie Williams was smoking heroin.

PR legend Chris, who was co-owner of publicity firm Poole-Edwards at the time, has worked with Prince, George Michael, Blondie and David Bowie during a stellar media career. He told me: 'He was smacked out. I went upstairs to his suite and there were all these people there just hanging out. There was a tent arrangement, in one room, like something out of Arabian Nights. There was a sickly sweet smell in the air. I thought, 'Oh, fuck. It is heroin' – they were smoking smack. He said: 'Hey, man, come in, sit down.' Someone tried to pass me a joint, which wasn't a dope joint. I was, 'No thanks.' Heroin's one place I've never even thought of going. There was a heroin scene going on at that point – I don't know who'd got him into it but he was smacked out. Next thing I know, the MD of EMI is telling me Robbie doesn't want to do any interviews, he just wants to chill. EMI had flown a load of journalists in, it was a big deal, and it wasn't exactly a great start to your career in Europe.'

Certain London cliques had moved from cocaine to heroin as the 90s wore on, with Suede's Brett Anderson and Justine Frischmann of Elastica becoming hooked on the drug. Blur producer Stephen Street also spoke to me of being furious when Damon told him, after the recording of 'Beetlebum' in Iceland, that he had written the song about heroin. 'It was the really early hours of the morning, but it was still kind of daylight, I remember walking through Reykjavík one evening and we'd been out for a couple of drinks. By this time, we had recorded 'Beetlebum', which we knew would be the first single, because it had turned out so well. It's so unconventional, such a great chorus. Damon was a bit full of himself that night and said: "Well, you do know Beetlebum's about my use of heroin." I was like, "Fucking hell, really? Damon, that's not clever, mate." I was really shocked. I was really quite upset. And I remember walking ahead of him. He was kind of boasting about it. He later said to me, 'No, I'm sorry, mate, but don't worry, I'm not hooked on it. I can take it or leave it.' I think he knew then not to talk to me about drug habits any more, perhaps. I know my reputation, a lot of people think Street's a bit squeaky clean, but it was a code of conduct I put myself under, when I first started in the industry. I was worried that if I got into it and liked it, I'd get fucked up. I'm very anti-drugs.'

Damon spoke about the period he used the drug in Q Magazine in 2014, explaining it was an 'incredibly productive' time in his musical career and said: 'I just thought, "Why not?"', adding that he felt the its freed him up and helped his creativity.

Just a few hours before Robbie's press conference began, as the 'Three Lions' refrain and the floodlights faded, we had consoled one another under the old Wembley Stadium's twin towers, wondering how many more years of hurt would have to be endured. It was miserable, that empty and ragged feeling which all football fans – particularly those of England and Bristol City – have experienced many times.

Our national team had missed again, once more the masters of heroic failure, but I didn't have time to wallow in collective misery. I had to go to work.

Anyway, back to the night in question. I was among the hundreds of journalists who had been invited to the Robbie post-match unveiling at the FA's hotel of choice, presumably hoping we could all celebrate an England victory together with Robbie riding the wave of positivity and optimism. Alas.

Perhaps a little like the England team, the hotel had something of a faded glamour about it, trading on former glories, a little ragged and dusty, but the scene of Football Association press conferences over the years, with rosy-faced, blazered windbags repeatedly announcing comings, goings, indiscretions and innovations. None of which managed to help England land any much-longed-for trophies.

After a schlep across town on tube trains full or inebriated, dejected and dead-eyed Londoners I arrived at the hotel. The function room was huge and packed with more than 100 journalists, photographers and TV cameras.

Chris Poole recalled the mood in the run-up to the game: 'England were in the semi-final and everyone was in jubilant mood. Robbie decided he wanted to go to the game, tickets in a box were obtained. EMI were obviously anxious to keep him happy so he went off to the football. I was a bit concerned but I couldn't do anything about it.

'I was busy at the hotel setting it up. I saw the result and thought "Oh God, I hope everything's going to go OK." Robbie and his little party of people turned up. Robbie was steaming when he got to the hotel – drinks in the box and whatever else went on. I thought "Fuck, this could be a disaster." He didn't arrive long before the thing was going to start. The whole point was that it was done at one minute after midnight, the moment they were allowed to announce the deal. It was rammed, refreshments were on hand all evening. I had to introduce the whole thing. Then Robbie got up. He looked really awful, but I don't think he came across as being completely out of it. He's one of those people who, when he gets on a stage, is a bag of nerves until he does, but once he's on there he's Mr Showbiz. And he was really good, he delivered what his new masters needed, he did his bit.'

Robbie strutted onstage at 12.01am with a comedic walk, like that old entertainer Max Wall. I distinctly remember being quite shocked by his dishevelled appearance and red eyes, clad casually in black trackie bottoms, white trainers and a short-sleeved 1966 red England shirt, bearing Bobby Moore's number 6 on the back. He looked like he'd been caning it, his tipple perhaps a little more potent than that of the assembled media, many of whom, admittedly, had been on the sauce.

He attempted to sing a verse of 'Football's coming home' before giving up and declaring: 'Oh fuck it. I suppose you all know the football result tonight. Well, it's a great way to go out. Losing graciously to probably the finest football team. Blah blah blah. Very unlucky for the guy Gareth Southgate but that's it now. Lose graciously.'

Robbie was here to announce his debut single, a rather below-par cover version of George Michael's 'Freedom', which would be released by Chrysalis Records in a £1 million deal, the following month. It was an inauspicious start to his new direction and many of us felt it a damp squib, which did not bode well for his future standing.

Robbie told us: 'I want to be seen and heard as an artist, in a professional light, and also have a lot of fun along the way. I'm dying to get out all over the place. And I hope to bring back fun into pop – charisma, a bit of a laugh, it's not all about being serious. There's a lot of fun to be had in any walk of life. I've got to write an album and there's big hype around it. I've got to write it. Music, schmusic. I am now a free artist. On Chrysalis. I'll be working with my manager and my record company and we work as a team. I have the final say, I push the button, whatever goes on, from now on because that's what I've fought for. When I was 12, I told me nan that I was going to be a millionaire and international superstar by the time I was 22. And I was. And I had no doubt in my mind that I was going to do it. And I also have no doubt now that I'm going to carry on being a huge star again. There is no doubt.'

Most of us in the room that night would not, at that moment, have believed how adored Robbie would become as a solo superstar. I certainly did not. He looked unprofessional and had clearly let himself go, haunted by demons and anxiety. It was like seeing a modern-day fat Elvis. Cut from the security bubble of Take That, he had run wild and fled to Glastonbury in 1995, hanging out with the Gallaghers. It may not have been planned that way, but, in retrospect, this was a superlative marketing move, signalling a new Robbie, free from the shackles of a squeaky clean boy band and playing with the big boys.

Out-of-control Robbie was officially out of the band on July 17 1995 and Take That would split on February 13 1996, with *The Sun* and ITV's *This Morning* offering counselling lines for distraught fans.

Chris Poole travelled to Barbados for the video shoot of the debut single in the company of a journalist from *Smash Hits*. The video was shot without any problems, but Robbie plagued him with bizarre telephone calls throughout the night. 'Robbie drove me crazy, phoning me up in the middle of the night saying there were ghosts in his room and all kinds of stuff. I didn't sleep. I had thought he could be a massive star, but I was concerned with his drug-taking, his obsession with ghosts and hauntings, he was a troubled soul is the truth of it. I'm not surprised by how big he became. Those early records and setting him up with the songwriter Guy Chambers was smart. The first few records after 'Freedom' were really good songs and he looked like he could be one of the biggest solo stars around.'

Robbie later admitted he had cleared the hotel mini-bar of all spirits and liqueurs before filming the promo, confessing he was in a 'bad, bad way', pre-rehab.

Figuring he would be a good influence, Poole introduced Robbie to clean-living EMI A&R guru Chris Briggs. And it

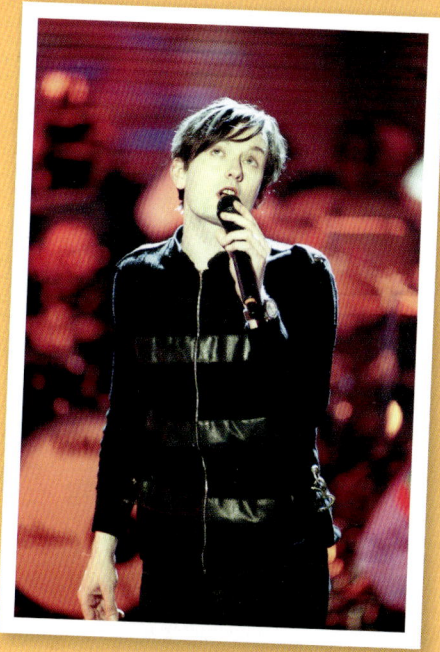
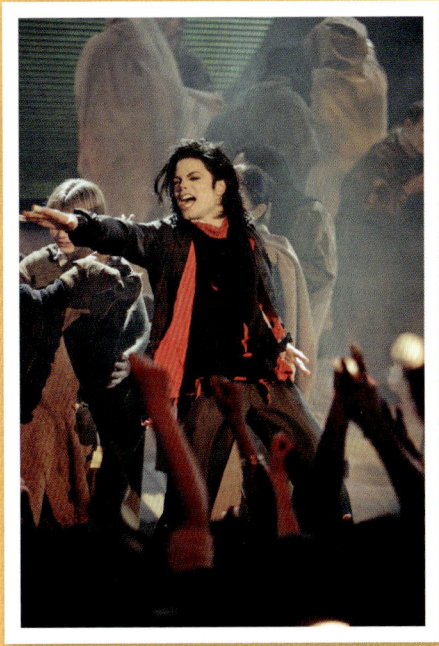

ABOVE: In one of 1996's most infamous incidents, Pulp's Jarvis Cocker stormed the stage at the Brit Awards during Michael Jackson's performance and wiggled his bum at the King of Pop. He was later arrested.

LEFT: The then leader of the opposition, Tony Blair, presents the prestigious Outstanding Contribution to Music award to David Bowie at the Brit Awards in 1996.

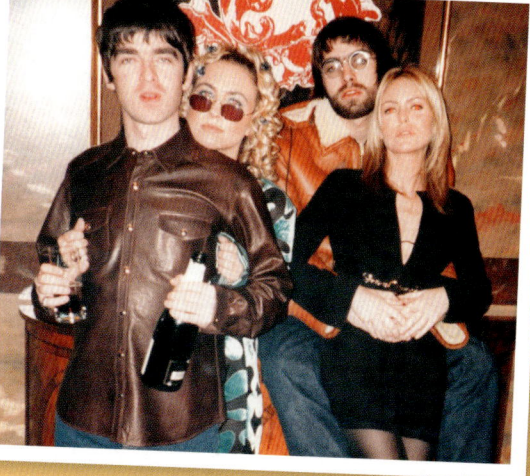

RIGHT: A rare photograph I arranged of Liam and Noel Gallagher with their partners Patsy Kensit and Meg Mathews, at a pre-Brit Awards celebration at London's Landmark Hotel in February 1996.

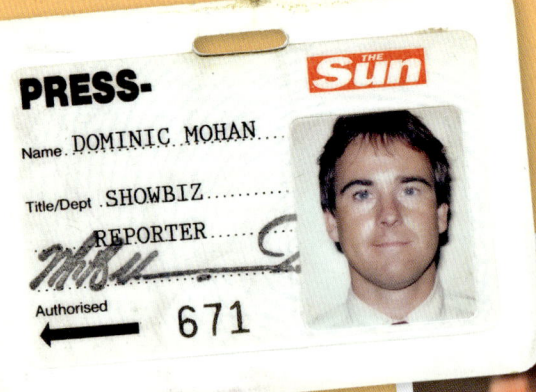

LEFT: My original *Sun* pass which was given to me when I joined the paper in January 1996.

RIGHT: Oasis singer Liam Gallagher clashes with Blur's Damon Albarn at the inaugural music industry Soccer Six tournament at Mile End Stadium, East London, on 12 May 1996.

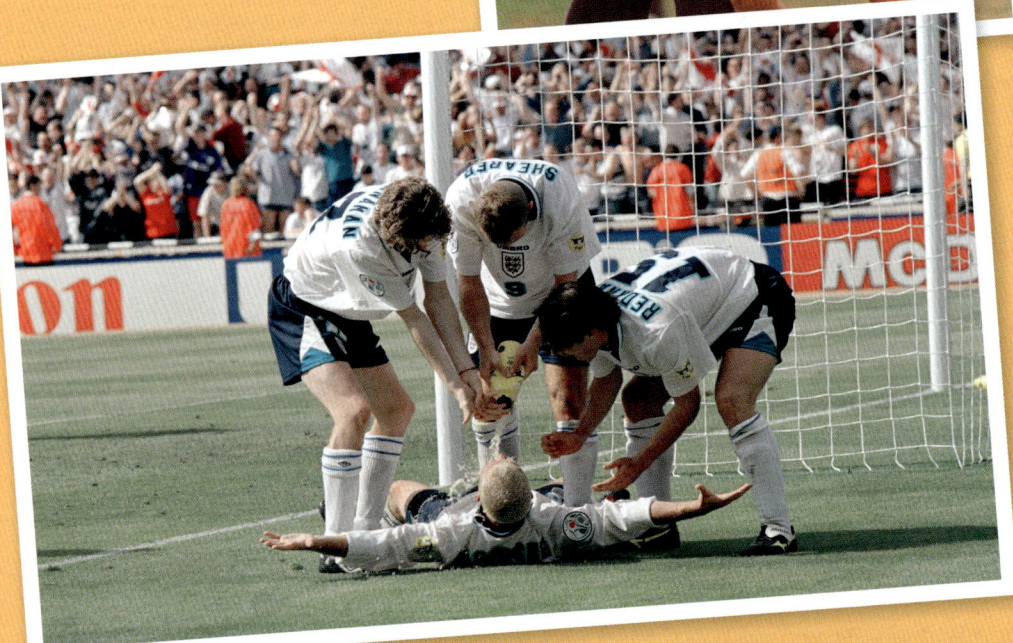

Gazza and his England teammates re-enact the dentist's chair at Euro 96.

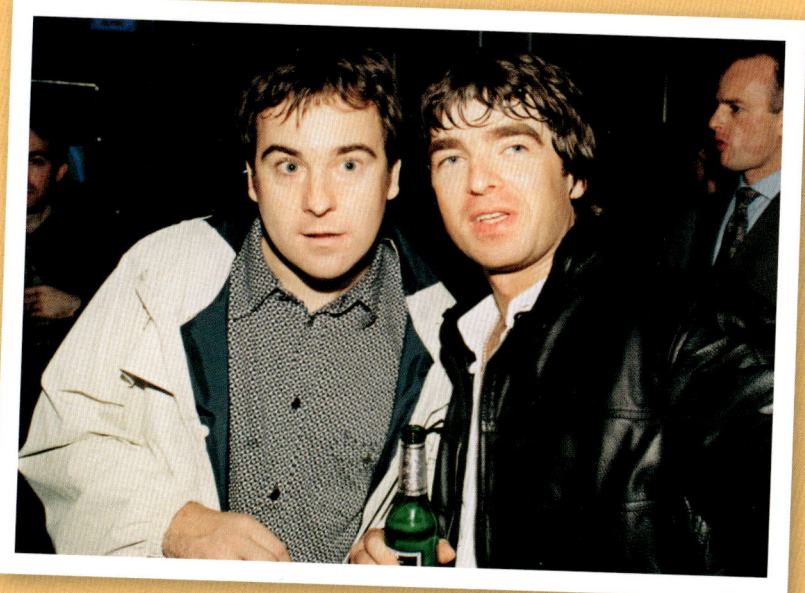

My late night encounter with Noel Gallagher at the Sound Republic venue in London's West End, after he had performed with The Who's Pete Townshend at a Rock the Dock fundraiser, 16 October 1998. Noel slapped the head of my boss, *The Sun*'s editor David Yelland, after I introduced them, during an amusing run-in.

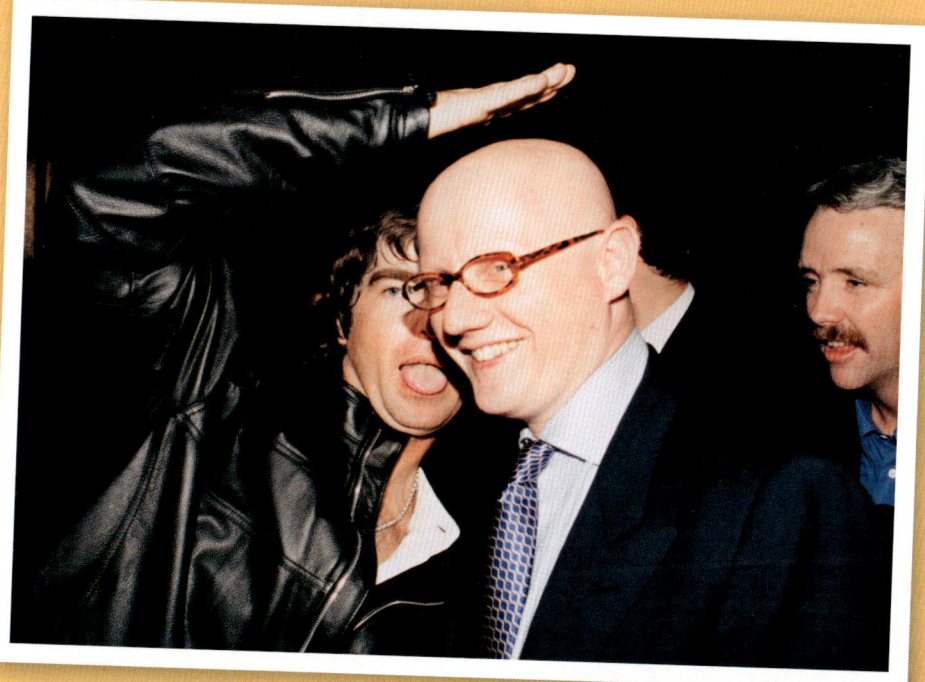

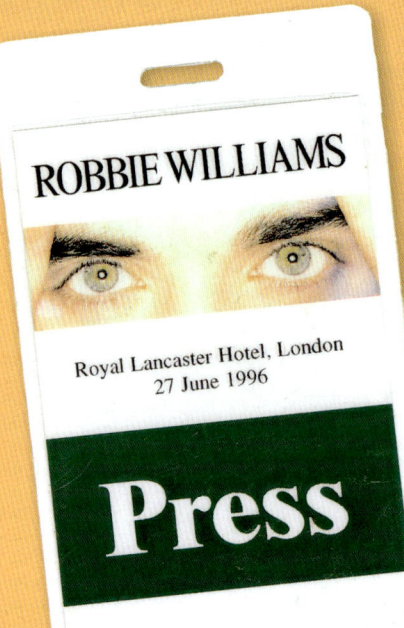

My original press pass to attend Robbie Williams' midnight press conference, straight after England's Euro 96 defeat to Germany, where he officially launched his solo career on 27 June 1996.

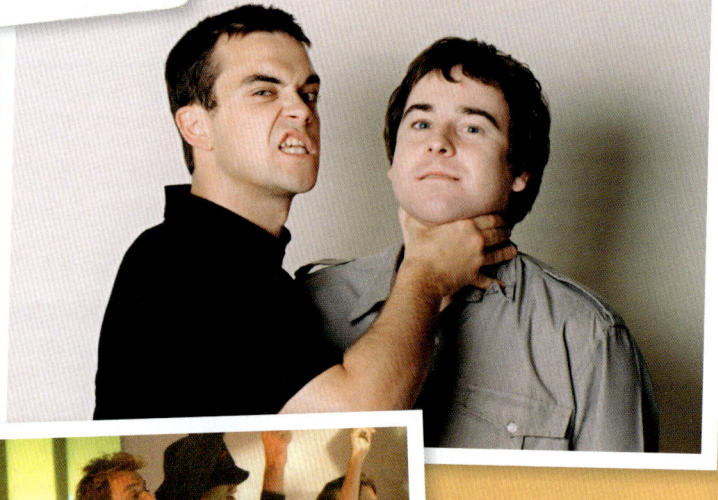

RIGHT: Robbie Williams strangles me during a photo shoot in Rome in February 1998.

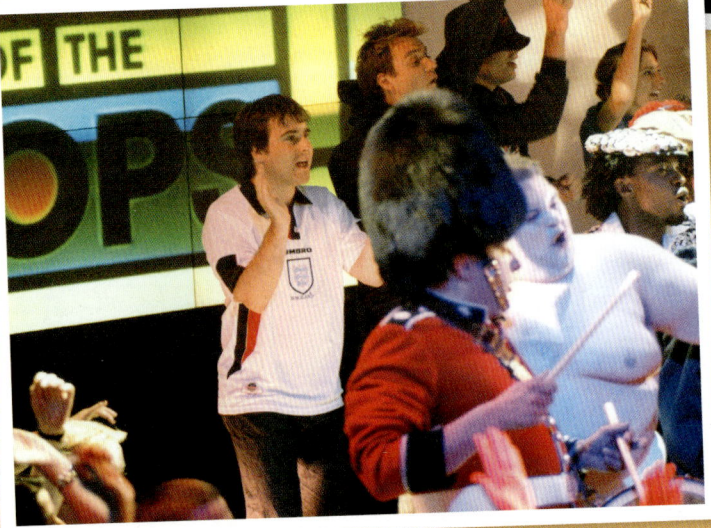

LEFT: On stage at *Top Of The Pops* in June 1998 with Vindaloo collective Fat Les. Blur's Alex James keeps a low profile in a blue bucket hat, while comedian Rowland Rivron bangs the drum.

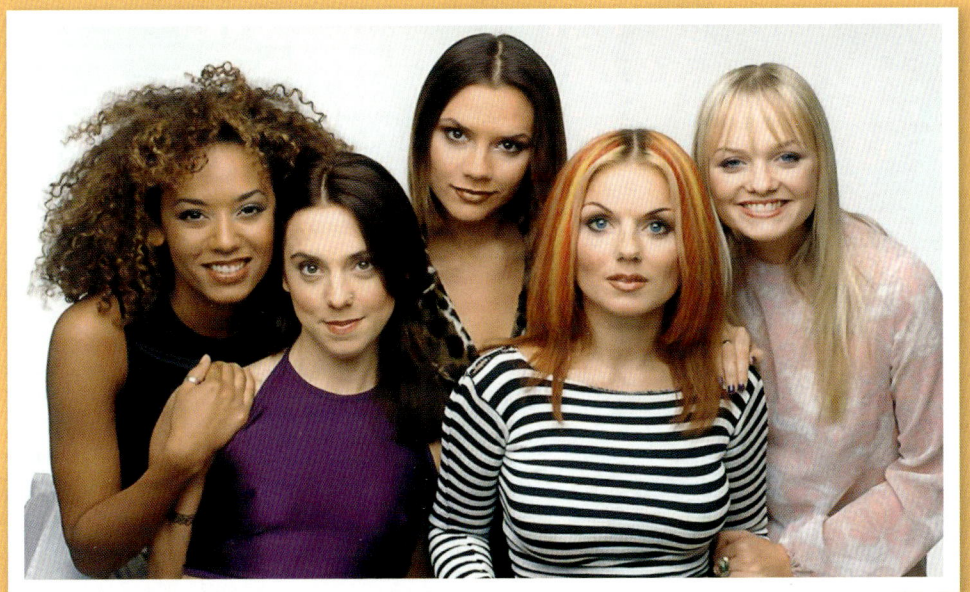

An early shot of the Spice Girls in 1996.

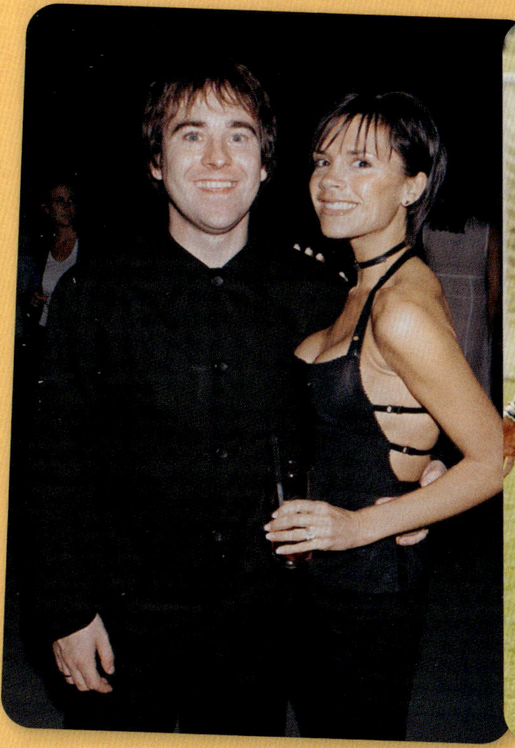

Me and Victoria 'Posh Spice' Adams, soon to be Beckham, at the VH1 fifth birthday party in London in 1999.

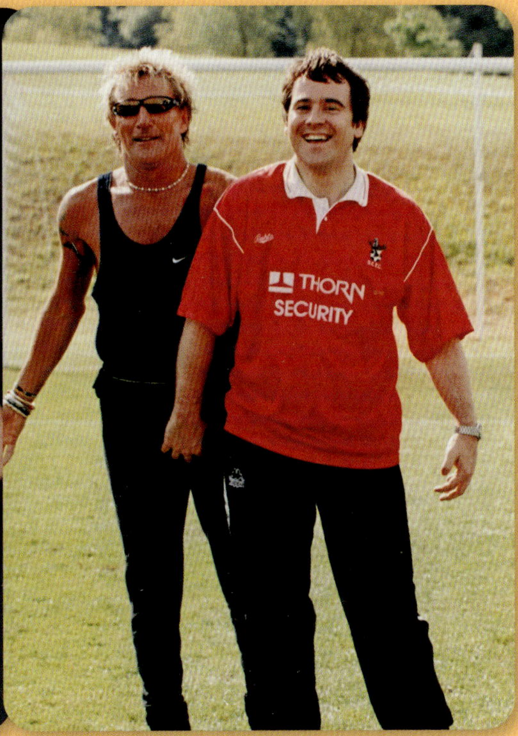

Rod Stewart and I re-create the famous Vinnie Jones and Paul Gascoigne testicle-squeezing photo at his home in Epping, Essex, circa 1999.

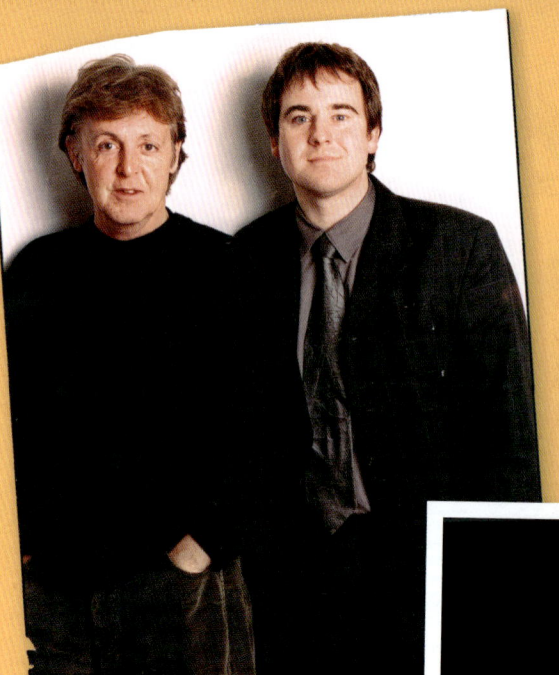

LEFT: Me and Sir Paul McCartney in London, 1998.

RIGHT: Noel Gallagher with his famous Union Jack guitar on stage at Manchester's Maine Road, April 1996.

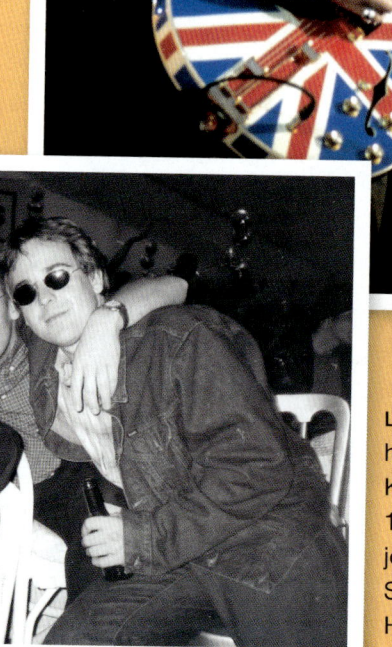

LEFT: In the Oasis hospitality tent at Knebworth, August 1996, with fellow journalists John Sturgis (*left*) and Rick Hewett (*centre*).

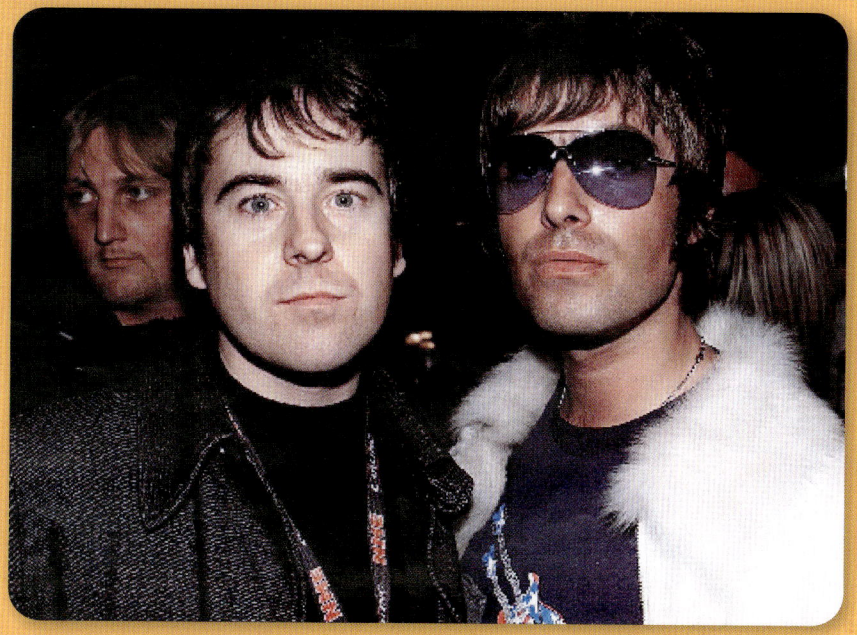
Me with Liam Gallagher at the NME Awards in London, 2001.

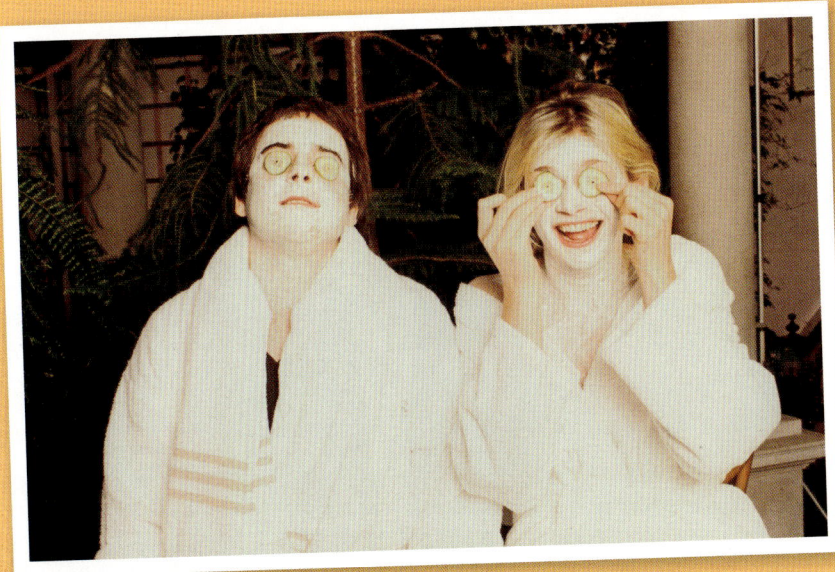
Having fun with Radio 1 presenter Zoe Ball at a health farm where she hosted her breakfast show.

I met Prime Minister Tony Blair at the 1998 Labour Party Conference in Blackpool. I interviewed him again in 2025.

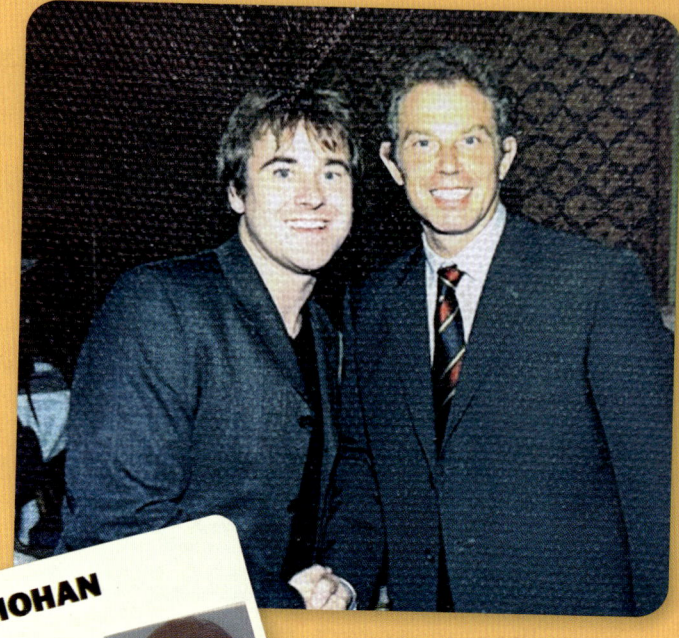

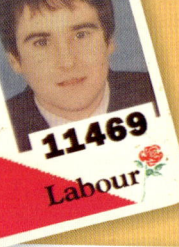

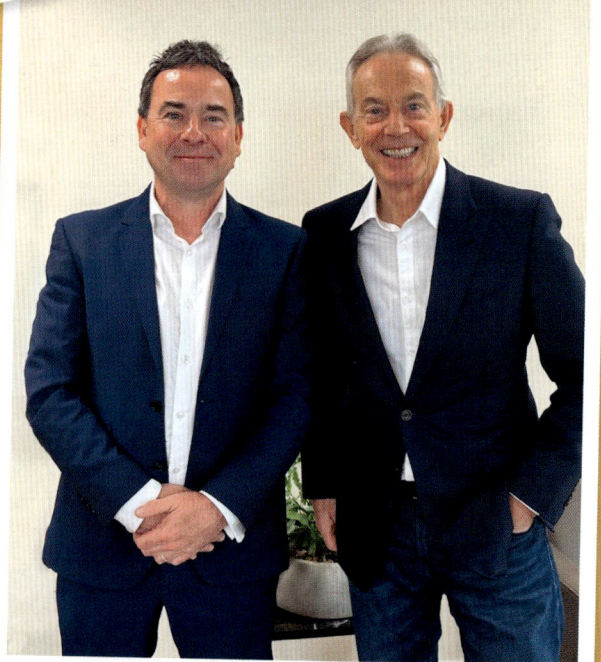

was Briggs who, in January 1997, hooked him up with songwriter Guy Chambers, who had worked with The Waterboys, World Party and had his own band The Lemon Trees. Chambers collaborated on Robbie's first five albums, as co-songwriter and producer, and all reached number one in the UK, hitting sales of over 40 million copies globally, with songs like 'Let Me Entertain You', 'Angels', 'Rock DJ', 'Feel' and 'Millennium'.

Surprisingly, 'Angels' failed to reach the top spot in the UK, peaking at number four following its release on 1 December 1997 but eventually shifting more than 1.5 million copies in the UK, with more than 656 million streams on Spotify. Robbie and Guy collected the 1999 Ivor Novello Award for Best Song Musically and Lyrically. Britons voted it the track they most wanted played at their funeral in 2005, the year it was also hailed as the best song of the previous twenty-five years at the Brit Awards. It was, however, kept from the number one spot by a single from children's telly characters Teletubbies with 'Teletubbies Say "Eh-Oh"', proving that not all music in the 90s was era-defining.

Briggs recalled: 'When we signed Rob, the cool people at EMI were laughing at us. They thought it could be career-ending for us. Chris Poole wanted me to talk to Robbie initially, not from a musical perspective but from a state-of-mind perspective. We put him together with Guy and it's great when things like that collaboration work. Nine times out of ten they don't, but it clicked. Serendipity really.'

Now a vocal advocate for sobriety, having been sober for over twenty years, Robbie would later speak of his heroin use around that time and, in 2025, admitted to Australian radio's KIIS FM's *Kyle and Jackie O Show* that he gave it 'a good go'. He has also spoken of staying awake for six full days and spewing up black bile after taking huge quantities of 'absolutely anything' at an MTV Awards ceremony.

But when Robbie started writing with Guy Chambers, musical alchemy was forged; they rustled up his signature tune 'Angels' in just 25 minutes. It was produced at London's Maison Rouge Studios. Britpop indie darlings Sleeper were also recording their second album there with The Smiths and Blur producer Stephen Street, who told me: 'So the first time I came across Robbie personally, face to face, was when I was working at Maison Rouge. He seemed quite stressed, highly strung, a bit agitated. You could tell he wasn't really, completely in a great place. Louise and Andy went outside to the shared kind of reception, kitchen area. And Robbie was there, and he was saying, "Oh, you must come in here and listen to what I'm up to," and they went in and listened to some work in progress of what he was doing on that debut album. And they came back in and said he's really buzzing. Louise said to me, he played me this ballad, it's an incredible song. Obviously it was "Angels". Then, basically, that album came out and they didn't release "Angels" first of all as a single. I think it was "Lazy Days". And they kind of panicked. The label reached out to me and said, "Would you be interested in working with Robbie?" I was quite surprised. I was like, "Really?" I'm not sure really. I don't work with boy bands. I'd been working for The Smiths,

Morrissey, Blur and Sleeper, "credible" indie bands. I didn't want to taint that. Then, sure enough, within two or three weeks, he did release "Angels" and then, well, the rest is history.

'I think Robbie was on the periphery of Britpop. If you think about it, the thing that really did make him huge is that one song. And it's a bit like James Blunt with "You're Beautiful". It's one of those songs that is so, so big – it's timeless. How much of it was written by Robbie? It's debatable.'

'Angels' is one of those soaring records that you immediately know is destined to become a national anthem the moment you first hear it. Its hymn-like quality and Beatles-esque orchestral flourishes follow a piano intro that is not dissimilar to that of 'Don't Look Back in Anger'. It's paced like a Gallagher classic but with a vulnerability that encapsulates Robbie's sensitivity with the refrain: 'I know that life won't break me.'

Noel would later declare: 'I've heard it and thought, "I wish I'd written that." "Angels" is Oasis by numbers. Add a fucking electric guitar on it and it would be.'

It was obvious that Robbie was going to become an even bigger name on the pages of *The Sun* and likely for many years, so I wanted to make him my friend and support him as a solo act. We'd all assumed Gary Barlow was going to become the Take That megastar, but this was the first indication otherwise. We flew to Rome together for an interview and a TV appearance for my debut Bizarre column, which I was to co-edit with *The Sun*'s current Editor-in-Chief Victoria Newton, following my promotion to Showbiz Editor. He pretended to throttle me for some photos, which may have betrayed his true feelings.

Each time I went to see a Robbie concert through the 1990s, I noticed the audiences would be more diverse in age and sex – it was becoming fine to like him if you were older or a bloke. His humour, demeanour, vulnerability and emerging brand of Gallagher-lite sounds chimed with the time, as his elders misfired. He was gradually morphing into the acceptable and palatable face of Take That, but with some gig-going males obviously attending only under the guise that they were there with their partners.

But another feud was brewing. Liam Gallagher said that Robbie should be hung, while Noel christened him the fat dancer from Take That. Robbie would soon become the one person who irked Liam and knew how to bash his Burnage buttons, despite them hanging out together not long before in those Somerset fields of Glastonbury in 1995 – the younger Gallagher famously kissing him on the cheek for the cameras.

Over the ensuing years, I would become something of a vessel for the warring adversaries to carry out their spat in print. Perhaps Robbie had seen the Oasis rivalry with Blur fade away and seized an opportunity to fill the void, land more column inches and sell more records.

Following the release of the Oasis album *Standing on the Shoulder of Giants*, I came into *The Sun*'s offices one morning to find a huge funereal wreath of flowers, maybe £200-worth, on my desk, envelope attached.

On the front was scrawled 'FAO Noel Gallagher c/o Dominic Mohan, Bizarre, The Sun'. I opened it up and the message within read: 'Dear Noel. R.I.P. Heard Your latest album. You have my deepest sympathy. Robbie Williams.' Now then. If that was the genuine article, I had an excellent scoop on my hands – and I was to be the conduit for the latest explosion in the Gallagher–Williams war. I contacted Robbie's representatives and they confirmed he had indeed sent the wreath, adding that he thought it would be a good bit of fun to do so. Fill your boots was their message to me. So I did, running the story big the following day.

When I later asked Liam – who would, of course, go on to marry Robbie's ex-fiancée, All Saints singer Nicole Appleton – about this during an interview, he flipped and growled: 'He'll regret that. I'll get him somewhere quiet when he's least expecting it. He won't be sending wreaths when he's in hospital. I'll send him some diet pills and a fat Elvis costume though.'

The wreath stunt felt like a symbolic shift of power between the warring parties, but it is something that would not happen today. Robbie would, most likely, simply post a picture of the flowers and note on social media and the mainstream media would then follow it up. *The Sun* and my column was the vehicle through which this feud was conducted and that put me at the centre of the conversation. The traditional media has lost that power in many ways, the ability to spark – and be at the heart of – the narrative as often, and the world is a less interesting place for it.

As bloated Oasis perhaps got too rich and started to falter, Blur didn't seem interested so Robbie began to step up. The country fell more deeply in love with his cheeky persona, natural wit, looks and sensitivity, in contrast to Liam and Noel's surly arrogance. Britain had known him as man and boy, witnessing him make terrible mistakes and hit rock bottom, clawing himself back up from the depths of heroin to become national hero and treasure. Forget not, Robbie began the decade flunking his GCSEs in Stoke in 1990. He closed it singing 'Millennium', as the country's leading male star.

Of course, he would later, in 2003, trump Oasis's Knebworth feat by playing three nights there and, as is his wont, sent Noel a pair of tap-dancing shoes with the message: 'Dear Mr N. Gallagher, you said two nights at Knebworth is history. Well, I guess three is just greedy. Yours, Rob. PS – Finding it difficult to find adequate support for my show. What are you doing on the 1st and 2nd? Oh, and the 3rd?'

Robbie's list of female conquests reads like the contents page of a lads' mag. He was a provocative interviewee too and made great copy, but it always felt that his demons weren't too far away. On one occasion I was flown over to Dublin ahead of a gig for an audience with him. A group of EMI executives and I awaited his arrival one evening in the hotel bar. On entering, Robbie fell flat on his face at our feet. We all turned away and acted as if nothing had happened.

One 1996 evening at Stringfellows nightclub in London, as I sat with the legendary owner Peter and some of Fleet Street's biggest names, a pale and slurring Robbie spent 45 minutes with his ogling face two inches away from a lap dancer's wiggling bum, before toppling headfirst from his chair, in front of us all. It was toe-curling to witness. Luckily, Robbie pulled through after the right people were assembled around him under the guidance of Chris Briggs, Chris Poole and his new management team at IE, Tim Clark and David Enthoven, who had himself successfully battled heroin, cocaine and alcohol dependency.

On learning the news of ex-One Direction star Liam Payne's death, Robbie wrote movingly: 'How to make sense of the Liam Payne tragedy? Obviously, my first feelings towards his passing were like everyone else. Shock, sadness and confusion. And to be honest as I write these words that's where I still am. Liam's trials and tribulations were very similar to mine, so it made sense to reach out and offer what I could. So I did.

'I still had my demons at 31. I relapsed. I was in pain. I was in pain because I relapsed. I relapsed because of a multitude of painful reasons. I remember Heath Ledger passing and thinking "I'm next". By the grace of God and/or dumb luck I'm still here. Even famous strangers need your compassion. What a Handsome Talented boy. What a tragic painful loss for his friends, family, fans and by the looks of the energy this moment has created.'

The Sun and I were firmly Team Robbie, much to the chagrin of his former Take That bandmate and songwriter Gary Barlow. My 'dismal rival' (as he would oft dub me) Matthew Wright on *The Mirror* and his editor Piers Morgan made a massive misjudgement and unwisely chose to write off Robbie and attack him. Schoolboy error.

1996

Robbie refused to talk to them so I was handed all the scoops. When he signed his record-breaking new EMI deal, I was fed all the exclusive details for a front-page splash. And, on the eve of Robbie's Irish dates, *The Mirror* was resigned to hiring vehicles with embarrassing billboards, which drove around Dublin, proclaiming: 'Sorry Robbie'. The rivalry between the two newspapers at that time was intense, often critical of one another in print and fighting tooth and nail over exclusives, all very tribal and antagonistic. That doesn't exist today.

The Sun's readers loved Robbie. He was the lad we'd seen grow up and he encapsulated the aspiration and dreams of a working-class boy done good. With *The Sun*'s – and my own – relentless backing for this underdog's solo career, his former bandmate and nemesis Gary seemed to disappear from view somewhat. Robbie was clearly trying to position himself as the new Freddie Mercury in many ways; at times, I almost thought he was angling for Freddie's old job as the reunited Queen's frontman. He even covered 'We Are the Champions' for the soundtrack of the film *A Knight's Tale*. But that wasn't to everybody's taste and a collaboration seemed remote after I bumped into Queen's drummer Roger Taylor backstage at some Hyde Park festival. I asked him how he felt about Robbie's aping of his old pal. 'He's no Freddie,' was the blunt response. Thanks Roger, that'll make a lead story for the column.

That's where the majority of my stories came from, hanging around backstage and chatting to stars at parties, club nights and premieres. If you'd have mentioned work–life balance back then, you'd be laughed at. The journalist's church is the ornate St Bride's on Fleet Street, the spiritual home of newspapers and, on visiting, I would always be alarmed by the young ages at which we lost the newsmen and women commemorated on memorial plaques there. But it is perhaps unsurprising.

The job was rewarding, of course, yet relentless. Knackering. Bags under the eyes and often out four or five nights a week until the early hours, but there was usually free champagne and canapés. It's not as if I was reporting from a war zone, but it took its toll. Back at the office desk at 10am, in preparation for conference with the editor at 11. Then, often, an expensed lunch with a contact or agent somewhere fancy like one of the Conran restaurants near Tower Bridge, back to work writing stories or conducting interviews for the next day's edition, then back out, usually in the West End, to do it all over again. Celebrities were certainly less guarded in the 90s and were unafraid of uttering something controversial for fear of being cancelled on a social media yet to be adopted. Once-underground stars like The Chemical Brothers and The Prodigy were themselves now at the top of the charts and fully-fledged slebs, hanging out at glam film premieres, propping up bars and telling me tales.

I certainly wouldn't want to do the job today, with journalists chained to their desks, rewriting stories from Instagram and TikTok when they'd be better off staying out late and being in the right places at the right time. Many publications are still full of celebrity content, but most fans will already be aware of it from following stars' social media platforms.

1996

But back to Robbie (or Rob, which is how his friends always name-drop him to show they are in the circle). He was clearly a super-talented live performer and lyricist and a dream interview subject. He would regularly lob hand grenades at Gary as he gained the upper hand in the Take That solo career war. I remember one particularly cruel column, where we mocked up one of those police 'Missing' posters, asking 'Have You Seen This Man?' with an unflattering image of Gary. This type of ribbing happened quite regularly.

One morning, I received a call from Gary's manager, a mobile phone in one hand and presumably a large olive branch in the other. Apparently, Gary wanted to straighten things out between us, treat me to dinner and play me some of his brand spanking new songs. A few evenings later, he rather decadently pulled up in a gleaming Bentley, complete with freshly starched chauffeur, at *The Sun*'s East London HQ, whence we were driven for all of ten minutes to the Butlers Wharf Chop House restaurant just over Tower Bridge. He popped a CD in on the way and I was treated to some of his new tunes, which clearly put him, at least, in a party mood.

On arrival – it was still before 7pm – I ordered a beer and he went for what would be the first of several large Southern Comforts with lemonade, which I felt was a bold move so early in the evening's proceedings. But I could sense he was a touch nervous, perchance embarrassed and rather unsettled. This conversation was to be all on the record, he assured me, and I recorded the exchanges over dinner, a small Olympus tape recorder whirring on my napkin. Rob's – sorry, Robbie's – success had clearly riled him and he started to rant. I couldn't quite believe what I was hearing from Take That's Mr Nice Guy or Mr Clean, as he was so often dubbed. Well, up until this point, anyway.

Without prompt, he began to open up about his sex life while in the band and the amount of drugs he had consumed. It was an interesting public relations strategy – to try and out-Robbie Robbie Williams. And perhaps one I would not advise. I believe the tabloid term would be that he, er, blew the lid off his squeaky clean image, as he told all. 'Oh yes, I've done cocaine, ecstasy and smoked dope. The problem was, if I took E, I'd feel like shit for a week and I just couldn't work. That's why I knocked it on the head. Everyone thought we were saints in Take That. I'm glad I tried them, but I got it out of my system when I was young. Drugs and pop stars don't really go together. I'd be so embarrassed if I ever took as much cocaine as Robbie has done. I'd be upset for my parents and so ashamed. For Robbie, it was inevitable. He was like a kid in a sweet shop. I don't know why he fell for it. I've got no respect for that. People like that are on the road to ruin. He seems to like doing things that destroy him.'

As the Southern Comforts continued to flow, he took further aim at his former bandmate and branded him 'a bastard' who had resembled a 'down and out'. It was one of those interviews where you are bursting inside, knowing that what you are hearing is live newspaper gold. I decided to simply give him the space to carry on speaking, while pondering how many front-page stories I would be able to mine out of this extraordinary conversation. There were at least three in the first half hour.

You could really sense the festering bitterness and there was a lot to unpack. At times, I felt like his therapist and he was off-loading years of private pain and gnarled anger. The interview made the front pages over the following few days and sailed around the world. Gary was greeted with ridicule in some quarters – he was just fortunate this interview took place in a pre-social media era.

It's the small vignettes that give people away when you meet them, not just in media interviews but generally in life. Like the very well-known conservative politician I once met, who treated a junior member of staff at a luxury hotel appallingly, verbally abusing him in front of me while we were waiting for our coats. He furiously smashed a brass bell on the oak cloakroom counter and vented his fury at the poor chap for having the audacity to keep us waiting for several minutes. I made a mental note of that and always kept it with me. When you catch people off guard like that, you can snatch a glimpse into their true persona.

Revelations aside, one of the most illuminating parts of the interview was when I asked Gary about his reputation as being even tighter with money than Rod Stewart. He explained: 'What I remember most is that the lads used to think I was mean with my money. It's true that I had a mobile phone when I joined the group, but I was on the dole so, when they used my phone, I admit I used to charge them to make calls.'

Then, at the end of the meal, I reached for the bill. But, as if to prove a point, Gary told me he'd take care of it. 'I want the receipt though, I'll put it on my expenses,' he added. I couldn't work out whether he was joking.

Gary's confessions sparked a huge reaction. After publication or, should I say, detonation, Gary would bump into work colleagues and badmouth me, telling them to deliver a warning that he was going to knock me out the next time we met and that he'd never grant me forgiveness. But he did forgive. After all, I had simply quoted him verbatim from the recording – he just didn't like the reaction, as happens so often with celebrities. It's quite common for many interviewees and their representatives to blame the vessel of communication for any fallout, when they should perhaps be looking closer to home. We later met at Wembley Stadium when our sons were both playing football in a tournament, shook hands and spent the day together. And yes, it was his giant son you may have read about and seen pictured – and he was excellent in goal.

Despite the bitterness, Robbie would, of course, go on to reunite with his old bandmates in 2010, recording the *Progress* album with them and performing live as a five-piece for the last time (to date). I think he wanted to help out his old mates in the band – the other three – who hadn't made as much money as him. I also believe being off the gear and his stints in rehab had encouraged him to be more tolerant and less feuding, particularly with Gary. The band sold 1.34 million tickets in less than twenty-four hours and played an unprecedented eight nights at the aforementioned Wembley, which earned them £38 million alone, and the equivalent residency at what would become the Etihad in their hometown, Manchester.

1996

Music industry bible *Billboard* placed it third on its highest-grossing tours of the year list, with 600,000 paying punters. Each band member received £7.9 million net.

So, long-term, the interview didn't do Gary any harm after all – and he would never again have to charge his bandmates for the use of his mobile.

One thing is for certain, by the turn of the millennium of which he sang, Robbie Williams was fortunate to still be with us, thanks to strong management and no small amount of luck. Robbie had gone from smoking heroin on the most crucial night of his solo career to becoming Britain's foremost male star, quite an achievement for the fat dancer from Take That.

Robbie's 90s began with flunking exams at school and ended with him selling more than 9 million albums, 4.3 million singles, winning two Ivor Novello Awards and three Brits – evidence that he had successfully inserted himself into a decade dominated by guitar bands and ingratiated himself with both the public – and the industry. The British populace and media were wooed by his charm, persona and very British lyricism, alongside cleverly constructed Britpop-lite sounds. Noel Gallagher branded his music Oasis by numbers, but it seemed to chime with the times and opened up new audiences for Robbie, taking grown-up Take That fans with him and appealing to increasingly male audiences.

The Britpop bands had taken indie music mainstream and now a boy band joker from the mainstream had stolen its jewels in an audacious cultural heist, in order to make himself seem cooler and more alternative.

ROBBIE

With the Blur vs Oasis so-called feud over, Robbie accelerated into the slipstream, leaving his Take That bandmates – and a particularly bitter Barlow behind – brilliantly utilising the media to stoke it all up and sell a lorryload of shiny CDs.

Robbie's solo career was born in 96, with his debut solo single, 'Freedom 96', about to be unleashed on 12 August. The media and industry were all expecting it to head straight to number one.

But the song was thwarted by a group of five young women, unknown just weeks prior (and a number of whom Robbie would later boast of seducing). So I'll tell you what you want, what you really, really want in the next chapter.

My Top Ten British Books of the 90s

1. *High Fidelity* **– Nick Hornby (1995):** Hornby's million-seller about a singleton record shop owner in North London ticked all my boxes and nailed being a 90s music nerd, full of lists like this one. A thing of beauty.
2. *Trainspotting* **– Irvine Welsh (1993):** This groundbreaking cult novel blew my mind – I'd never witnessed writing like it. Welsh is a modern-day James Joyce with stream-of-consciousness prose and veering from Scottish to English language, with nothing taboo. Heroin, alcoholism and violence. Game-changer.

1996

3. ***The Beach* – Alex Garland (1996):** The captivating tale of a young backpacker's quest to find the perfect beach caught Britain's imagination at the moment we felt our nation could do no wrong. Nick Hornby described Londoner Garland's classic book as 'a Lord of the Flies for Generation X'.
4. ***Harry Potter and the Philosopher's Stone* – J.K. Rowling (1997):** The one that started it all. The magical 90s escape into the world of the young wizard was instantly addictive and spawned one of the UK's greatest exports. An unputdownable debut for grown-ups and their offspring.
5. ***Fever Pitch* – Nick Hornby (1992):** Hornby again with this autobiographical essay about the ups and downs of being an Arsenal fan and one which spawned two films. Another million-seller.
6. ***Bridget Jones's Diary* – Helen Fielding (1996):** A thirty-something single working woman in London, Bridget's diary records musings on a troubled personal life, loosely based on Jane Austen's *Pride and Prejudice*. Originally a newspaper column, the novel is laugh-out-loud funny and became a hugely successful film franchise.
7. ***About a Boy* – Nick Hornby (1998):** Another vote for Hornby (my favourite author of the 90s and beyond) goes to this coming-of-age classic. It is a romp through 90s culture, music and sex and captured the epoch ingeniously. A beautiful thing.
8. ***The Buddha of Suburbia* – Hanif Kureshi (1990):** The struggles of living in London as a mixed-race teenager

in the 1970s are excellently captured by the author in this highly autobiographical debut. An important and special book.

9. *Mr Nice* – **Howard Marks (1996):** This humorous volume was the one to be seen with in the mid-90s. A captivating trip with the jailed drug-dealer, who once had forty-three aliases and eighty-nine phone lines, dealing with MI6, the CIA, the IRA and the Mafia. Hard to put down.

10. *Man and Boy* – **Tony Parsons (1999):** A TV producer's life unravels after he cheats on his wife and loses his job. Parsons writes with such elegance and this is a very moving romantic novel that always touches me. It seems as if Tony has been with me, man and boy, from those early music paper musings to today.

CHAPTER 6

Spice

'You've shagged Dominic twice? Yuk.' What Posh Spice told my wife when I first introduced them

Up until now, 1996 had been dominated by the lads. Then, suddenly, BOOM! Some breathless bunch called the Spice Girls, of whom few had heard, blasted out of absolutely nowhere and detonated, shifting the narrative and exploding on to the nation's – in fact make that the world's – front pages.

It was hard to keep up with 1996, with seemingly never-ending revelations and cultural phenomena dropping on to our messy desks weekly as the greatest year stomped on.

Oasis had to slog it on the road before coming to prominence while Robbie had gone through his Take That apprenticeship – but this was an instantaneous taste of Spice: five working-class girls and a dose of Girl Power jettisoned into our consciousness.

1996 may be remembered for indie lads with guitars and a boy band superstar but it was the Spice Girls who sold the most records. Their debut album *Spice* shifted 21.9 million copies globally while the follow-up *Spiceworld* sold almost 14 million in 1997. This was coupled with outrageous single sales of 11 million in 1996 and 6 million the following year, proof that they conquered the world like no other British band in the 90s.

But Mel B believes the Spice Girls' and her most enduring legacy from that decade is helping to abate racism in schools and usher in an era of acceptance for a generation of young mixed-race girls in society.

Scary Spice, with her trademark afro, superlative dance skills and no-nonsense attitude, became a defiant symbol of a transformative, modern Britain. She felt that her role in the biggest girl band of all time heralded a remodelling of the nation, giving schoolgirls from ethnic minorities the courage to stop straightening their hair and emboldening them to join in playground dance routines with accepting pupils from different backgrounds.

She also told me she believed the group, who would burst into the global pop charts from July 1996 with a devastating series of infectious singles – 'Wannabe', 'Say You'll Be There' and '2 Become 1' – also brought power and recognition to the LGBTQ+ community, stimulating a more inclusive Britain – and world beyond.

I've interviewed Melanie Brown, now MBE, many times and, behind that brash exterior, she is always thoughtful and lends intelligent insight into subjects in a way that her bandmates sometimes cannot – tackling issues around racism, sexism, the music industry, domestic violence and sexual orientation head-on.

In a fresh and powerful interview, she told me: 'We stood for Girl Power. We were all very proud of that. Our first official fanzine had an article about Emmeline Pankhurst.

We were telling people to be who they want to be and there are so many LGBTQ+ people who still come up to us and tell us it gave them the strength to follow their own path. I have mixed-race ladies coming up to me telling me that because I wore my hair in a big fro, they stopped straightening their hair. They got to be part of the dances in the playground. Those are the things that mean the most to me.'

Melanie, who has spoken previously of what she described as an abusive relationship, explained how she has channelled the band's Girl Power mantra into her work as a Women's Aid patron and vowed to fight against domestic abuse.

'For me, Girl Power has grown into my work with domestic violence and to stop abuse. I got an MBE for my work with survivors and women suffering from abuse. It's an epidemic and I won't stop fighting. Girl Power made me stand up for what I believed in – but fighting abuse is my passion.'

Today, Mel still has a fondness for the optimism of that pre-social media age – particularly its fashion and music – but with some reservations about the era.

'The 90s was a great time to be young and it feels like yesterday to me. I love the 90s. It just happened. It was in the air and you can't force anything like that to happen – it either does or it doesn't. When you are in the eye of the storm, it's actually calm, but you don't always have a sense of the hysteria around you. There was great music, a great spirit of optimism in the country, no social media – or very little – and great fashion. The greatest moment was being with my girls and having my girl Phoenix – a 90s baby.

Britain was a cool place to be but I'm a northern girl and I like to think me and Mel C helped make the north pretty cool – Leeds and Liverpool.'

But she admitted she felt it was important to look at that period holistically and confessed many women like her had to deal with misogyny and laddish sexism – much of which has disappeared from society today. 'I think there are pros and cons. You can't wear rose-tinted glasses. It was also the era of The Lad and women were expected to put up with a lot of crap that just wouldn't happen today. I think we have moved on in some ways but gone backwards in others. I'm glad I'm a performer and not a politician. But, as a mixed-race, working-class survivor and Spice Girl I'm not afraid to speak out about issues which are important to me.'

Mel was born in Harehills, Leeds, in 1975, the daughter of the late Martin Brown, from Saint Kitts and Nevis, and English wife Andrea Dixon. She has happy memories of the beginning of the decade, before she found fame; as a teenager, she harboured ambitions to be a performer.

'I was always pretty happy. I was a dance kid trying to make it,' she recalled. 'I'd danced in Blackpool as a 16-year old in my first professional job and I loved it. The height of my ambition was to be in an Andrew Lloyd Webber musical or *Miss Saigon* – my mum thought I'd be perfect for that. I also thought it would be great to become a dancer on a cruise ship. Then I did the audition and met the other girls. We all moved into a house in Maidenhead and worked our backsides off, but the managers who took us on wouldn't sign us. The only people who really believed in us was the five of us.'

1996

Mel attended the 1996 Brit Awards with bandmates Geri, Victoria, Emma and Melanie C, just months before their debut single 'Wannabe' exploded globally; at the following year's ceremony they scooped two awards, becoming its focal point.

So, I ask, as she sat in Earls Court as an unknown, did she have any inkling then that the 1997 awards would be their night and was she confident that could happen? 'I thought we were amazing and I always believed anything could happen. Obviously, none of us realised exactly how big it would become, but I always believed in us.'

The 90s image of Geri, clad in a Union Flag mini-dress, is considered one of the defining symbols of the Cool Britannia period, so does Mel wish she had worn the celebrated attire? She barked back: 'Are you kidding? Leopard print is my signature – I wore it then. I wear it now.'

As one fifth of Britain's biggest 90s pop band, Mel recalled that her first interaction with the country's most celebrated rock act, Oasis, also came at the Brit Awards. Scary too revealed she had witnessed one of the band's Live '25 reunion shows in their hometown: 'I became friendly with Meg – who is still a dear friend today – so I'd see them around at parties. I went to their Manchester concert with my husband, Rory, and Phoenix. It was fantastic. Good on them.'

At the 1996 Brits, a champagne-swilling wannabe Mel C was almost booted out of the band before it was officially launched, after sharing a table – and a few bottles – with rocker Lenny Kravitz. Sporty was rebuked by manager Simon Fuller the following day after telling bandmate

Victoria to eff off. He threatened Mel with being ousted from the band if any such behaviour was repeated.

The Spice Girls would go on to sell a total of more than 100 million records after forming in 1994. They fused a feminist spirit under the Girl Power ethic with a playful sexiness, and fiery Geri Halliwell was soon christened Ginger Spice, fresh-faced Emma Bunton became Baby, scowling Victoria Adams' became Posh, with footie-mad Melanie Chisholm cast as Sporty and Mel, Scary Spice.

The band was assembled after the quintet responded to a 1993 advertisement in a trade magazine for a manufactured female pop group. The girls all had talents and backgrounds in dance and acting and became housemates. They signed to Virgin Records in 1995 after dumping their management and came under the control of Svengali Simon Fuller, who would later create the *Pop Idol* and *American Idol* TV formats. I remember having lunch with Simon Cowell, then an unknown executive at BMG Records, and he mentioned he had been offered a role as a judge on a new talent show series called *Pop Idol*. They wanted him to be a Mr Nasty pantomime villain figure, he explained, before claiming he was probably going to turn it down because he had no urge to be famous. I laughed directly in the face of the same man who had a mirror on his office wall, emblazoned with the words: 'Yes, Simon, you look fabulous.' Cowell also shared that he had put me forward as a fellow judge, which he claimed ITV later vetoed, believing that my presence would hinder coverage in rival publications. Perhaps they were right. Them's the breaks.

1996

My first encounter with the girls came in the early summer of 1996, around the release of 'Wannabe', not long after Oasis at Maine Road and just ahead of Knebworth, when the girls visited *The Sun*'s offices. They were a whirlwind. The riotous quintet ran wild around the editorial floor – there were kisses, cuddles, executive tie-pulling, mocking, lipstick, laughter, legendary photographs, the heavy scent of perfume, loads of cleavage and a bit of acapella – it was a smart way of endearing themselves to the entire *Sun* staff on production, features, news and picture desks, and winning over employees young and old, back room and front-of-house, getting company-wide buy-in for the Spice brand at all levels, early doors. Who are these maniacal wannabes, we collectively pondered, but it was apparent they were going to be a force to be reckoned with and an onslaught of coverage ensued. Their high-intensity, no-nonsense personalities, their striking and contrasting good looks and distinctive fashion styles were intoxicating and 'Wannabe' – not my music of taste, but obviously I wasn't the demographic – nonetheless became a stone-cold classic pop song and feminist anthem.

The promotional coming-into-the-office trick was one that would be replicated by many pop acts and entertainers from that point on, and a steady stream trickled in to see us: Hearsay, Ant & Dec, Jason Donovan, comedians Harry Enfield as Kevin the Teenager, Rowan Atkinson as Mr Bean and Sacha Baron Cohen, memorably in character as his four blockbuster alter egos over a number of years: Ali G, Borat, Bruno and then The Dictator. He even signed a photo of us together with the message: 'Keep da beast clean.' Wicked innit.

Rowan was the only one who ever refused to break out of his persona. He parked his Mini millimetres from the glass office door and then, once inside the newsroom, spent an age picking up papers and screwing them up, plucking random objects from desks and scrutinising them up close, while making strange gurgling noises, but not once uttering a single, decipherable word. When I addressed him as Rowan, asking what other projects he might be working on in order to construct some sort of salient interview from this peculiar encounter, he gurned at me, looking confused and rubber-faced, before grunting: 'Wooo. Maaa. Bleee. Noo. Oooo.' (Or something not too dissimilar.) I'm not even sure how to spell such absurd utterances – but he landed loads of coverage for his latest film.

Spice were ubiquitous and 'Wannabe' inescapable, on TV music shows and radio. Girls would dress as their favourite Spice, something I hadn't really observed before, and certainly a precursor to the cowboy-hatted modern-day Swifties and Beyoncé-botherers. The song topped the charts in the UK for seven weeks – keeping Robbie Williams' debut off number one – and did the same in Australia, Belgium, Denmark, Estonia, Finland, France, Germany, Holland, Hong Kong, Hungary, Ireland, Israel, New Zealand, Norway, Spain, Sweden, Switzerland, the US Billboard Hot 100 and even Zimbabwe, shifting 1,269,841 copies worldwide. The band has spent 179 weeks on the UK chart, 135 weeks with their albums. Sorry to be such a statto.

1996

In the first two years, the girls' empire was estimated to have pulled in half a billion pounds and they were the first act to propel its first six singles to number one and the only group ever to spawn five solo hitmakers. Even Chancellor Ken Clarke tried to get in on the act when he gave a rather dull speech outlining his hopes for the very economy they had spiced up, employing the line: 'I'll tell you what I want, what I really, really want. I want to see healthy sustainable growth and rising living standards.' Zig-a-zig naaah.

Looking back, it seems like I was interviewing one or other of them every few months, with (usually Page One) headlines such as: 'I Speak to David 40 Times a Day, Says Posh', 'Life with David Is Everything I Wanted, Says Victoria', 'Becks in Fury Over Posh Boob Taunt', 'I've Taken a Vow of Celibacy Says Geri', 'My Love for Chris, by Geri', 'I Got a Belly Tattoo After My Grandparents Died ... I Feel Like They Are My Guardian Angels: Mel C Exclusive', 'Football's Too Scary for Baby, Says Posh', 'Exclusive: Posh and Becks Made Me Believe in Love Again: Emma Talks to Dominic Mohan' and, one of my favourites, which graced the front page, no less: 'Geri Rushed to Hospital with Fingernail Stuck in Ear'. Ginger had to be seen by doctors after a false nail became lodged in her lughole during a video shoot. That one didn't quite land the Pulitzer Prize we were hoping for.

Geri stunned us all by walking out of the group in 1998 following a row with the girls after she granted an exclusive interview to my colleague Victoria Newton following a cancer scare. It came just hours after our infamous meeting at *Top of the Pops* with the crew from Vindaloo.

SPICE

Geri later told me: 'It all started off when *The Sun* did an interview about my breast cancer fears. I knew I had to do something about the issue and maybe I did get overemotional about it. The girls were behind me to a point but then an interview I was doing with ITN was cancelled. I was furious. I don't really want to get into who made the decision, but I would have felt a liar and a hypocrite if I hadn't done anything about it. I felt I was losing my soul and integrity, and I had to get my priorities right, so I left.' She then revealed that she hadn't been invited to David and Victoria Beckham's wedding later that year.

Posh and Becks, as they had become known by then, of course, pulled off a deal rumoured to be worth £1 million with *OK!* magazine. I travelled to Ireland to cover the 'sumptuous nuptials', as the mag might call it, and tried to get a glimpse of the happy day. The security was off the scale. The magazine even had its own helicopter to protect airspace around medieval Luttrellstown Castle, near Dublin, which would chase off rival choppers trying to invade its territory. This meant the noise overhead on the happy day was deafening and it sounded like something out of *Apocalypse Now*. How romantic.

But someone who shouldn't have leaked to *The Sun* exclusive pictures of the couple on their regal thrones at the fairy-tale wedding banquet, both dressed in white, and surrounded by bouquets of flowers and ivy that would have made Elton John blush. Near-nude figures of the couple were iced on their spectacular cake. Coverage extended to six pages and ITN interviewed me about scooping *OK!*. There obviously weren't any hard feelings because, when my wife gave birth to our first child in 1999, the first bouquet to arrive – literally within the hour – was 'With love from Victoria and David'. Or from their publicist, at least.

David Beckham had become a household name in 96, scoring a spectacular halfway-line goal against Wimbledon on the first day of the season after breaking into the Manchester United first team. He made his senior England debut a few weeks later on 1 September, aged 21, in a 3–0 away win against Moldova and scooped the PFA Young Player of the Year award that season.

Just after Geri left the group, I travelled to Italy to watch the four-piece perform with tenor Luciano Pavarotti in his hometown Modena. Pavarotti was everywhere in the 90s, bringing opera to the masses after his classic 'Nessun Dorma' was chosen as the BBC's World Cup theme tune in 1990.

Mel B told me: 'It was a huge shock at first, like we had all lost a limb. But if someone wants to move on you can't hold them back. We're all growing up and wanting to do our own things. Geri's growing up too and if she wanted to go in another direction that's up to her.' And Victoria added: 'We've all known each other for so many years and been through so much. The band is so strong. We all love each other and we all love Geri.'

I would later bid for Geri's epochal Union Jack dress at a Sotheby's charity auction: after Chris Evans (who briefly dated Geri in the late 90s) folded at £31,000, I battled against the Las Vegas Hard Rock Hotel, but they gazumped me at £36,200. I must stress that this was *The Sun*'s money, not my own, but the dress wasn't my size anyway. I felt like I'd lost the Cup Final but did get my hands on Geri's Girl Power dress for £1,500, the one she wore in *Spiceworld: The Movie*, and we gave it away in a competition. This raised funds for the CLIC Sargent Cancer Care for Children charity; afterwards Geri said: 'You were brilliant, Dominic. I'm so pleased with how things went. It's incredible the amount we raised. It was really exciting but nerve-wracking.' Chris Evans rang me later that day and said: 'I really wanted the dress. It was you and me from £15,000 to £31,000, but I decided to pull out. Those Hard Rock bastards.'

The Spice Girls were helping to mould young British fashion, as were a slew of new British designers who were rising alongside the YBAs. Stella McCartney helped make her dad cool again while Bowie had read about an up-and-coming British fashionista by the name of Alexander McQueen and, in 1996, commissioned him to design his now iconic Union Jack frockcoat, which he showcased at the VH1 Fashion Awards that year.

It felt like these radical and fearless designers like McQueen, Vivienne Westwood and John Galliano were prepared to go to extremes and take risks in the 90s, regardless of any criticism they might receive. Zero flying fucks given back then. When asked for her memories of the 90s, Stella admitted she didn't recall anything of the decade because it was so wild.

Spice budgets were wild too. When Geri launched her solo career in New York, I was the sole British journalist flown out there with her for an exclusive chat, in which she spoke about her sex life: 'I have taken a vow of celibacy. I've squeezed out all my emotions for my solo career – it's been a sacrifice. I haven't been in a serious relationship for five years.' Not long afterwards, that sacred chastity was swiftly jettisoned, when she hooked up with broadcaster Chris Evans. And, when she later returned to *The Sun*'s London HQ, she confirmed they were lovers, telling me: 'He is great and very sweet. Everything has come together and it's fantastic.' Geri would also go on to date Robbie Williams, aristocrat Henry Beckwith, while laughing off reported flings with Russell Brand and David Walliams, before settling down with former Red Bull F1 team principal and later a client, Christian Horner, with whom she has a son, Monty, born in 2017.

Geri could be unpredictable. On one occasion, when I started asking her some tricky questions during an interview, she jumped up and lay on top of me, pinning me down quite aggressively on a chaise longue, her face up close to mine and screeching repeatedly: 'Why are you being so horrible to me?' She rarely had much of a filter – another time, we met up at London's St Pancras station and her opening words to me were: 'Ooh. This is exciting. It feels naughty, like we're having an affair.'

Victoria equally so. When I introduced her to my wife Michelle, mother of our two boys, Posh immediately snapped: 'Yuk! You've really had sex with Dominic twice?' Husband David chuckled at his wife's sharp tongue – she may look moody but she can be very witty and harsh. Of course, Victoria, sorry Lady Beckham, now leads a very refined bucolic life, of luxurious tweeds and the Cotswolds, sipping on fine vintage wines. Quite a contrast to the young woman I once took to a bar where she ordered a Sancerre and lemonade. Very posh, Spice.

The girls were pretty media-savvy and rarely put a platform-heeled foot wrong, until one infamous interrogation. Geri praised Margaret Thatcher in *The Spectator* magazine and boasted that the band were all true Thatcherites. This went down very badly with scouser Mel C and, in 2001, Geri took part in a Labour Party political broadcast for Tony Blair. 'She saw the light,' Mel declared.

The band would limp on without Geri into the new century dawned but finally imploded in March 2001. I wrote the front-page Spice obituary, under the headline 'End of the Spice Girls'. It was an odd feeling writing it, I remember. This global phenomenon had exploded on to our streets and newspapers and now it was no more. The story-machine had failed to viva forever. Well, until 2007 actually, when all five members reunited for The Return of the Spice Girls Tour. Tickets for the first return show in London sold out in 38 seconds as five million people worldwide signed up for the ticket ballot on the quintet's website. Each member earned £10 million from the dates. It was fun enough but felt rather meaningless and irrelevant by then.

Five years on from that, the group performed a medley of 'Wannabe' and 'Spice Up Your Life' at the closing ceremony of the London 2012 Olympic Games. And, in 2018, the girls would reunite again for another tour, without Victoria Beckham scowling at the side, however. They still pocketed £12 million each for that one.

1996

In another emotional interview, Geri told me about her very close friendship with George Michael and described him as her saviour when she quit the band. She said: 'He's been a pillar of strength for me. When I left the group I was meant to be staying with him for three days, but I ended up staying three months. He knows me really well and can sometimes see through me, which is kind of scary. We have a lot in common and it's a real and honest friendship. He gives me advice and criticism and really helped me with my confidence.'

This was about the same time that the world was searching for George, who'd gone AWOL. The troubled former Wham! singer/songwriter disappeared off the face of planet earth after being arrested in April 1998 for committing a lewd sex act, in front of an undercover police officer in a Los Angeles public toilet.

Many assumed he was lying low in a different corner of the world until the furore died down. *The Sun* had rather memorably covered the story with the headline 'Zip Me Up Before You Go Go', which would scoop front page of the year. It wasn't one of mine, annoyingly. I'd tried to arrange an official interview with George, who I'd met previously, but to no avail. He was staying shtum.

After a typical punishing week at *The Sun*, Friday nights were a moment to let go and forget the stresses of the job. It was a dream role for sure, but one which would often cause difficulties in one's personal life. Missing birthdays, Valentine's Days and anniversaries were customary, as I was sent around the world or stuck in the office late, trying to crack a story. One particular evening, not long after

George's arrest, I was out in the West End. Exhausted, I had a squabble with the missus and decided to go home to our top-floor flat in Swiss Cottage for an earlyish night. In September the previous year, we had watched Princess Diana's rose-covered funeral cortège slowly travelling up a mourner-lined Finchley Road from our roof terrace, with a feeling that this was the symbolic end of Swinging London and the feelgood 90s.

Arriving home alone, I checked my pockets. Pen and paper? Yes. Phone? Of course. But where the hell were my keys? I was locked out with no one in the building. It was a pleasant evening and, assuming she'd be home soon, I sat at the top of the steps leaning against the front door. Alas. Nothing – and she wasn't picking up the blower either, as was (and still is) rather common.

Opposite the flat, at the bottom of Fitzjohn's Avenue, just off the Finchley Road, was a rather handy 24-hour shop called Lobins, perfect for late-night booze and food runs. They did a lovely chicken baguette. To kill some time, I wandered over and flicked through the magazine racks, grabbing a pack of Red Stripe. I was alone in the store with the owner but both of us turned around suddenly as a bell rang and the doors flew open. Two men, themselves rather refreshed, crashed in from a stretch limo parked outside. It was 2am.

I recognised the first chap as he entered. It was Andros Georgiou, the cousin and confidant of a certain George Michael. And, behind him, was an absolutely flawlessly dressed, goateed gentleman, wearing an immaculate black suit and blue baseball cap.

1996

In a rather familiar voice, he asked for a dozen Diet Cokes, mineral waters and a packet of Camel Lights. Um. Er. What? This cannot be really happening, I said to myself. It was only George Chuffin' Michael, the Wham! genius the world's media had been searching for. In my corner shop. Opposite my flippin' flat. Had I entered some kind of parallel dimension of journalistic paradise where scoops were served aplenty? Or had my drinks been spiked earlier in the evening and I was hallucinating? Was the stress getting to me at last and the plot being lost?

He and Andros sidled over to the magazines themselves, poring over the glossy pages of *Arena* and *GQ*. George exclaimed, 'Ooooh! Look, it's Beckham, we must get that one.' When Andros called him Yog, this was my absolute confirmation of the duo's identity, as I knew Yog was the affectionate nickname only George's closest friends used for him, a shortened version of his Greek name Georgios. This was obviously the easy-to-stop-at, all-night store before travelling up the hill to Yog Towers.

I needed to seize the moment. I approached him and proffered my palm and we pressed the flesh. I was touching *that* hand, possibly the most famous hand on the planet at that moment in time. I can confirm he had a very firm grip.

'George, it's Dominic. How are things?' I enquired.

'Hi. Yes. It's been a weird couple of weeks but, you know, things are settling down a bit. I've just been out with a few mates and we're going back to mine.'

'Thank you, George,' was my reply

'Goodbye,' he said.

And that was it. The pair exited and I made my way back to the flat, pulling the cheap pen and paper, which I always carried, from my pocket. I immediately scribbled down the admittedly rather brief exchange.

I waited a while on the steps before checking my watch and abandoning ship. Fortunately, there was a reasonable hotel a few minutes' walk away and I was soon checked into the Marriott. I crashed out and woke up fully clothed on the bed eight hours later. I'd initially forgotten the night's encounter but, as I sipped one of those nasty hotel instant coffees, it hit me. I scrambled for my pad and discovered several scrawled paragraphs of notes on a crumpled page. It had really happened. I needed to tell the office.

Each morning on a daily newspaper, the heads of departments (news, sport, features, business and showbiz) prepare a list of topics and ideas they would like to propose for the next day's edition and present them in a late morning conference to the editor. On a Sunday and bank holidays, there is an approved rota of executives who are permitted to sit in the editor's chair.

It was approaching 11am and I called the news desk. I told them I had something for the list – an exclusive interview with George Michael. They refused to believe me. When I explained the circumstances they asked me if I needed a lie-down.

I filed over the piece and it made a fun addition to the following day's paper. It wasn't quite as in-depth as many of my interviews, granted, and Michael Parkinson would later probe a little deeper, but I had got the first newspaper words with George, however brief, since his arrest.

1996

Journalism is often about being in the right place at the right time, often through planning and design and deliberately inserting oneself there, but this was a completely random encounter sparked by a chain of arbitrary events.

The next day, the headline read: 'George Speaks: Dominic gets interview of the year ... at 2am in 24-hour supermarket off the Finchley Road'.

The copy said: 'It's the showbiz exclusive of the year – the big one they ALL wanted. George Michael has opened his heart to Bizarre's Dominic Mohan in his first newspaper interview since being caught by an undercover cop in a Los Angeles public loo last month.'

Okay, so it wasn't your conventional interview. Not a suite at the Metropolitan Hotel or the Dorchester for this one.

When Parky interviewed George later that year, the singer said he felt privileged to be on the show, explaining how his mother would allow him to stay up late to watch the programme. At the beginning of the exchange, George memorably quipped: 'She probably wouldn't have been quite as thrilled that I had to take my willy out to get on here. I mean really, would I have been on for an hour tonight without that incident?'

It was a textbook example of how to handle a crisis. If there is an elephant in the room, take ownership of it as early as possible, defuse the interview with humour and address the issue head-on. It is precisely the approach I use with clients in tricky situations.

The following year, George would conduct a considerably longer interview with *The Sun* – and *The Mirror*,

Express and *Daily Star* (although, pointedly, not the *Daily Mail*) after another strange turn of events.

I was back at the Landmark Hotel, three years after my Oasis encounter there, for a press conference to promote George's appearance at the Wembley Stadium charity NetAid concert the next month, alongside Robbie Williams, Stereophonics, Bono, Eurythmics and a revived David Bowie – raising money for the poor and highlighting the plight of Kosovan refugees. The oft-reclusive George, immaculate again in green suit and a rather fetching orange shirt and tie number, told us: 'If we get sufficient and respectable and compassionate coverage of today's conference, I will personally speak to the editor of each of the tabloid newspapers tomorrow on the phone about anything they like.' We had never heard anything like it and were taken aback, but not quite as stunned as George's own PR team.

I swiftly rang the office and explained all, urging the paper's editor David Yelland to adhere to George's wishes and give the event the coverage it deserved. I knew Piers Morgan, now Editor over at *The Mirror*, would be all over it and was concerned David would be contrary. He saw himself as a more upmarket editor and, by his own admission, didn't really have a nose for celebrity, once splashing on a story about Ed Balls on the day I had landed Madonna's first-ever interview with the paper. That was a tough one. Fair play though, he gave the launch a good showing (as did our rivals) and George duly rang around and confronted his demons the following day. It must have been his most dreaded nightmare.

It's intriguing to study those lengthy interviews today, as they not only give compelling insight into George himself – but also shine a light on the editors themselves, their personalities and those of their newspapers at that moment in time.

The *Mirror* headline roared: 'I'd like to bed Tom ... and Nicole'. When George was asked if he could choose any woman from any time, he admitted he would sleep with Elizabeth Taylor. Piers, a former Bizarre editor himself, of course, then asked him a series of quick-fire questions about threesomes, playing Grant Mitchell's boyfriend in *EastEnders* and stuffing shuttlecocks down his pants.

Yelland, who generously stuck my byline on the interview, chose to quiz him in depth about political issues and figures, such as married top Tory and ex-Defence Secretary Michael Portillo, who had opposed lowering the age of consent for homosexuals, despite having admitted gay flings as a student. And a disgusted George didn't hold back, claiming Portillo's confessions were only 'half-truths' and branded him a hypocrite. 'I am very surprised that someone who claims to be a politician is stupid enough to think that he can tell half of the truth. And I think anyone who has supported differing ages of consent for men and women, when it is very obvious that he was having sex with men when he was a young man, is a complete hypocrite. He disgusts me, to be honest with you.'

This emphasised the paper's more progressive and liberal attitude towards politics and sexuality, with some of the more rumbustious hallmarks of its past being shed, perhaps becoming more in tune with the times, echoing new PM

Tony Blair's outlook. This was something future editors like me would later try to embrace and carry on, with campaigning and compassion remaining central pillars – but alongside sparkle, wit and world-beating headlines, naturally.

Yelland's intelligent, in-depth questioning had revealed George's more cerebral nature, highlighting his profundity, knowledge and comprehension of such political and social issues, and less of the wild man of old perhaps, although his premature death would suggest otherwise.

In the preceding decades, George had been a regular at hedonistic nights at fabled club Stringfellows, attending Rod Stewart's legendary birthday party there in 1986, alongside Paul Young, Cliff Richard and Ronnie Wood. It held fond memories for him because his band Wham! had made early appearances there. It was during one such performance there that a BBC producer discovered the group, and thought they would be perfect for *Saturday Superstore*, a weekend children's TV programme, before cooking shows ruled the sabbath schedules. Their performance on the programme put them on the radar of *Top of the Pops* and, when another act pulled out at the last minute, George and Andrew were booked to perform 'Young Guns', in November 1982. And bang! Wham! exploded.

George and his pop contemporaries were regular guests at the venue and throughout the 80s and, certainly, the earlier parts of the 90s, maverick Peter Stringfellow was the country's most famous club owner, a TV personality and, on occasion, a rather publicity-seeking, indiscreet,

1996

mullet-flicking ball of raw energy, with a penchant for youthful dancers and his 'n' hers leopard-skin G-strings. Every time I was in his company, he would call me 'Dominique', as if I went under one of his pole dancers' monikers.

His club was founded in 1980, housed just off Leicester Square, and would eventually feature what he called 'table-side dancing' from 1996. In many ways, the club was a 70s and 80s cultural throwback that bled into the 90s and became quite outdated – it was certainly something of an anathema to me. Guests included Prince, Marvin Gaye, Tom Jones, Jack Nicholson, Colin Farrell, Oliver Reed, Simon Cowell, Chris Evans, Mel B, Rihanna and even Professor Stephen Hawking, who loved a lap-dance from Peter's Angels. Actor Kiefer Sutherland was memorably snapped in a ripped shirt there and was ejected by bouncers in 2010. There were always photographers about, helping to feed Stringy's appetite for publicity.

But, in those heady early days, it was part of the job description to worship weekly at story-machine Stringy's leopard-skin throne – and he was an intriguing and jocular host. You'd always come home with a belly full of gratis champagne and ropey chicken and chips – but, most importantly, an exclusive. Fortunately, I had a strong constitution and a very tolerant missus.

One generous evening, Peter dangled his golden locks close to my ear, as his nubile showgirls wiggled their oiled buttocks close to the other one. He then revealed that Simply Red's Mick Hucknall had been an enthusiastic visitor, just days earlier, but Peter complained that the ginger crooner was a little stingy when it came to tipping the girls and simply lapped up free dances. Thank you very much, a page lead in my lap and in the next edition, under the headline 'Mick's Too Tight to Mention'.

After another 3am encounter, Peter insisted that his personal chauffeur drop me off at home in his baby-blue classic Rolls-Royce, with antique wooden steering wheel. I was a little embarrassed by my humble two-bedroomed ground-floor flat and asked the driver to drop me around the corner.

Stringfellow was a relentless, column-packing story-magnet and he was extremely media-savvy, feeding celebrated Bizarre editors with gossip and indiscretions over decades and ensuring continued focus on his increasingly controversial establishment. At a celebration dinner for the column's 20th birthday at London's Café Royal, alumni from this academy of tabloid excellence assembled, and Stringy was introduced as the guest of honour. He paid tribute to Bizarre editors old and new, all of whom were present, including inaugural editor John Blake, eulogising about its journalists and their vital role in the explosion of his nightclub business. Bizarre really had become a byword for popular culture. Never have so many egos been in one room without there being violence, but back-slapping and back-stabbing were served up in equal measure.

'I want to thank every one of you and give something back to Bizarre,' Stringy proclaimed, before clicking his fingers and uttering the word: 'Ladies!' At that precise moment, a foxy phalanx of a dozen underwear-clad strippers emerged from the shadows and began to bobble,

Stringfellows-style, at the booze-laden tables. An uncomfortable-looking Victoria Newton was close by, but I happened to be sitting next to former Bizarre editor, and now LBC host, Nick Ferrari. As a blonde, clad in very little, wiggled close to his rosy sweating head, he provided an accidental Alan Partridge-style commentary throughout proceedings. 'Ohh I say,' he muttered, followed by 'Extraordinary' and 'Absolutely remarkable,' punctuating Stringy's girl's jiggling, writhing and teasing. As she moved to peel down her thong, Nick could barely contain himself and blurted: 'Suuuurely not?'

At the other end of the scale, Le Caprice and The Ivy were two of the classiest restaurants in London, where you'd also often stumble on interesting stories and couplings, lavish rooms packed full of media folk and celebrity. You never knew whether you were going to bump into Princess Diana, Smokey Robinson, Alex from Blur or Christopher Biggins. Entrepreneur Nick Jones opened Soho House in 1995 too, not far from Oliver Peyton's buzzing Atlantic Bar & Grill, which had launched in April 1994 and was always brimming with beautiful people – and journalists. Robert De Niro, Bono, Björk, Robert Downey Jr, Bill Murray, Damien Hirst, Tracey Emin, Liam, Steve Coogan and Jonathan Ross were all spotted there. But, not long after, in 1998, chef Marco Pierre White launched Titanic above in the same building, prompting a legal dispute. The idea was that it was the Titanic floating atop the Atlantic (geddit?), but this hadn't gone down well. Marco had become the youngest chef to win three Michelin stars after he had been appointed chef-patron of The

Restaurant Marco Pierre White at the former Hyde Park Hotel. In 1997, his protégé-turned-rival Gordon Ramsay won his second Michelin star at Aubergine in Chelsea.

One frequent visitor to Titanic was Vernon Kay – his career was on the up and he was snapped by paparazzi leaving the restaurant not long after moving to London in the late 90s, where he had landed work as a model after being randomly spotted by an agent in Manchester. He lived with a group of similar lads, who were unsure about how they should tackle their new life on the catwalk, before collectively deciding to just 'walk like Liam Gallagher'.

'There's one picture of me coming out of Titanic, actually,' said Vernon. 'And it was in the paper and it was in a couple of magazines. I flipped the fingers to the paparazzi. My mum saw it and went apeshit. Thought it was disrespectful. My mum said: "You're not one of them Gallagher boys." So, that's why I'm like, "I'll leave it to Liam."'

But the establishment to be seen at in the mid-to-late 90s was the Met Bar on Park Lane, which served the Metropolitan Hotel upstairs. It was next to the infamous Nobu restaurant where, in 1999, tennis champ Boris Becker had sex with waitress Angela Ermakova in a broom cupboard, five minutes after they met, resulting in her pregnancy. But the Met Bar was sometimes tricky to blag your way into, and it was minuscule. Thursday night was when it all kicked off, the shenanigans organised by Meg Mathews's best pal Fran Cutler, dubbed the Party Rottweiler. She could certainly organise a soirée and wasn't afraid of barking at revellers and booting them out.

1996

You'd often see faces like the Kates Winslet and Moss, Johnny Depp, Kylie Minogue, the Spice Girls, Huey Morgan from Fun Lovin' Criminals, Leonardo DiCaprio, Michael Douglas, Jay Kay from Jamiroquai, the Manic Street Preachers, Blur, England players like Beckham, Teddy Sheringham and Darren Anderton – who had a meltdown one night when the missus tackled him about his 'Sicknote' nickname. Bon viveurs packed like pickled sardines into the confined space, with a mirrored wall at the far end, one which I walked straight into during my first visit, disbelieving that the place could be so minute. On another occasion, I spotted Liam and Patsy and bowled over to chat, then accidentally knocked over his beer, which toppled into his lap, staining his light-coloured trousers. He was surprisingly OK about it but flipped when I dared to offer to replace his lager. 'Why would I need you to buy me a drink?' he jabbered while jumping like a small ape, some weird northern macho nonsense, before Fran told him to be calm and sit down, like a mother attempting to placate a moody toddler who is past his bedtime. Not long after that, All Saints were in, with rumours swirling about Nicole Appleton's closeness to Liam. One night, she collared me in there and kept over-insisting: 'Liam and I are just really good friends. There's nothing going on, I promise you.' They went public with their relationship in 2000 after Liam divorced Patsy – and the couple married on Valentine's Day 2008.

But, perhaps, the greatest celeb spot there was witnessing Madonna strutting her stuff on the makeshift dancefloor with *Easy Rider* actor Dennis Hopper. It was Cool Britannia

HQ, not a smartphone or camera in sight, just pure, unbridled fun. Another late night there, I watched Mel B chewing the face off actor and musician Max Beesley, in a rather excessive and nauseating PDA. I rang Mel's publicist the following day and explained that I was running the story in the next edition. Even though I myself was witness to this snogfest, she denied it had ever taken place and threatened to issue a denial via the Press Association if it was printed. Undeterred, I went ahead. And so did she. I received a bollocking from the editor and defended my position vigorously. A few weeks later, Max and Mel adorned the front cover of *OK!* magazine enthusing, presumably quite lucratively, about their new-found love. When I telephoned the aforementioned, denial-issuing publicist for an explanation, she had the audacity to declare: 'It wasn't true at the time.' I informed her that, with my new-found capacity to predict future events, I would be applying for the job as *The Sun*'s astrologer forthwith.

I've always thought it's a very short-term and blinkered strategy for a publicist to knowingly lie to a journalist. I understand they are on occasion deceived by their client's instructions, but celebrity clients come and go while the more meaningful and useful long-term relationships can be with journalists and those in the media. If a PR lied to me, I would never trust their word again, especially as I rose up the executive ranks to Editor, and they would lose the power and influence of that bond. That's how a publicist's currency and relevance fades.

Such mad moments and, um, bizarre interactions with celebrities and their gatekeepers happened on a daily basis, and became part of my working life, providing an endless stream of colourful copy for my bosses, documenting Britain's wildest decade and a thronging and decadent London. But my own – and later my editor's – encounters with the most powerful celebrities of that era would rarely be straightforward, as you will learn in my next chapter.

The Spice Girls assault in 1996 seized power and dominance of the British – and worldwide – media, as the year and decade dazzled on. They were fun to be around and began to steal column inches from all those guitar bands, their outlandishness, fashion and love lives an enduring curiosity – still evident today.

Spice would inspire scores of young girls and boys to audition and follow their platform-booted path, with hungry entrepreneurial managers circling. The quintet sparked a record company and televisual revolution and stampede for the next manufactured pop group, transforming the popular culture landscape and gradually shifting the narrative away from guitar music – and on to our TV screens.

But, as 'Wannabe' sat atop the UK charts throughout August 1996 and, furthermore, most of the world, there was the trifling matter of two of the most significant concerts in British music history about to take place somewhere in a field in Knebworth Park, Hertfordshire. Come with me.

SPICE

My Top Ten Singles of the 90s

1. **Oasis – 'Live Forever' (1994):** The song that put Noel on the map as the most gifted songwriter of his generation. Liam's transcendent vocals combine with his brother's spine-tingling guitar solo. Inspired by the Rolling Stones' 'Shine a Light'. If a man is tired of 'Live Forever', he is tired of life.
2. **The Verve – 'Bittersweet Symphony' (1997):** Listened to this back-to-back fifteen times the day it was first released. Genius sample and soundtrack of the late 90s, with Richard Ashcroft's apt lyricism. The song that saved the 90s. Bring back The Verve!
3. **Oasis – 'Wonderwall' (1995):** Liam's greatest recorded vocal performance. The world suddenly sat up and realised what we'd all been banging on about.
4. **Nirvana – 'Smells Like Teen Spirit' (1991):** Had never heard a thing like it and this angst-laden anthem spoke for a generation. Kurt Cobain – what a loss.
5. **Pulp – 'Common People' (1995):** To many, this is the apex of the 90s Britpop single. Such a statement and Jarvis at his lyrical highpoint. An unforgettable Pulp concert favourite.
6. **Faithless – 'Insomnia' (1995):** *The* dance anthem of the wildest of decades. The alchemy of mystical murmurings from much-missed Maxi Jazz seared with the wizardry of Rollo and Sister Bliss is proof that dance music bands can work. Breathtaking live.

1996

7. **Blur – 'Girls & Boys' (1994):** I love 'The Universal' and 'Parklife' too, but this typifies the 90s in so many ways with its upbeat, Club 18–30 holiday theme. It's laddish and all that malarkey but hints at sexual fluidity and a more modern gender view, which was beginning to chime. Take a bow, Damon Albarn, you visionary.
8. **The Spice Girls – 'Wannabe' (1996):** Has to be in any 90s top ten as this is a definitive and groundbreaking pop moment that played its part in transforming British society and ushered Girl Power into the homes and playgrounds of contemporary Britain – and much further beyond.
9. **The Prodigy – 'Firestarter' (1996):** The pioneering pop soundtrack to a nightmare, 'Firestarter' took the band to a new, hellish level. Keith its haunting face yet such a kind, softly spoken and gentle man in person. RIP Keith Flint.
10. **Massive Attack – 'Unfinished Sympathy' (1991):** There hasn't really been another record like it before or since. The Bristolians' mesmerising moment with Shara Nelson's timeless vocals is mixed with a sense of anxiety and loss – and those strings, good Lord.

CHAPTER 7

Knebworth

**And the night Noel insulted *The Sun*
editor then slapped his head**

Knebworth was the Oasis moment to surpass all others.

1996 was the zenith of the 1990s and those two concerts, their jaw-dropping scale and cultural significance, was the apex of 1996. This is why, as we chronicle the year moving forward, we must now revisit Oasis and their further ascension in August of that year – those twin, epic, balmy, mythical nights with more than 250,000 in attendance. *The Sun* printed a souvenir poster to mark the occasion and Radio Supernova broadcast on 106.6 FM within a 20-mile radius of the site.

We had collectively lurched from Kentish Town, August 1994, to Earls Court, November 1995, via the Brit Awards, February 1996, to Maine Road, April 1996. Next on this unheralded horizon were the unprecedented outdoor shows at Loch Lomond in Scotland and, of course, the pre-eminent Knebworth spectacles four months later on 10 and 11 August. As 1996 snowballed on and intensified, the unparalleled rise of the Gallagher brothers had become a relentless journalistic – and then, by extension, national – fascination, obsession even.

1996

The Spice Girls may have been perched at the chart pinnacle, queens of the world for a bit, but two and a half million of us meanwhile were scrambling for tickets (that's nearly 5 per cent of the population) to stand in a field near Stevenage for the decade-defining moment. And, yes, I paid for mine.

Models, footballers, artists and authors mingled backstage. Kate Moss, Jarvis Cocker, Simply Red's Mick Hucknall, Stuart Pearce again with his Nottingham Forest teammates, actresses Anna Friel and *EastEnder* Martine McCutcheon. Broadcaster Chris Evans was there but does not remember so. We watched the band's helicopter landing backstage from the crowd and Liam christened this weekend the Woodstock of the 90s.

The missus and I were gathered with a growing group of friends and I'd managed to snaffle two stick-on VIP passes, courtesy of a certain Mr Johnny Hopkins, which granted access to the complimentary bar. There were 7,000 on the guest list over that weekend and Alan McGee reckoned the bar tab alone cost him more than £250,000. With some furtive sticker swapping, we were able to sneak twenty-two people into the hallowed, now-mythical area, perhaps in some way helping to facilitate the ushering-in of a novel and more draconian VIP wristband system to prevent such skullduggery. We took black and white photos on a disposable Kodak (no cameraphones then). They offer a blurry insight into a more innocent time of joy, freedom and happiness, not quite up there with Oasis official photographer Jill Furmanovsky's peerless shots but an indelible monochrome memory of magical moments.

KNEBWORTH

The vast hospitality marquee, emblazoned with a mammoth banner reading 'Creation Records. World Class' really was a carnival-like promised land, lined with bars, all fully stocked with pretty much any drink you wanted. Hooch even, I recall, which was the drink of the moment. There was a barbecue, which sizzled all day long. We saw caricaturists sketching free portraits for punters and magicians doing tricks for the soon-to-be sozzled and staggering guests.

The atmosphere was lively but super-friendly, as at the Live '25 concerts I experienced later, and the sunshiiine shone. There were only ten arrests over that fairy-tale weekend. Gangs of girls in cargo trousers and England tops, their partners clad in the Oasis uniform of bucket hats, chequered shirts and Clarks Wallabees. On the Saturday, we witnessed a stellar line-up of support from The Chemical Brothers, Ocean Colour Scene, Manic Street Preachers and The Prodigy. Sunday's line-up was a touch weaker, with Cast, Dreadzone, Kula Shaker, the Manics again and The Charlatans. Either way, those alone would have been a bargain for the £22.50 ticket price. But the Oasis set was momentous. Liam snarled pitch-perfect through all the classics and then gave a monumental rendition of 'Champagne Supernova', when the brothers were joined by their guitar hero, a flu-ridden John Squire of The Stone Roses.

'This is history. This is history. Right here. Right now. This is history,' Noel chirped. He was not wrong. As a 20-something journalist on the UK's bestselling paper, it was a privilege to be the chronicler of such halcyon times and momentous events, I thought to myself, as I dictated copy from my landline home phone the following day. I was only six years into my career but was now being not-badly remunerated to postulate about super-talented homegrown talent, helping to articulate the transformative zeitgeist for a mass audience and record those memorable days in print. When I approached broadcaster Zoe Ball about her recollections of the era, she told me: 'You might remember more than me.' And Happy Monday Shaun Ryder also told me: 'I don't remember anything from the 1990s but I can remember the 1970s.' And, in 2015, Noel himself told Kirsty Young on Radio 4's *Desert Island Discs* that he could not actually recall walking on stage at Knebworth.

At this juncture, the Oasis schedule was relentlessly punishing and, in retrospect, perhaps the band should have been granted a prolonged break after the all-conquering Knebworth shows.

But just twelve days after their triumph, on 23 August, Oasis were booked to play at a prestigious *MTV Unplugged* gig at the Royal Festival Hall, a rite of passage reserved for the world's biggest artists, the greatest performances coming from The Cure, Nirvana and – one of the band's heroes – Neil Young. For *Unplugged*, the group would be filmed, stripped down, on London's South Bank in front of 2,700 fans. But, as they ambled on stage, one of them was missing in action. 'Liam ain't gonna be with us tonight 'cause he's got a sore throat,' Noel told us all in the slightly disheartened crowd, as he picked up his acoustic and sat down on a stool. 'So you're stuck with the ugly four,' he quipped.

KNEBWORTH

It was a laid-back, classic acoustic performance, which suited Noel's vocal style, in complete contrast to the screaming mega-shows less than two weeks earlier. This is how he wrote such classics after all. Enhanced by strings and horns, Noel nailed it with a poignant and intimate performance. The drama was intensified by a drunk, champagne-swigging Liam, who heckled from a box and made us all feel embarrassed for Noel who, it appeared, was being publicly humiliated from the posh seats. He later admitted his younger brother was 'shit-faced'.

The *New York Times* review said that it was almost Shakespearean, the brothers' rivalry condensed into a single performance. Yet another drama to add to the Gallagher canon and, indeed, more copy to be written to fill the pages of *The Sun* and to satisfy a voracious audience, desperate to read of every abusive twist and violent turn of the band's dynamic.

And, over the following days and weeks, there were many more of those to come. Less than 100 hours after the *Unplugged* debacle, the brothers were due to fly to Chicago for the start of a US tour. Liam refused to board the plane, claiming he needed to buy a house for him and his then-fiancée Patsy Kensit, telling reporters: 'I can't go looking for a house in America while I'm trying to perform to silly fucking yanks.' It sparked the memorable *Sun* front page: 'What's the Story? Liam Quits the Toury'. I'm not certain when the last time a story about a band member walking out on a tour had made the front-page splash and this is illustrative of the Oasis feeding frenzy in 1996.

1996

Gallagher Jr resumed the tour, but then it was Noel's turn to quit, resulting in the 'Blowasis' front page in September 1996, as he headed home on Concorde. This constant attrition and conflict made us fear that Oasis was over for good, but the biblical brothers patched it up once again and the band resurrected. The group and its management had pushed 96 too far and the wheels of the burning Oasis truck had come off as it hurtled downhill, to borrow an analogy used by manager Marcus Russell from Ignition (this according to the group's former tour boss Iain Robertson).

There was no better place to be than London at this moment in time – and word was getting round. At the end of that tumultuous year, Liam and Patsy posed for the cover of American glossy *Vanity Fair* wrapped in Union Flag bedding, and the mag proclaimed Britain the coolest country on the planet, screaming: 'London Swings Again'. However, Johnny Hopkins, along with Noel and the band's management, was against taking part in the shoot, as he explained to me: 'Oasis were no fans of Cool Britannia. They were not cheerleaders for it. Cool Britannia was a con-trick. It was a convenient term used by politicians and the media to paste over the cracks and to bolster their agendas. Just as the whole thing was dying. The nationalism lurking there in plain sight was a major concern for me. While there were fashion people within their circle like Kate Moss, Naomi Campbell and Stella McCartney, footballers like those at Man City, as well as the author Irvine Welsh, there were no real ties with anyone else within Cool Britannia. The Cool Britannia "scene" was never as connected as it was made out. The links between people were quite tenuous.'

But comedian Mike Myers would create his buck-toothed James Bond spoof character for the film *Austin Powers: International Man of Mystery*, starring woman-of-the-moment Liz Hurley and showcasing a swinging London. And we had some of the best authors on the planet – Nick Hornby had just penned *High Fidelity*, while Alex Garland wowed with groundbreaking *The Beach*, later turned into a hit film with music by a William Orbit-produced All Saints. Released in February 1996 and based on Irvine Welsh's 1993 novel, *Trainspotting* is Danny Boyle's frantic, heroin culture classic, which launched the career of Ewan McGregor. It was shot in Glasgow over seven weeks on a budget of £1.5 million. The sparkling soundtrack is Tarantino-esque but mixes alternative rock, old and new, and dance music to great effect. Iggy Pop's 'Lust for Life' became synonymous with the epic, as did Underworld's 'Born Slippy' and Bedrock's club anthem 'For What You Dream Of'. Blur and Pulp were also featured. Danny Boyle approached Oasis about contributing a song, but Noel turned down the invitation because he mistakenly thought the film to be about actual spotters of trains. In 1999, the film was ranked tenth by the British Film Institute in its list of Top 100 British movies of all time and won oodles of awards. We'd never seen a British film of its ilk. It certainly depicted the country a little differently to soppy 'Four Weddings and a Funeral' and 'Notting Hill'. The truth is that the best films that year and decade came from the US, but *Trainspotting* and *Lock, Stock* were the exceptions.

1996

Creation's Johnny Hopkins is generally more cautious in his assessment of the creativity of the 90s, across the arts: 'Apart from *Trainspotting*, British films were pretty poor then. But in America, Tarantino consistently made great films. I query the idea of a creative explosion in the 90s. Was there really a creative explosion? No! Much of it was rubbish – most Britpop bands were lame. The creative explosion was overrated. Creativity is always going on. It's just in the 90s creatives sought sensation and commercial success and the media wrote more about them all, pulling the strands together, selling it as the new Swinging Sixties.' Does he mean me?

Johnny's right though, most of the 90s best films were American, specifically by Quentin who was spitting out golden celluloid classics just as Noel was in song. He was, disappointingly, a bit of a miserable tosser when I later interviewed him, however.

Workaholic Noel, meanwhile, had begun working on the songs for 1997's *Be Here Now*, just after the Maine Road gigs, when he travelled to stay at Mick Jagger's home in Mustique in the Caribbean and when he bumped into Phil Collins. It was the most-anticipated record for decades following the success of its twin, earth-shattering predecessors.

The spectacular cover art for it was to be photographed and we received word of its staging at Stocks House, a Georgian mansion in Aldbury, Hertfordshire, directed by Microdot's Brian Cannon and photographed by Michael Spencer-Jones, who had both worked on the previous two albums. A snapper was promptly dispatched and captured an uncannily similar image to the one that would ultimately appear on the sleeve of a record that shifted over half a million copies in the first week. In the unlikely event that you haven't seen it, the band are depicted mooching around a swimming pool in stunning gardens. In the pool is a partially submerged Rolls-Royce, in tribute to The Who's Keith Moon, who reportedly once drowned his own Roller. There's a moped, a gramophone, a globe and other curiosities, including a calendar that displays the date of the album's release. I dissected the sleeve and explored the meaning of each object for one article, linking some to The Beatles, The Who and others. Noel later claimed they were simply chosen randomly from a prop store, debunking any supposed significance.

At £75,000, Cannon estimated that the cover was probably the most expensive record sleeve art ever created and this figure apparently didn't include the bar bill, either. Such an audacious piece of journalism caused major ructions and ended up in the High Court, with Creation Records suing for breach of copyright over the photograph. They lost.

Details of the album itself were scarce and label Creation was guarding its crown jewel more closely than the royal treasures themselves. It wasn't to be released until 21 August 1997 – so when it was announced that the band would be supporting U2 on their PopMart tour in the US in June, tickets were duly booked. Again, I'm not certain it would happen today with shrunken newspaper budgets and foreign travel curtailed. It was, unquestionably, a more relaxed Oasis, basking in their support slot in front of

1996

curious Americans at Oakland Coliseum in California. One idiot asked me: 'Which ones are the brothers?'

But we got a chance to hear the album's wonky title track for the first time and a menacing live debut of single 'D'You Know What I Mean?'. That day, photographer Dave Hogan captured some of my favourite images of Liam, who had married Patsy Kensit just a few weeks previously. We had been booked into the same hotel as the band, the Pan Pacific in San Francisco's Union Square. Predictably, there was no sign of them the following morning but, as we were checking out, I bumped into Massive Attack, Björk and Madonna producer and fellow Bristolian Nellee Hooper, who I'd always see out and about in London clubland, sometimes with Robbie Williams.

We chatted about the epic show and he introduced me to the bewitching woman at his side, who I half-recognised. 'This is Lisa Moorish. Lisa, meet Dominic,' he grinned. The model and singer looked a little coy, as we politely discussed the previous evening's shenanigans. I thought little of it. Almost exactly nine months later, Lisa gave birth to a daughter, Molly, whose father later turned out to be a certain, er, Liam Gallagher.

And so the hugely hyped third Oasis album *Be Here Now*, recorded at Abbey Road Studios (where else?) was finally released – on a date that would turn out to be ten days before the hideous car crash in Paris that killed Princess Diana – and, ultimately, the record itself. But it was an overblown mess of an LP, with layer upon layer of crazy and unhinged grating sounds.

KNEBWORTH

Alan McGee decreed that the album's downfall was because of the cocaine consumed during its recording and described the band as a runaway train and uncontrollable. Oasis was such a bank-rolling machine at that moment, and the sycophancy around them was off the scale. Would anyone really have told Noel that the band's album wasn't good enough and that he needed to go back and work on it further?

Broadcaster Chris Evans mocked the record on his Channel 4 TV show, opening up a *TFI Friday* episode with a defibrillator trying to resuscitate the album and bring it back to life. The pair didn't speak for several decades but have since made up.

Anyhow, radio stations were preoccupied with playing calming and mellow music to chime with the national mood. On 8 September, just eight days after the Parisian tragedy, I was the only British journalist who flew to Norway alongside Liam – who was alone and suffering with an ear infection – for the opening of the *Be Here Now* tour at the Oslo Spektrum. Something had changed – and for the worse. Epics such as 'Rock 'n' Roll Star', 'Columbia', 'Slide Away', 'Cast No Shadow' and 'Morning Glory' had been unceremoniously dumped from the set for weaker new songs, while 'Wonderwall' and 'Don't Look Back in Anger' were dispensed with too early. Liam dedicated 'Live Forever' to 'The Princess', but the tour debut didn't receive anywhere near the coverage one would have predicted just a few weeks earlier. Usually, one would expect such an event to be on the front pages, but my review was relegated way back in the newspaper, to accommodate the mountains of Diana coverage.

The tour landed in Exeter five days later, with support from the newly emerging and exceptional Scottish band Travis but, again, the reception was muted. The stage design was itself as overblown with cocaine-induced abandon as the album and its sleeve, the group emerging from a giant red telephone box, its door held open by a besuited *Quadrophenia*-style bell boy.

The show came to the band's favoured Earls Court venue on 25 September for three nights, scene of their transformative gigs in 1995 and their ascendancy at the Brits in 1996. Triumphant support came this time from Wigan five-piece The Verve, whose own illustrious album *Urban Hymns* was just days from release. The record company kindly couriered over an advance copy of the CD to our home late on the previous Friday. We listened to it over and over again with our friends until the early hours in disbelief. It sounded immense, a record to reclaim the 90s, eclipsing *Be Here Now*, with anthems such as 'The Drugs Don't Work', 'Sonnet' and 'Bittersweet Symphony', which ingeniously incorporated a Rolling Stones' string sample alongside Richard Ashcroft's pleading vocals and forthright lyrics. I'd reviewed and rated the album in the morning's newspaper and, as Ashcroft introduced 'Lucky Man', he proudly told the crowd, '*The Sun* gave this song ten out of ten today'. He later thanked me at the aftershow party at the Roundhouse in Camden and admitted he couldn't believe how well the record had been received. The Verve were on the periphery of Britpop, both before and after it, but they were carrying its torch, in a post-Diana Britain.

KNEBWORTH

Let me, if I may, move on to the following big Oasis world tour which was to open in Tokyo. The band were unveiling their eagerly anticipated *Standing on the Shoulder of Giants* set in Asia after a hiatus, following that insane, all-conquering period. I hastily arranged a meeting with my editor David Yelland and explained that I thought we should cover it.

He asked if the band was paying for the trip and whether I had arranged an interview. I told him that it didn't quite work like that with Oasis. You just had to put yourself in the right place at the right time, and something would usually happen. I'd done it many times.

It was certainly a long way to travel, and at considerable expense on the off chance, for what might end up being simply a concert review, but I told him I was confident I could deliver something more meaningful and implored him to trust me.

The trip was then agreed and myself and man-mountain photographer Dave Hogan were booked on business class flights to Tokyo, a city I had never visited. I'd obviously been fortunate enough to chronicle a slew of other mind-blowing performances by the band, but this felt different. It was a long way from home and I had put myself under considerable pressure to return with more than just a report of the gig and a hangover. The trip was costing over £7,000 in expenses.

I rang some music industry contacts and enquired about where the band might be most likely stationed. They all agreed on the capital city's Hotel Okura. John Lennon holidayed there with Yoko not long before his death, and it was the rock stars' hotel of choice.

1996

If you've been to Japan you will know that the jet lag is particularly punishing, as famously captured in the Bill Murray film *Lost in Translation*. We flew in and were ferried to the hotel at around 8pm, bleary-eyed and knackered, but there was work to be done. We dumped our bags and headed for the bar. And, guess what, Liam, drummer Alan White and their entourage were all there in a corner, knocking back draught Guinness. We discreetly approached the barman and ordered a couple of pints of the black stuff ourselves.

Within moments, I felt a sharp poke in the back. 'What the fookin' hell are you doing here, Mohan?' Liam snarled at me. I told him we had flown over for the band's opening night at the Yokohama Arena to cover it in the paper. 'What, you've come all the way over here just to see us?' Of course, I offered. 'Come and have a beer with us,' he uttered in a softer tone, and we joined the gang. He seemed to be delighted that the band still mattered to the media after some criticism of their recent albums and was chuffed we'd made the effort.

After a few minutes of boozy chatter, Liam turned to me and said: 'Do you want to do an interview? Have you got a tape recorder?' I tried to play it cool and insisted that we were fine just having a drink and relaxing. 'I want to do an interview and I want to do it here, right now,' he bellowed. I couldn't believe my luck and the jet lag wore off immediately. I asked him where Noel was and he declared, somewhat disparagingly, that his brother was tucked up in his hotel room watching Beatles videos.

We sat on a crumpled sofa and talked for an age. Nothing was off limits. Noel did most of the interviews – Liam had done them before, of course, but never so lengthy or lucid, nor with a mainstream and populist journalist like me. We discussed his marriage to Patsy Kensit, drugs, fatherhood, his relationship with his stepson, his brothers, the Beckhams and, naturally, his music. He had just become a dad to Lennon and wouldn't stop talking about him. He revealed he'd written a song about his son, called 'Born on a Different Cloud', which was news to me and would appear on the band's *Heathen Chemistry* album, years later.

He told me: 'I realise I'm blessed. He's alive, healthy and happy and smiles all the time. He sleeps with me in bed and I stay up all night just staring at him and realising how lucky I am. As long as I can sing and look after him, I'm happy.'

This was a rare, softer side to Liam which, at this point, few had glimpsed nor read about. There was less bravado about him. He seemed a nicer person. It was a fantastic interview.

As my audience with Liam concluded, he asked: 'Do you think you'll run any of this?' I assured him the newspaper would and, within days, the exclusive was splashed across the paper. I was desperate for the loo and he followed me in, wielding a video camera, hurling a pint of Guinness in my direction and then scarpering with a manic laugh and a chorus of 'Go let it out' from their recent single.

The trip had certainly been worth the gamble and a bit of stout on my Evisu jeans, but it is indicative of the complex nature of his personality. You never know which Liam you're going to get – whether he will hug you, pin you up against a wall, try to undress you or politely enquire about the family.

1996

We've always lived near one other in North London and whenever I bumped into him alone with my young son on Hampstead High Street, he would be charm personified, playing and talking to him and showing great interest and empathy. After the birth of Lennon, he asked me to join him in a pub close to the hospital to wet the baby's head, just near the site of the old Heavenly Sunday Social, and he granted another exclusive interview, admitting: 'Lennon's a good-looking baby but not as good-looking as me.' Inevitably, it made the front page.

But at other times it could be quite different. Chatting politely backstage at the Royal Albert Hall to The Verve's Richard Ashcroft, after he had ably supported Oasis at a Teenage Cancer Trust show, I suddenly felt a stranger firmly grab my privates from behind. Ashcroft looked mortified as Liam yelled over and over again: 'Get your cock out. Get your fookin' cock out now.' Grimacing in pain, I explained I was trying to have a civilised conversation with one of the country's most talented songwriters and he scuttled off. 'Is it always like this between you two?' Richard asked, and I had to admit that it often was. 'That's Liam,' he chuckled.

The most hedonistic event on the 90s calendar though was the Q Awards, where champagne was served at midday and we'd finish off about 3am. It certainly brought out the best (or worst, depending on how you look at it) in Liam and Noel. Anyone who was anyone went to it in those days. A vote-seeking Tony Blair was at a few of them, due to his Oxford University friendship with the mag's founder Mark Ellen. Their student band Ugly Rumours featured a shaggy-haired Blair on vocals with Ellen posing on bass, and it was the latter who had first introduced Blair to Noel at the 1994 Q Awards, notably just after the Oasis man had hoovered up a fat line of cocaine in the toilets of the Park Lane Hotel, according to ex-tour manager Iain Robertson.

At one such event, I witnessed Liam strutting back from the toilets smoking a cigarette. As he passed Mick Jagger, who was angled with his back to him, he flicked ash on Mick's hair, who sat throughout the awards, blissfully unaware that his famous head had become a makeshift Gallagher ashtray.

At another, Liam's feud with Robbie Williams took yet another tabloid twist. Robbie left the bash after just an hour following a tirade of abuse from Liam, who was by then dating his ex-fiancée, All Saint Nicole Appleton. At the Brit Awards the previous March, Robbie had challenged the Oasis man to a televised bout and asked the audience: 'Would anyone like to see me fight Liam? Are you gonna pussy out, you fucking wimp?'

I watched as the pair sat twenty yards apart at the Park Lane Hotel, exchanging stern glances throughout the ceremony. Liam publicly heckled a chain-smoking Robbie as he took to the stage to receive the Classic Songwriter award with pal Guy Chambers. The singer booed and shouted, 'Get your fucking hair cut.' Robbie refused to be drawn, saying only, 'I'm going to keep my gob shut.' When I spoke to him afterwards, he seemed on edge and, uncharacteristically, snapped, 'I don't want to get involved,' before making a sharp exit. Later on, I asked Liam about the feud. 'I think

1996

Robbie's a queer,' he told me. 'He was three tables away from me and he was eyeing me up. I'll fucking have him.'

But Robbie wasn't the only target of abuse for Liam that day, who once again offered us a disasterclass in yobbery and laddism. He yelled, 'Get your tits out' at host Davina McCall, who was wearing a daring dress. Then he screamed at Kylie Minogue, 'Get your tits out too, you lesbian, and write your own songs for a change.' As Blur's Alex James gave an award to The Clash's frontman Joe Strummer, Liam shouted: 'Oi! Fat boy, you fat bastard.' It wasn't exactly Oscar Wilde stuff, but it was great copy. Mad incidents and rock star clashes like this just don't seem to happen like this any more. I long for the day that Ed Sheeran lamps Tom Grennan in a row over Raye.

I fell victim to the brothers too. When it was announced I had helped judge the Q's best producer category, Noel took to the stage. 'How can anyone let Dominic Mohan be on a voting panel?' Later, Liam ripped my shirt and tried to pull off my trousers screaming, 'I want to see you naked,' in front of disbelieving guests and media. Another quiet day at the office.

There's an element of performance and pantomime villain with the youngest brother in certain situations, and it seems as if he's never really had to grow up. Now over 50 years old, he has been in the public eye since he was 21, but I think he employs such bravado to compensate for the fact that he knows he isn't as sharp or quick-witted as his older brother.

One of the most memorable nights in the company of Noel came as he was partying hard after he and Ocean

KNEBWORTH

Colour Scene's Steve Cradock had joined their hero, The Who's Pete Townshend, on stage at London's spanking new Sound Republic club, in London's Leicester Square.

To celebrate, we had retired to a small, backstage bar area, he accompanied by wife Meg, actress Anna Friel and models Kate Moss and Helena Christensen. It was rather late and everyone had been on the sauce – but there was good humour, jollity, friendly banter, cigarettes and alcohol in the air.

Then, suddenly, a side door burst open and in stumbled *The Sun*'s editor David Yelland – out of nowhere and completely unprompted – accompanied by a large proportion of *The Sun*'s newsroom, all in suits and ties. They'd blagged their way in, looking for some action after a night out on the company. It was something of a wild culture clash, with me caught slap bang in its messy middle. On one side of the room lounged the hedonistic tastemakers and fashionistas of the Primrose Hill set, the country's bestselling newspaper's ruthless newshounds standing on the other. I sensed danger.

I continued my wise-cracking contest with Noel, whose rapier wit was at full throttle by that hour, when I felt a hand repeatedly tugging on the sleeve of my Columbia Sportswear hooded cream rain jacket, as was the fashion of the time. I turned casually to find my bespectacled, belted-and-braced editor at my side. He asked whether I would introduce him to Noel, with assurances he was an enthusiastic fan of his songwriting. I counselled that perhaps this was not the most rational idea as many of those in the vicinity were somewhat intoxicated. But he insisted. And then he insisted again.

There I was, in the early hours of the morning in a London nightclub, faced with a startling, and potentially career-damaging, dilemma. The socially awkward editor of the flippin' *Sun*, my employer, wanted me to toss him into a lion's den, gone midnight, where he would be forced to joust with one of the most bombastic and acerbic characters in rock, who was sweating profusely in a leather jacket and clutching a bottle of Beck's.

But I had no choice. Unwillingly, I made the introduction and sputtered: 'Treat him gently, Noel. He's my boss.' Alas, this would not transpire to be the case.

'What? You're the actual editor of *The Sun*? You bald cunt,' was his opening gambit. Oof.

Yelland, who has been open about losing his hair through alopecia aged 11, made a valiant attempt to establish common ground: 'I actually love Oasis, Noel. Until recently, I worked for the *New York Post* and saw you perform live at Madison Square Garden.'

'Oh really?' Noel retorted. 'What did we open our set with that night?'

'Er, oh, um, I can't, er, remember. I think I got there late because I'd got stuck in a meeting at the office,' he stammered. It was as if I were witness to a helpless and struggling, drowning man. But it wasn't about to get any easier.

'Ha ha. I'm also a massive Manchester City fan like you, Noel …' To be fair to him, he was giving it a bit of a go, but Gallagher Sr wasn't having any of it. 'Are you now? In that case, who scored the winning goal when we were last promoted to the top division?'

Yelland paused and put his palm to his cheek, as was his wont when grappling for an answer to a sticky question. 'Oh. Let me think. I'm, um, not sure, er …'

With the palm of his hand, Noel then began to slap the head of the editor of Britain's biggest-selling newspaper, arguably the most important person in the country's print media, even leaning in to take a pretend bite of his skull, before strutting back to his adoring throng.

It had been a bruising encounter. And, as my boss dusted himself off, I explained that, if he thought that was bad, he should meet Noel's younger brother, Liam.

In all fairness, a chortling Yelland took the confrontation in his suited stride and never bore a grudge, acknowledging the amusing side of the close encounter. But the incident, in many ways, highlighted why the media, and the public, adored Oasis so much, and continue to do so. They just don't give a toss about who they offend or insult, and that's why the brothers' interviews are so riveting, Liam's brutal early sexism aside. Media-trained boy bands would always be sycophantic and all over someone in such high office. Believe me, I know.

Oasis certainly seemed omnipresent at this time and I was penning stories about them on an almost daily basis. I'd not witnessed a media feeding-frenzy like it as a working journalist, but it was refreshing to be writing about super-talented musicians, rather than boy band puppets. Believe it or not, it was front-page news in *The*

Sun when both siblings had their hair cut short, under the headline 'The Brothers Trim'.

The Gallaghers happen to be Catholic brothers – and their complex relationship had begun to resemble something of a holy fable, albeit latterly played out via Twitter and X, rather than the scriptures. Human beings have always been fascinated by sibling stories of jealousy and antagonism, not least in the Book of Genesis, with tales of Joseph and his feuding brothers, chronicling betrayal and ultimate reconciliation of the main man with his family. Sound familiar? Indeed, as Liam might say, biblical.

At this time, as the band's publicist, Johnny Hopkins was overwhelmed with media enquiries from around the world. I would talk to him on an almost daily basis, the conversations not always smooth and straightforward. We were both under intense pressure and Johnny told me: 'Dealing with the tabloids is obviously different to working with the music press – different types of stories, different audiences. Overall, I enjoyed it and dealt with some interesting characters. I had some previous experience of the tabloids, so it wasn't new to me. Also, as a music obsessive, I was aware of how the Rolling Stones/ Andrew Loog Oldham and the Sex Pistols/Malcolm McLaren and their PRs had played the tabloids and also been turned over by them. That shaped what I did. The enquiries came through 24/7. It was exciting. I was dedicated to Creation and Oasis, so I was up for it. The success of Oasis brought in more financial clout to Creation, more staff, and more leverage in the music industry and the media. With Oasis and the other mid-90s bands, there were more stories, more personalities. The bands were more focused and ambitious. The politicians and the mass media saw the potential in so-called Britpop to support their own agendas. Britpop's use of the Union Jack was key to this.'

But one of the most disrespectful and abhorrent pieces of media behaviour and coverage about the Gaelic-blooded brothers came as the band played two triumphant shows at Dublin's Point Theatre, a sort of homecoming.

How anyone at the *News of the World* had ever thought that attempting to force an unwanted reunion between the siblings – all three, in fact – with their father Tommy was a good idea, I shall never fathom. Their mum Peggy had walked out on violent drunk Tommy, who had beaten Paul and Noel as children. But he never laid a finger on little Liam, who was just ten years old when he was taken away from the Irish labourer-turned-DJ.

In fact, if there is a filing cabinet somewhere with a drawer labelled The Stupidest Ideas of All Time, then this hideous stunt would be somewhere near the top of the pile within. I would not have gone anywhere near it.

Reporters turned up with the estranged Gallagher at the band's city centre hotel, The Westbury, and sat together in the bar, waiting for the brothers to spot him. Eldest boy Paul Gallagher later admitted that he felt the incident was the worst invasion of privacy in the band's career and that their dad was simply looking to stir up trouble. Label boss McGee was with the group in Dublin that night and agreed, revealing that the band became less approachable after the incident and security was scaled up.

1996

A maniacal Liam exploded with rage and, unsurprisingly – quite justifiably actually – unleashed a battery of expletives in his father's direction. Earlier, they had also set up a phone call from father to youngest son, which the *News of the World* taped, of course. To compound their misjudgement further, a recording of the unsettling exchanges was placed on a premium rate phone line. Outbloodyrageous.

I was working a Sunday shift in the *Sun* office the morning that ugly story dropped and was tasked with finding a follow-up. I discovered Liam was still staying in the hotel under the alias Louis Cyphre – borrowed from Robert De Niro's devilish character in one of my then-favourite films *Angel Heart*. I called up the hotel and was put straight through. We exchanged pleasantries, but when I asked Liam about the close encounter of a paternal kind, he responded with memorable menace. 'If he ever approaches me again I'll slit his throat from ear to ear.'

This is Johnny Hopkins' take on the incident: 'It was never an attempt to reunite the brothers with their father. It was a stunt to sell newspapers. It should have been a major moment of triumph in their career. A homecoming to Ireland. Up until that point, Oasis world had been quite accessible, a rolling tour/off-tour party. The incident led to more security around the band. It also had a significant impact on media access, even for the music papers and magazines – which understandably annoyed those publications.'

My work as one of the popular media's interviewers and chroniclers of such devilment and roguery in print, digital and broadcast media, during a period of such creativity and cultural shift, would ultimately help contribute to my rise to running the paper's features department, being made an associate and then deputy editor before becoming a Yelland successor as *The Sun*'s editor, an appointment announced on 26 August 2009. Strange timing because, two days later, Oasis would implode and split up in France, dominating those early newspapers I edited.

But, in a 2017 interview with *GQ* magazine, Liam would claim that it was, indeed, my presence in the band's dressing room, before the Paris show, that sparked an incendiary row with Noel, ending the band. Dead for ever. Or so we thought.

'All of a sudden I saw Dominic Mohan and some other fucking clown from *The Sun* waltzing around backstage, necking our champagne. Not having it,' he recalled. As if I would be on a Parisian freebie, sipping the Gallagher bubbly, just as I'd landed the biggest job in British journalism. *GQ* never put the allegation to me.

Yes, I've been fortunate enough to witness Oasis live across the planet on around thirty occasions – but never in Paris. The bloke he was talking about is Scottish and a little younger than me but sometimes sports a similar haircut. It was, in fact, one of my Bizarre successors, a certain Gordon Smart, now a BBC radio and TV broadcaster. I don't know what Liam was thinking. It was a case of mistaken identity. That's the story.

My Top Ten Gigs of the 90s

1. **Oasis – Knebworth Park, 1996:** 'This is history,' declared Noel and that's what we were witnessing. By no means hyperbole, Knebworth was our generation's joyous happening and the bill encapsulated mid-90s Britain. This was the Oasis juggernaut hitting top speed, yet always feeling as if it could crash and burn at any moment. My mad favourite.
2. **Oasis – Maine Road, Manchester, 1996:** This was the moment the madness truly went stratospheric, a star-studded crowd and Mancunian crowning glory with a better setlist than Knebworth. Mesmeric and intoxicatingly unforgettable riot on home turf. 5–0 Oasis. A privileged witness.
3. **The Verve – Haigh Hall, Wigan 1998:** The hazy homecoming for Richard Ashcroft, Nick McCabe et al., a crowning moment to celebrate the joy and success of the all-conquering *Urban Hymns*. The Verve's career was bittersweet but this its zenith. A joyous singalong in a frothing field of dreams.
4. **Oasis – Kentish Town Forum, London 1994:** The moment the 90s ignited for me. I'd never witnessed such power and fury, the band edgy and on the verge of violence. The debuting of the songs that powered the 90s and a jaw-dropping, life- and career-changing moment, never to be forgotten.
5. **The Stone Roses – Cambridge Corn Exchange, 1995:** We'd seen them at Ally Pally as the 80s burned

out and this was the much-anticipated comeback. *The Second Coming* gets lost in time but boasts half a dozen tunes for which other bands would kill, showcased here – 'Love Spreads', 'Daybreak', 'Breaking into Heaven', with virtuoso guitar work and tragic Mani's bass.

6. **The Verve – Glasgow Barrowlands, 1997:** It's the beginning of the *Urban Hymns* tour at one of the country's most lively venues and The Verve were on fire. And what a setlist. 'History', 'The Drugs Don't Work', 'Sonnet', 'This Is Music'. Ashcroft was at the toppermost of his most maniacal genius.

7. **U2 – Oakland Coliseum, 1997:** A spectacular preview of the band's PopMart tour before it reached the UK and with a relaxed Oasis in support on this date only. An incredible double bill with a mind-boggling consumerism-themed stage set featuring a giant lemon and a yellow arch and all the anthems you would expect. An unforgettable band on fire.

8. **Blur – Kentish Town Forum, London, 1993:** Blur's Sugary Tea 1993 tour saw them perform surrounded by sofa, lampshade and cooker on stage and showcasing the breakthrough collection of songs which made up *Modern Life Is Rubbish*, including 'For Tomorrow', 'Chemical World' and 'Sunday Sunday'. That night, you could feel the talent bursting through – it was obvious that these cheeky chappies were on the cusp of coronation.

9. **Music for Montserrat – Royal Albert Hall, London, 1997:** Arranged by Beatles producer George Martin to

1996

raise funds for victims of a volcanic eruption on the Caribbean isle, the line-up featured Paul McCartney, Eric Clapton, Elton John, Phil Collins, Carl Perkins, Mark Knopfler, Sting and the London Community Gospel Choir. Many highlights but the climactic closing sequence from Abbey Road of 'Golden Slumbers'/'Carry That Weight'/'The End' and then 'Hey Jude' will never leave my soul. George Martin conducted and Clapton and Knopfler traded guitar licks.

10. **Neil Young & Booker T. and the MGs/Pearl Jam – Finsbury Park, London, 1993:** Another great double-header with grunge riding high and Eddie Vedder's voice the most pre-eminent on the planet at that moment. All the Neil Young classics including 'Like a Hurricane' and 'Southern Man' but the explosive encore of 'Rockin' in the Free World' with all artists on stage is a magical mosh pit memory. Mind blown. A final Americana hurrah before the game changed …

CHAPTER 8

Macca, Townshend, Bowie and Rod

The elder statesmen join the party – and that time I nearly broke Elton's Oscar

As Britpop swept away the nation throughout 1996, dominating the charts and the media, rock's elder statesmen wanted to get in on the act.

Many were eager to be associated with Cool Britannia, Blur and Blair, and to insert themselves into this nationalistic narrative as the Labour leader had. Fortunately, I had persuaded many of them and their representatives that an effective way to do this would be via the pages of Britain's biggest-selling newspaper.

What the ageing Brit rockers were realising was that this was an opportunity to re-market themselves and hitch a ride atop Britpop's magic bus, many being name-checked and praised by the new young pretenders. In 1995, *The Help Album* had highlighted this intersection of the musical generations, raising money for the War Child charity – which was co-founded by producer and Roxy Music wizard Brian Eno – and provided aid to conflict-stricken areas, such as Bosnia and Herzegovina. All the songs were recorded in a single day and the album featured Paul McCartney, Blur, Paul Weller, Radiohead, Oasis, The KLF,

1996

The Stone Roses, Suede, Andrew Weatherall, The Boo Radleys, Sinead O'Connor, Orbital and the Manic Street Preachers. It included a version of The Beatles' classic 'Come Together', by newly formed supergroup The Smokin' Mojo Filters, comprised of McCartney, Weller, Noel Gallagher, Steve Cradock, Steve White and Carleen Anderson.

At the 1996 Brits, elder statesman Eno and a youthful Thom Yorke from Radiohead collected the special Freddie Mercury Award for the project, presented to them by Queen drummer Roger Taylor. Yorke told the audience: 'For one day last year, we stopped fighting and actually did something decent for once.'

There was considerable mutual backslapping between young and older generations, which I was reporting on regularly and was then being given access to some of the most celebrated names in British music, specialising in interviews with rock's elder statesmen – including Pete Townshend and his singer Roger Daltrey – who were trying to stay relevant, and because of my extensive work with the Britpop movement. They were mostly artists I'd familiarised myself with from an early age, via my parents' record collection. In fact, The Who were their band – my co-creators' first date was at one of the band's early shows in Bath. The Who was in my blood.

But it was late in 1996 that Townshend switched on his computer and made the most devastating mistake of his career, and, thus, derailed his life.

Just as his profile and success were more buoyant than they had been for decades, due to his role as one of the founding fathers of the Britpop movement, the songwriter chose to enter his credit card details into a website featuring child sex abuse images, a decision which would threaten to taint his incredible musical legacy for ever more.

Then 51, he viewed these heinous photographs on a number of occasions after stumbling across them, driven – he would later insist – to research what sort of material such sites contained and born out of a fury at how simple they were to access.

His actions seem inexplicable. They came just after he had handed over the Best British Group gong to Oasis at February's Brits, and following an appearance with the event's host Chris Evans, as a star guest on *TFI Friday*, on 8 March, where Evans introduced him to millions of viewers as 'the father of Britpop'. And few would argue with the moniker bestowed. After all, it was Townshend who penned rock operas *Quadrophenia* and *Tommy*, helping the band sell more than 100 million records during a sixty-year career, an inspiration to the 90s crop.

But the British police would soon launch an investigation into online rape and abuse images of minors and established Operation Ore. It was then the UK's largest ever computer crime investigation and began after police received information from American law enforcement about Landslide Productions, a Texas-based online platform that provided access to images featuring minors. More than 7,000 suspects were identified, alleged to include two former Labour ministers, a senior teacher at a leading girls' private school, military personnel, an official with the Church of England, doctors and a slew of university academics. This led to 3,744 arrests, 1,451 convictions and the suicides of 33 suspects.

I am deliberately avoiding the term 'child porn', which many in the media choose to use, after discussions over the years with fearless safety campaigners Shy Keenan, founder of Phoenix Survivors, an advocacy group for victims of sexual abuse, and Sara Payne, whose daughter Sarah was abducted and murdered, aged eight, by a convicted paedophile. They believe the term 'child porn' trivialises such images. I agree.

Permit me to fast-forward to Saturday 11 January 2003, when the *Daily Mail* ran an exclusive story revealing that an unidentified rock star was one of the 7,000 UK citizens suspected of viewing such images online. The slow wheels of justice were catching up with a celebrated name in the public eye. It was a shocking revelation.

This prompted huge speculation about the musician's identity and I received calls over the weekend from my superiors, who wanted to know the name of the man in question. I was stunned and sickened to discover that Pete Townshend appeared on the list. When his business manager Nick Goderson called him about the anonymised story, Townshend told him: 'That'll be me then.' And how severely must he have regretted recruiting Gary Glitter to perform with the band in 1996, just before he was convicted of child sex offences.

My immediate instinct was that Townshend had to come out publicly and discuss the revelation – preferably with me. If he did not, there would then be a void waiting to be filled with speculation about his guilt across the world. I rang his representative, actually The Outside Organisation founder Alan Edwards, for whom I would later work as CEO. I wanted to leverage my previous interviews with Townshend and support for The Who and felt that, if there was any journalist he should talk to, it was me.

I put forward my case for interview and we discussed Townshend's predicament at length on the Sunday morning. I conveyed my belief that he needed to come out fighting and put his version of the story forward immediately, no delay, however painful that might be. In such moments of crisis, many individuals, famous or not, choose to bury their heads and hope the story just goes away. This one certainly would not.

I waited patiently for a response, before receiving a call back in which it was politely explained that the episode was too raw and that Townshend was devastated. He would firmly not be commenting. I reiterated my position and explained that I thought he would be making a, perhaps irreversible, mistake if he didn't say something quick and, importantly, to an outlet as powerful and influential as *The Sun*. In a last-ditch attempt, I suggested that I send over some questions that the guitarist might consider responding to via email, presumably after a legal representative had analysed his words forensically. I hastily sent over a selection of tough, gut-instinct and searching questions, which I knew *The Sun*'s readers, the country – the world – would want answered. But, if I'm honest, I didn't hold out much hope, thinking this front foot media strategy would be torpedoed by some over-cautious lawyer and

1996

it would all get lost in legal land, as is common in such circumstances. I told my editor such in order to manage expectations.

Hours went by. And then an email arrived. I opened the message with some trepidation, but Townshend had answered every single question, and in not inconsiderable detail. The quotes were powerful and I knew I had a white-hot scoop on my hands, which would resonate across continents.

In the email, Townshend explained that he had been 'stupid' rather than sinister, insisting that he was not a paedophile. 'I am not making any excuses. I am angry about child porn on the internet and deeply wounded at the inference that I might be a paedophile. I have looked at child porn sites maybe three or four times in all, the front pages and previews. But I have only entered once using a credit card and I have never downloaded. With hindsight, it was very foolish, but I felt so angered about what was going on it blurred my judgement.

'I have never purchased any forms of child pornography or wished to own any. I saw the first awful photo by accident. It repelled me and shocked me to my very core. I was not breaking the law at the time. This was the winter of 1996/1997. It was then illegal to download, which I did not do, not to search and view.

'I'd be prepared to have my computer hard drive analysed. Chasing after people like Gary Glitter and Jonathan King is important, and it is important that the police are able to convince themselves that, if I did anything illegal, I did it purely for research. I am not a paedophile.'

Townshend also revealed he believed that he himself had been a victim of child sex abuse and had previously contacted the National Crime Squad about his concerns over internet images and hoped to work with Scotland Yard and the NSPCC to front a campaign to warn of such online dangers. He signed off the interview with the words: 'Thanks Dominic for giving me this chance to speak.'

Importantly, I also managed to interview Townshend's bandmate Roger Daltrey that day who, strongly and swiftly, said in his defence: 'Pete was very angry about how easy it was to get hold of child pornography on the internet. I believe his innocence will be proven. My gut instinct is that he is not a paedophile and I know him better than most. If he was Gary Glitter, I'd tell you and I'd say he deserves everything he gets. Pete has perhaps been a little naive the way he has gone about it, but I believe his intentions are good.' Townshend also received support from industry friends, including Bono, Sting, Jerry Hall, David Bowie and Bob Geldof.

And, so, the front page was cleared for the exclusive interview, under the headline: 'Cops Can Come and Get Me'. And they did. Later that day, in fact. In his autobiography, *Who I Am*, Townshend revealed that his lawyer told him police had intended to interview him informally but, because he had admitted to using a credit card in his statement, they were now forced to arrest him. Detectives arrived at his London home, just hours after the story dropped and removed eleven computers, videotapes, family photos and dozens of optical and zip drives, before interviewing him at nearby Twickenham police station. He was then bailed. Incidentally, the paper carried a particularly memorable cartoon that day – depicting Townshend angrily smashing up his computer with trademark guitar. This was also to be David Yelland's last ever edition as my editor. He quit that day to take a management role and go to business school in the US. He was replaced by Rebekah Wade.

It would take four months of investigation before Townshend was asked to meet with the police once again, this time at Kingston police station in Surrey. News had started to leak that he would be offered a caution but, in reality, there was an uncomfortable twist and added caveat. The Who man would have the choice of being cautioned and going on the sex offenders register – or going to court. He opted for the former.

Long-term, the incident doesn't seem to have affected Townshend's career or The Who's standing, greatly enhanced by the Moddish Britpop association but very nearly wrecked. There was a limited protest at the 2010 Super Bowl in Miami where the band performed, but I hold on to the belief that his swift actions in coming out and addressing the allegations head-on are what saved him. Had he hidden away and uttered nothing, he may have been doomed and the public and press would have presumed his guilt. It is a lesson in public relations and dealing with crises – something I would have to address later on, many times, from the other side of the media fence.

Significantly, 90s Britpop artists such as Oasis, Damon Albarn and Stereophonics alongside Paul Weller, Muse, Coldplay, Paul McCartney, Ed Sheeran, The Cure and Kasabian, all flocked to support the Teenage Cancer Trust and play on bills alongside Townshend and Daltrey. And two years after being put on the register, Townshend and his band were incendiary at the mesmerising Live 8 concert in London's Hyde Park.

I also believe that Townshend's openness and willingness to confront the allegations was down, in part, to the major therapy he had been through, to conquer his alcohol and drug addictions over the decades. From my experience, interview subjects who have undergone such treatments are often more inclined to lay themselves bare in the media, less afraid to tackle sensitive or taboo personal issues. Years earlier, Townshend had opened up to me about sleeping in skips in New York after he started drinking heavily again. Similarly, with Robbie Williams, there are few areas he is afraid to go. That honesty can make such characters more endearing to a curious public, in many cases, and a contrast to over-media-trained micro-celebs with little of substance to say, many eager to cultivate a cancellation-cautious social media image

But the interactions between the old guard and the new Britpop stars would continue regardless. Noel Gallagher had played with The Who during the inaugural Teenage Cancer Trust shows – the first of many – at the Royal Albert Hall. His band would also record a cover of 'My Generation', which would often become a live Oasis favourite. And Townshend would go on to say: 'When we hear Liam's voice, it's our voice. It's everyone's voice.'

In 1996, The Who performed on a *Quadrophenia* tour with drummer Zak Starkey, son of Ringo and later a member of Oasis. At the Hyde Park show on 29 June, they were joined on stage by David Gilmour of Pink Floyd and singer Gary Glitter – it wasn't the greatest performance and I was perturbed by Glitter's appearance as I had started to hear some seedy rumours about him. The weather was patchy and bassist John Entwistle was struggling with his equipment, Daltrey wearing a Mod-themed eyepatch after Glitter had accidentally hit him in the face in rehearsals the previous day. Three years later, in 1999, Glitter was convicted and jailed. This was an unnerving precursor to related events, which would occupy and trouble my journalistic career in the years to come, and that is something I will address in my next chapter.

There was certainly a Who and Mod revival, with the band in vogue once again, re-releasing 'My Generation' themselves as a single, and a mastered *Quadrophenia* album, alongside a new hits compilation which peaked at number eleven in the charts in August 1996. This was the same month Townshend's protégé Paul Weller would have a top five hit with 'Peacock Suit'. The group would collect a Lifetime Achievement gong at the rowdy Q Awards the following year.

Weller had, of course, guested on *(What's the Story) Morning Glory?* in 1995 as his own solo revival soared with his quintessential album *Stanley Road* hitting the top of the charts. He contributed a guitar solo and backing vocals on the monumental closer 'Champagne Supernova' and admitted 1996 made him excited again and reconfirmed the power of music in British culture.

I built up a strong relationship with The Who as the years wore on, because of my personal love of their music but also because their Britpop revival made them interesting newspaper subjects once more. Before Sir Roger Daltrey launched the Teenage Cancer Trust shows at the Royal Albert Hall, he took me for a rather memorable lunch and asked for my support for the project. 'What would you need from me to make it work?' he boomed, as he fiddled with his hearing aid – a not altogether unsurprising aural accessory, given the deafening, epic power of The Who's live performances over the previous decades. I said that if he and Townshend could offer me one hour of interview time each and then take me for a tour of the TCT hospital ward at University College Hospital, London, I could probably tee up the announcement with a trio of double-page spreads in a three-part series, perhaps featuring on the front page. 'Done!' he thundered, crushing my hand with a powerful shake and bursting into that familiar belly laugh of his, sounding like a triumphant East End villain who'd just pulled off the bank job of a lifetime. I always liked Daltrey; he was no-nonsense and his word is true. But I wouldn't want to be on the wrong side of him.

The following week, I was invited to the band's West London rehearsal space where they treated me, and me alone, to ear-twitching versions of 'My Generation', 'Pinball Wizard' and 'Baba O'Riley'. Nice work if you can get it – my hearing aid probably isn't far off either. This was the fun side of the job, having the privilege of spending time with, and witnessing, a band like The Who, up close and cranked to eleven.

The interviews were jaw-dropping, particularly Townshend's. He talked about his lapse back into alcohol-

1996

ism: 'I had *Tommy* on Broadway and it went to my head. I thought "Even if I have got a bit of a problem with alcohol, it doesn't matter," but of course it did. It doesn't matter how much money I had, I still ended up coming out of a club, seeing a builder's skip and thinking, "Oh, what a lovely place to spend the night." My head went completely. I used to do that all the time. My limo driver would be waiting for me to wake up. There were probably people walking past saying: "Isn't that the bloke from The Who asleep in that skip?"

'There was one day when I just said: "That's enough." I didn't go to a clinic, I just stopped. What I'd managed eleven years before, I thought I could manage again. It was messing up my life. But I've certainly had help over the years. I've had counsellors. I had a therapist for three years. I just know I'm all right now. I don't think about alcohol but I know I wasted a lot of money on it.'

One of the finest proponents of this no-holds-barred school of post-therapy media interview technique is Sir Elton John, who himself battled crippling drug and alcohol addiction. Elton once invited me to his beautiful home Woodside, close to Windsor Castle, for a lengthy interview. I'd met him a few times before, but we hadn't sat down properly together. I drove to the sprawling mansion, stuffed full of priceless artworks by YBAs Damien Hirst and Tracey Emin among others, before being ushered by one of his staff and shown into a small library-type room. Its shelves were stacked full of fascinating books, including *The Sun*'s Hold Ye Front Page history guide, which brilliantly covered significant moments through *Sun* front pages, such as Christ's birth under the headline 'A Star Is Born'. I don't know whether it had been placed on the shelf specifically for my benefit, of course. As I bent down to pick up a glass of water from a coffee table, I accidentally knocked something to the floor, with a concerning thud. As I picked up the object, I realised it was Elton's Oscar for his *Lion King* theme song 'Can You Feel the Love Tonight?'. Whoops-a-daisy.

Elton is a fine subject and host, a relentless gossip with razor-sharp wit, even granting me an audience with his music room, packed with glorious reams of alphabetised vinyl, CDs and memorabilia. I could have spent weeks in there. He has himself shifted 300 million-plus records globally, including an astonishing 33 million copies of his Diana-tribute single 'Candle in the Wind' in 1997.

It was a curious interview, his first with *The Sun* for twenty years, in which Elton admitted he still fancied women – thirteen years after he last slept with one. Perhaps wanting to play up his own laddishness, so fashionable at that time of course, he told me: 'I can be driving along and see a woman walking down the street. If I like the way she walks or dresses I think, "Phwoar! She's gorgeous." The other day an incredibly good-looking woman was interviewing me in Spain. She was unbelievable, astonishing. She was only about 22. Even though I'm gay I don't just fancy men. A woman can walk in the room and I'm like, "Cor!" I'll do the same with men though. But will I sleep with a woman again? Probably not. I'm very happy with David.'

Elton, then 54, singled out actresses Nicole Kidman, Liz Hurley and Julia Roberts as the women he fancied most.

1996

And he also opened up candidly about his drug-taking. He had kicked the gear a decade previously after, quite astonishingly, attending more than 1,400 therapy meetings in three years but, at the peak of his addiction, binged on coke every four minutes. 'The problem I have is with cocaine. If anyone had cocaine in the room, I'd go nuts. I can smell it and I'd be out. I have dreams I have a white nose, it's all around my mouth and I'm trying to get it off my nose and my mother's coming in the room.'

Elton always had a strong sense of mischief. At one BAFTA Awards aftershow party not long after that interview, I attempted to reach the V-V-VIP section of the bash, as is always a celebrity journalist's desire, even though the final destination could often be somewhat underwhelming and you'd end up being stuck with an *EastEnder* and a member of S Club 7 chewing your ear off at 1am, it was all about the mission, the quest. Suited-up, with razor-sharp haircut and polished shoes, I developed a successful – yet simple – technique back then whereby, on attempting to enter such hallowed ground, I would pretend to talk importantly on my mobile phone, as if on a vital business call, and security would often simply wave me through. This worked particularly swimmingly at an FA Cup Final several years previously where, despite having only a bog-standard general admission match ticket, I managed to navigate my way through four security cordons, before entering the players' bar at Wembley Stadium and ending up drinking alongside Sir Alex Ferguson, Andy Cole and Denis Irwin, consoling themselves after a 1–0 defeat to Everton.

MACCA, TOWNSHEND, BOWIE AND ROD

So, at the BAFTAs, I employed an identical masterplan and strutted straight into an intimate, plushly dressed corner, a welcoming bosom of hand-picked and carefully vetted celebrities in the exclusive inner sanctum of the lavish aftershow bash, sponsored by a snooty American style magazine. I was behind enemy lines and immediately scrutinised my surroundings, military-fashion. Among the fifteen or so guests within, Elton and David Furnish were at 45 degrees east, maybe Russell Crowe and that could be Bryan Ferry 90 degrees south. I homed in on a clear and present danger in the form of a petite, neurotic-looking blonde at 180, firmly clutching a highly confidential clipboard of important names, her penetrative eyes locked solely on me. I casually sidled up to the canapés and played with a limp cocktail sausage, before the hard-faced hostess tapped me on the shoulder and hissed: 'I don't think you're meant to be in here.' I don't quite know why, but I immediately responded with the blurt: 'I'm with Elton.' This last-minute, high-risk strategy could go one of two ways. My short-term future lay in the diminutive, twinkle-fingered hands of the Rocket Man himself. Would he admire my daring chutzpah or revel in seeing me frog-marched out and exiled from the holy land?

Blondie slinked over to Reginald Kenneth Dwight for his verdict. It was zero hour. 12am. And I didn't think it was gonna be a long, long time. She muttered in his ear and he turned purposefully, offering that familiar, gap-toothed grin in my direction, then muttered the unforgettable words: 'Send Dominic over a glass of champagne.' My humiliation had been spared and it was a walk of shame for crestfallen Madame Clipboard, delivering my bubbles in her manicured hand. I was still standing. Mission accomplished.

Elton enjoyed his post-dependency life to the full and admired wit, sparkle, creativity, audacity and adventure, his knowledge of modern music unmatched. When I spoke to him about Oasis, he fired back: 'They could have been the biggest band in the world but they blew it. It all came down to the fact that they were not prepared to work. And the drugs didn't help during their aborted trips to America. Having said that, I would never write Noel's future off.'

He consumes emerging music like no other and has injected longevity into his incredible career by continually working and performing with young artists. A valiant hallmark of his life and work is that he would often put a protective arm around emerging talent to try and prevent them from falling into the same dark holes that swallowed him up, decades before. In one of our interviews, he said of Robbie Williams: 'I worry about him. I always feel he's a bit of a loose cannon. He's only 27 and can't have a drink and that scares him, you can see. He has that self-destruct button which we all have, but he wears it on his sleeve. He has self-esteem problems and seems to hate himself. He has cemented himself as the number one male artist in Britain but he's like a little deer caught in headlights. I just worry.'

Probably my favourite interviewee of the rather more vintage variety would have to be Elton's close mate and sparring partner, Sir Rod Stewart. When he spoke about Rod, he would always giggle. 'When me and Rod get together, I truly believe we are the funniest two people in the world. We just insult each other – but in a great way. We came up at the same time and have always been rivals.'

Rod has forever been a lad, perhaps the ultimate British lad, but he definitely saw an opportunity in the 90s to remind people of that reputation and jump aboard that speeding Britpop bandwagon. He even recorded covers of Oasis's 'Cigarettes & Alcohol' and Primal Scream's 'Rocks', moulding them both to sound like Faces classics. He is one of the most enjoyable subjects with whom to spend time and he generously invited me into his homes in Essex and Los Angeles and took me on his (borrowed) yacht in Monaco for a trip around the Mediterranean, chortling when I turned green and was seasick. We played football on his full-sized pitch in Epping on a number of occasions and I was even permitted to squeeze his legendary privates, Vinnie Jones-style, for a photo.

In one interview, I christened him King of the Lads as he told me: 'I've got more in common with Liam Gallagher than Eric Clapton. I'm a good laugh. I love a drink and I hate people who can't stop talking about rehab. Rehab bores, I call them. I have always been a bit of a tearaway and I'm like the young generation.'

Rod honed that voice for decades, in homes close to mine – North London council houses with freezing outside toilets – but went on to sell over 250 million records worldwide, 50 million of them in the US. In 2024, he sold his catalogue for $100 million but, in one 90s interview, explained to me: 'People call me an old fuck all the time but I'm young at heart. I'm the opposite of Eric, Elton and all my so-called contemporaries. Oasis are like the Faces were in the 1970s – the same attitude and I think I've still got that. I try to cut my intake down but I still take drugs now and then socially. I've never paid for them in my life but I'll have them if they're around. The most important thing is to use any stimulants when you're in a great frame of mind, in a social way. So many people of my generation are boring about drinking, but I just get on with it. I'm quite proud of it, not afraid of it.' When I enquired about which drugs in particular, he chuckled. 'Mind your own business.'

It was clear Rod was aligning himself with the drug-bingeing, lager-swilling, leering and promiscuous lad movement, which was sweeping across Britain. He embodied that lifestyle anyway and had done so for many decades. So, while Townshend, Bowie and McCartney were perhaps the more serious, musical figureheads, Rod became the lifestyle hero. I remember once asking him what his hobbies were and he answered, 'Basically, shagging the wife.'

By covering the Gallaghers, Primal Scream and Skunk Anansie on his new record, *When We Were the New Boys*, playing footie with and talking to the lad from *The Sun* in lengthy, often bawdy interviews, enhancing his drug-taking and sexual credentials, working-class Rod was inserting himself into the 90s narrative and attempting to procure album and ticket sales from a younger generation caught up in the Cool Britanniamania.

There was certainly little mention of his love for model railways and his spectacular, secret toy train collection, In fact, when I enquired about this particular hobby, I was given short shrift and he refused to let us photograph this less riotous side of his life and personality. Over twenty-three years, he built a massive and intricate model of a US city, based on 1945 New York and Chicago. He unveiled it, not in the pages of *The Sun* or *Loaded*, but for the cover of *Railway Modeller* magazine. Rock and, indeed, roll.

When he guested on *TFI Friday* in the 90s, I was invited to join him backstage in the West London studios, where fellow guests included England's Euro 96 hero Teddy Sheringham, who ridiculed me for wearing Clarks shoes. This was at the height of Evans's and the show's co-writer Danny Baker's friendship with Teddy's teammate Paul Gascoigne, and the trio tore up London together, providing us with many a headline. One of my favourites was under a drunken photograph of the unholy trinity: 'The Three-Must-Have-Beers'.

We were all in the raucous green room together when a family approached with a very young baby. Rod was brilliant and attentive with them and patted and hugged the young child. Gazza then leant in and asked if he could say a hello too. He held the baby and began to playfully jig it up and down before Rod chipped in: 'Careful, mate, you could damage the kid.' Gazza looked crestfallen and handed the little 'un back, but the nipper didn't seem too bothered. Afterwards, we lost Gazza and all cabbed it across town to the Met Bar on Park Lane for a memorable night with his Rodness.

During another interview with me, this time in Los Angeles, we drank rather too many bottles of Chablis Premier Cru, in his hangar-like lounge, which itself dwarfed my entire flat of the time. Then, dinner at The Ivy via a chauffeur-driven Bentley – quite a leap from the Archway Road where he grew up. Over many hours, he spoke about his romantic relationships quite intimately and personally, which surprised me. This was clearly the best angle from the interview – certainly from my perspective. As a decent tabloid journalist, you develop an instinct, an ability to instantly home in and identify the strongest angle, which you intuitively perceive will make a *Sun* headline, whether that be Townshend in the skip, Gary Barlow on ecstasy or Alex James in women's lingerie.

The following morning, I received a call from one of Rod's representatives inviting me to watch a tour rehearsal later that day somewhere in the Hollywood Hills. I was picked up and ferried to the studio where, a bit like The Who experience, I was treated to a private performance of some Faces classics and 'Maggie May'. Always an effective way to win over and impress a journalist. I wasn't naive.

When the band took a break, Rod approached and asked me if he could have a word outside. After a smattering of small talk, he got to the point. 'It was a great night with you last night, but I fear I may have made a few comments which I shouldn't have, and the wine was talking a little bit.' I said I understood and enquired which section of the interview he was objecting to, but I had an inkling. He outlined what he felt may be problematic. Now this could be tricky, I replied, as I had already informed London of the interview on the way over. 'Please, Dom,' he begged. I didn't want to put him in a difficult position as he had been so hospitable and generous of his time with me over the years, so I thought for a moment and conceded. 'The only way I could really make that work would be if you might be able to tell me something that trumps that line, a better story and angle. Then I can see what I might be able to do.'

'Well, there is one thing I didn't mention to you,' he said, before handing me the startling revelation that he had recently undergone throat surgery for deadly thyroid cancer, which he feared would cost him his famous raspy voice for good or, worse still, his life.

'It was scary – and it could have been very nasty. It was only because of a CAT scan that it was spotted. If I had left it a couple of years, it would have been a very different story. I didn't realise it would be devastating for my voice. They cut you right through the neck. They cut through the muscles, and they go through memory loss, and you forget how to sing. The muscles just shrivel up. I woke in the hospital, and the doctor said, "Don't worry, your voice will be back in six months." Six months came up, and no voice. Seven months, no voice. Eight months, no voice. I could talk, but I could not sing.

'It only came back to its former glory about four weeks ago – about nine months after the operation. As far as my voice is concerned now, it's really weird. It has a new warmth to it – that's the upside. It's like I've gone back to the 1970s rasp. When you have a scare like that, it puts things in perspective. I said, "Jesus Christ, I'm lucky. This must have happened for a reason."'

Now that was clearly an enviable front-page scoop, which would propel itself across many continents from the moment of publication. It was as if Rod had kept the story up his silken sleeve for use only in an emergency. A seasoned and savvy media master, he naturally knew that this revelation would smash any other headline to smithereens. And it was exclusively mine.

I was learning fast that the old-timers knew exactly how to play the media. The Who, Elton, Rod, McCartney and Bowie, who I would all interview on multiple occasions throughout my career – they wanted to be seen in the pages of *The Sun* alongside the Gallaghers and Blur. And I always felt that Rod Stewart loved and enjoyed his fame more than most. His lifestyle was probably akin to the one that many of my newspaper's readers would want to emulate, if they had the fortune, which is why they were so intrigued and fascinated by him. I felt the same.

Figures like Rod have seen journalists, editors, trends and movements come and go for decades. But, with that experience, of course, comes a knack of knowing how to flatter and engage with young writers like I was then, welcoming us into their homes and on to their yachts, knowing, and feeding them, what they want, identifying and tapping into their own passions and interests. Rod would always arrive at interviews with a relevant scoop in mind and that, along with decent (but sometimes patchy) music over the decades, has kept him in the spotlight – and the lifestyle – in which he is so comfortable. That's how the pre-digital, celebrity media game worked back then. His label had flown me business class to LA and accommodated me in the one of the city's finest hotels, Rod entertained me at his own home and took me out to one of LA's most celebrated restaurants. I'd got what I wanted and he and they had too.

MACCA, TOWNSHEND, BOWIE AND ROD

Rod and his representatives could see I was reporting on the most significant popular culture movement in Britain since the 60s he inhabited, for Britain's most popular newspaper, which was, in turn, taking some ownership of it. They wanted Rod to be written into that era, exploit the scene and, as a music-loving twenty-something, I was happy to oblige, gaining enviable access to him and his contemporaries across the planet, securing acres of interviews, revelations and confessions and being the journalist to whom a legendary figure like Townshend would turn when he found himself in times of trouble.

In the 90s, Paul McCartney also wanted to be seen in *The Sun*'s pages alongside his young pretenders – and I was, of course, happy to oblige. He granted me his first interview since wife Linda's death at his MPL Communications HQ in Soho Square. When he posed in front of a giant image of Linda, he pulled some sad faces and looked at the image, with his thumbs down. He was clearly still buried in grief.

He would later tell me: 'I feel better now. I thought I would take as long as it takes to get through the grief, and that was a long time. After Linda died, some people told me to get busy, but I thought "No, I'm not going to." I thought, "How long would Linda want me to get over it, to be down? Month? Maybe two?" Once you get to three or four months, she would have been, "Come on, snap out of it. Get on with your life."'

In another chat, I asked him about Liam Gallagher's choice of name for his son, Lennon, and he responded: 'I think it's a cool name. It's a nice tribute. Liam has obviously been a mega-fan of John's. I suppose it's like calling your baby after the Liverpool football team. I think it's a good name – but then I would, wouldn't I?'

I'd spend unforgettable times with him, not least when we played piano together in New York and he gave me an exclusive preview of a song he had written about 9/11, before performing at the legendary charity gig at Madison Square Garden, with an audience packed full of servicemen and women, many of them victims of the terrorist attacks. It was harrowing.

Macca basked in the spotlight as one of Britpop's elder statesman, had a late solo career flourish with his 1997 record *Flaming Pie*, promoting it on *TFI Friday*. When Chris Evans asked Macca which band he would have loved to have been in other than The Beatles, he said Nirvana. Since his 60s heyday, he had never really gone away, of course but, in the 90s, his image changed and he was regarded as a much cooler figure, because of his association with the new generation of rock wannabes, who worshipped at his vegan leather-clad feet – not to mention the emergence of his daughter Stella as a highly talented fashion designer. He started making better records again too, seemingly re-energised by the 90s, 'The Frog Chorus' and 'No More Lonely Nights' a distant memory. At his gigs, you'd start to see The Chemical Brothers, Fatboy Slim and members of Oasis and All Saints, proof his image had been boosted.

Noel first met the Beatle when he was invited to his home near Abbey Road in St John's Wood, north-west London, to celebrate Stella's first fashion show in 1994. Twiggy answered the door to a stunned Noel, clad in a

Rubber Soul-era brown suede jacket. Macca greeted him with the words: 'You look like a Beatle.' Noel retorted: 'So do you.' Then, Sir Paul praised his protégé's songwriting, singling out 'Slide Away' particularly.

Like McCartney, David Bowie's career would revive around this time too. Post-Tin Machine, his much ridiculed rock side project, Bowie had started to lose his way a little, struggling to land magazine covers and rejected by condescending editors, something that seems to have been somewhat airbrushed from history. But his interviews rarely disappointed and he famously told me how, unlike Macca and pal Sir Mick Jagger, he would never accept a knighthood. He hinted that the Palace had already offered him a New Year's honour, but he turned it down because he believed the gongs were a waste of time. When I asked if he had been approached, he said: 'Might have. I would never have any intention of accepting anything like that. I seriously don't know what it's for. It's not what I spent my life working for. It's not my place to make a judgement on Jagger, it's his decision. But it's just not for me. Am I anti-monarchy? I'd only have a serious answer to that if I was living in this country.'

Bowie, then 56, died in 2016 and the world seems to have fallen apart since we lost him. He admitted to me that he feared death: 'I feel bitterly angry that I won't be doing all this for the rest of eternity. Rage, that's what you get more than anything else. You get a bit angry, because it's good down here. I made a real decision not to disappear or die. I was very ill, but I made a decision to pull myself out of that abyss.'

When Bowie played at London's Astoria in 1999, guests included Fatboy Slim, Boy George, Joseph Fiennes, Mel B, the Pet Shop Boys, Cerys Matthews, Jimmy Page, Jagger and Townshend, who revealed he had written to Liam Gallagher to warn of the dangers of drink and drugs. Townshend told me that mad night: 'I know what he is headed for and I've written a letter to him because it's my duty. You have to tell people like that that you value them and love them. I've met him a few times and it wouldn't be too strong to say that I love him – he's adorable. His mum pats him on the head and says he's just a lad and lads get drunk. Well, yes, but at some point they have to stop.'

I posed for a picture with the holy trinity of Townshend, Jagger and Bowie at the aftershow party at my friend, entrepreneur Brenhan Magee's club Pop. The ensuing headline read: 'Jagger. Age 53. Worth £150m. Bowie. Age 52. Worth £100m. Townshend. Age 54. Worth £50m. By Mohan. Age 30. £276.50 overdrawn.'

Preparation is one of the key tools for any journalist and interviewer. Do your research. Know your subject. Never enter the lion's den without having read up on your interviewee or you can be made to look a fool, like MTV's Donna Air who, in the mid-90s, asked pouting Irish siblings The Corrs where they first met.

Before I conduct interviews, whether for print, radio or on camera, I always have an idea of what sort of revelation or headline I feel I want to prise out of my subject. This matters less in broadsheet print journalism as they are not as headline-driven and have acres of space for their interviews to run.

My Top Ten Favourite Interviewees Over This Period

1. Sir Rod Stewart (Hilarious and generous)
2. Sir Paul McCartney (The Godfather)
3. Liam Gallagher (Unpredictable but eminently quotable)
4. Sir Elton John (Nothing is out of bounds)
5. David Bowie (Cerebral but also bloody funny, something many overlook)
6. Madonna (Opinionated and straight-talking)
7. Robbie Williams (On his sleeve is worn a heart)
8. Ronnie Wood (Wonderful company and loveable raconteur)
9. Alex James (Expletive every four words but full of life, spirit and humour)
10. The Who (Townshend and Daltrey are so contrasting but interview gold)

The worst is probably John Squire, of my beloved Stone Roses. I interviewed John, a man of few words but many guitar notes, on my Virgin Radio show and, to quote one of his song titles, it was The Hardest Thing in the World. He's one of the most transcendent 90s guitarists, as we were witness to at Ally Pally 89 and Knebworth 96, but as we, er, 'chatted', he was more interested in the football on the studio telly than my questioning. When I asked him about his guitar prowess, he looked at me blankly and said: 'United are one nil up.' On bloody air.

1996

My Top Ten Worst Interviews (and They're Not All with Blokes Called John)

1. John Squire (Monosyllabic telly-watcher)
2. John Lydon (A nightmare mauling after the abusive punk's lunchtime sake binge)
3. Jon Bon Jovi (Tricky, although I think hungover)
4. Mariah Carey (Fruitloop)
5. Quentin Tarantino (Prickly and obtuse)
6. Beyoncé (Hard work)
7. Blue (Buffoons)
8. Avril Lavigne (Offish, but I probably shouldn't have asked who she'd slept with)
9. Ricky Martin (Talks bollocks, start to finish)
10. Gareth Gates (Challenging – and I still can't believe he pulled Katie Price)

At a tabloid like *The Sun*, you probably have around 1200–1500 words for your story and interview over a double-page spread in print, unless it's running over several days, so the words need to be crisp and tight. I was always taught that a good populist journalist's copy could be cut from the bottom up and still make sense, in just one paragraph. Today, that is a skill more precious than ever and the ability to do so is valuable, in a social media world of soundbites, low attention spans and character-restricted posts.

In the fast and intricate world of tabloid wordsmithery, there are two things it is particularly important to avoid, that is repetition … and repetition. This has given rise to a phenomenon known as 'knobbly monsters'. A knobbly monster is red-top slang for that awkward second reference to a subject when the obvious or only term has already been deployed. It originated after a *Sun* journalist wrote of a crocodile attack and was unable to rustle up another word for the animal, opting instead for the term 'the knobbly monster' as his alternative. Other mighty fine examples since include Julius Caesar described as 'the tyrannical toga lover', 'the popular orange vegetable' for a carrot, Westlife as 'the stool-loving man band', 'cod digits' once (and only) replacing fish fingers, while 'the horizontal sleeping surface' came in place of bed.

A howler of a slightly different breed surfaced in one report about an overseas trip with the England football team. Attributed to the senior sports writer at the *Daily Mirror*, his report began with the words: 'Here in Jerusalem, birthplace of the legendary Jesus Christ …' There was another intro which read: 'From my hotel room overlooking Mount Everest …'

The *Daily Mirror* held a party when *The Sun* was first launched for 5d in 1969 – the year of my birth and the moon landings. Mirror chairman Hugh Cudlipp declared: 'That's no threat to anybody,' when he read the first edition. But within three days sales had doubled and hit 1.6 million. It was an intoxicating mix of sport, glamour, news, politics and humour, which was then breaking new ground.

But it became famous the world over for its headlines and that is what first attracted me as a news-hungry teenager, drawn to the sparkle of red-top wordplay and its directness. Tabloid headline writing is an art and I have worked with some geniuses throughout my career, who have rustled up some corkers, many of which have slipped into modern parlance.

Digital journalism and the race for search engine optimisation and clicks has led to an erosion in standards of headline writing – with many online editors shunning puns and cute linguistic gags, because they fear such word trickery won't be pushed up the Google rankings. The problem with that is it can homogenise news brands and they all start to look and feel the same.

One example of this came in May 2025 when *The Sun* ran an online story with the headline: 'TRANS FOOTIE BAN: FA will BAN trans women from women's football next season after "win for common sense" Supreme Court ruling'.

The print version, however, rather memorably, read: 'They Think It's All Ovaries … It Is Now'. Cue applause.

Some of the most glorious headlines are often those born out of simplicity. When a story landed about an old British boozer being turned into a mosque, I went with: 'Imam Walks into a Bar …' But perhaps the most magnificent example of this approach came in 1983, in the Murdoch-owned *New York Post*, the planet's other most smartly headlined newspaper. Following a grisly murder in a Queens strip club, the *Post*'s managing editor Vincent A. Musetto, who died in 2015, wrote the following five words on the front page: 'Headless Body in Topless Bar'. Genius.

'Arizona Psychic Hit by Car Says He Never Saw It Coming' was spectacular in a 2017 edition of Arizona's *The Republic*, while *The Times* penned a 1986 tale about the former Labour politician Michael Foot leading a committee to look at nuclear disarmament in Europe with the line: 'Foot Heads Arms Body'.

Kelvin MacKenzie's 'Freddie Starr Ate My Hamster' in 1986 aside, as far as *The Sun* goes, the top-rated headlines throughout my career in the 90s and beyond are assessed here in yet another Nick Hornby-esque list:

'It's Paddy Pantsdown' (1992) – The Lib-Dem leader's fling with secretary.

'I Was Carlos the Jackal's Driving Instructor' (1994) – Londoner taught international terrorist how to drive. Straightforward but irresistible.

'Zip Me Up Before You Go Go' (1998) – George Michael arrested after exposing himself in LA public toilet. Doesn't get much better than that.

'I'm Only Here for De Beers' (2000) – World's biggest jewellery heist foiled at Millennium Dome.

'Super Caley Go Ballistic Celtic Are Atrocious' (2000) – Scottish football giants tamed.

'World's Tallest Bloke Lives in Neasden' (2002) – Does what it says on the tin.

'Tyrant's in His Pants' (2005) – Jailed Saddam Hussain snapped in his undies.

'How Do You Solve a Problem Like Korea?' (2006) – Geopolitical special on East–West diplomatic relations.

England
Algeria
Slovenia
Yanks

(2009) – Initial joy at England football team's supposedly weak World Cup group. Oops.

'Sunny Outlook in Many Areas But Depression Over Heathrow as Shower Drifts in from South Africa' (2010) – Weather map, indicating England team returning in disgrace from aforementioned World Cup.

'Bin Bagged' (2011) – Osama bin Laden dead. Two words. Top-drawer.

'Munchkin Fury at Maggie Ding Dong Song' (2013) – Wizard of Oz star slams musical Thatcher slur. Cue formation of indie band named Munchkin Fury.

But the front page that would get me noticed by those in, what we then called, deep carpet land – heralding the next stage of my career – came when I was Associate Editor (Features) in 2005. Brackets felt important then, you know. The death of Pope John Paul II that year coincided with a new election cycle as Cool Britannia's political face, Tony Blair, aimed for a third term and eyes were on which party the paper would endorse. Pope John Paul had been in the Catholic top job for so many years that most were unfamiliar with the fascinating and intricate procedure employed to choose a successor – and we were obsessed with watching the Vatican's Sistine Chapel chimney on live television for hours – waiting for that decisive plume of white smoke.

A somewhat industrious reporter, Harry Macadam, somehow managed to locate a very similar-looking chimney in East London and a fine selection of coloured smoke bombs in blue, red and yellow. Health and safety goons seemingly absent from their posts back then – happy days – we clambered up on to the precarious roof of the Wapping HQ and erected the smokestack, put out a photo call notice and announced that *The Sun*'s political allegiance would be revealed, Vatican-style.

BBC News broadcast the stunt live on *News at Six*, as did *The Sun*'s website, and the declaration went around the world as plumes of red smoke bellowed from the East London rooftop, signalling a third term backing for Blair. And so the 'One Last Chance: Sun Smoke Goes Red for Blair' front page was born. From then on, for me things would only get better …

CHAPTER 9

Blair

The Labour leader, Oasis and ounces of cocaine

As Cool Britannia's glorious night of coronation at the 1996 Brit Awards drew to an exhausting close, the Blairs tentatively approached all-conquering Oasis's table at the front of an emptying Earls Court.

The soon-to-be Prime Minister Blair and high-flying lawyer wife Cherie were eager for the group to sign memorabilia for their Britpop-loving children but were blissfully unaware that they were within touching distance of perhaps thousands of pounds worth of illegal Class A drugs.

The MD of Creation Records, and latterly manager of the brothers' nemesis Robbie Williams, was with the award-winners and confessed: 'There were literally ounces of cocaine, just a couple of feet away from them.'

And rhythm guitarist Paul 'Bonehead' Arthurs recalled: 'They were very sheepish. Cherie Blair was like, "Would you mind awfully signing something for my kids? They're very big fans." We just went, "Waaaargh." We were fucked.'

Blair agreed to speak to me for this book at his Institute for Global Change in London. He's starting to show his age a little more now but is slimmer than when he was PM, that familiar beaming grin and his hair now completely grey – and less of it. He's wearing jeans and a crisp white shirt and his words are measured but sometimes a little staccato. He is probably the most approachable prime minister with whom I have interacted, alongside David Cameron, and he has both warmth and humour.

I asked him about the illegal drugs stash, the fact that Noel had binged on ecstasy that evening and whether he'd twigged. 'Absolutely not,' was his response, 'but I was probably a bit naive about these things. I always liked Noel Gallagher actually, I didn't really know Liam. But I always liked Noel because I felt that he had a toughness about him and also an intellectual rigour that, let's say, was not always present in all the pop guys.

'I remember being really nervous about the Brit Awards in 1996. David Bowie was a hero and, actually, he was a really nice guy – at least, he was very nice to me. The thing you always know as a politician, stepping out in front of an audience like that, it's always got the capacity to go horribly wrong.' I don't think Blair could resist the lure of sharing the stage with those Britpop heroes and their elder statesmen, speaking to the youth whose vote he craved so, on balance, it was worth the risk.

Blair had, of course, presented Bowie with his lifetime achievement award that night and then rode the Cool Britannia wave, becoming the political face of it, despite the movement emerging under a previous government. He's obviously written and spoken about his time in office extensively but never in this detail about the cultural force of Britain at this time, his role in that movement and his encounters with the protagonists of the period.

In July 1997, Blair famously held a reception at Downing Street for the creative industries and was joined by actors Ralph Fiennes and Ross Kemp, Wallace and Gromit creator Nick Park, comedians Eddie Izzard, Lenny Henry, Harry Enfield and Ben Elton, fashion designer Vivienne Westwood, author Nick Hornby and Creation's Alan McGee, along with Noel and his wife Meg Mathews. Noel would also write a lyric around this time, which would borrow from a Blair speech. An election was called for the beginning of May 1997, one thousand days before the new Millennium and Blair referenced this in an evangelical speech to the Labour Conference in October 1996. On *Be Here Now*'s 'Magic Pie', Noel sings: 'There are but a thousand days preparing for a thousand years.' Incidentally, in a prescient passage of that speech that resonates today, Blair warned: 'A spectre haunts the world: technological revolution. Ten years ago, a fifteen-year-old probably couldn't work a computer. Now he's in danger of living on it.'

Blair told me: 'I had no idea that Noel was going to be at the Downing Street party. From my albeit limited knowledge, I didn't think he was someone who was going to behave badly. I had actually no idea about the party until I walked into it because, believe it or not, you're running the country, so there are more important things to think about. But that's gone down in folklore. We made a great deliberate decision to have all these people there and I literally had nothing to do with it.'

The image of Noel, clad in an ill-fitting jacket and shirt, hair freshly trimmed, shaking hands with a grinning Blair, while clutching a glass of champagne in his left hand, pinged around the world, a celebrated public relations moment for the PM, but perhaps less so for the Oasis chief.

Was Blair shocked at how prominent the image featured in media across the globe? 'Absolutely, I was surprised because, as I say, I can't remember what thing I was dealing with at the time, but I was dealing with something and I remember coming through one of the doors from the flat that led into Downing Street proper, bumping into a whole lot of people and thinking, "Mmmm." It was fine.

'Britpop was a big thing for sure. I was listening to bands like Blur and Oasis. I was aware of all of this, but you're also running the country! It's more a thought at the end of the day rather than sitting there at Cabinet table thinking about Oasis or Blur.

'I was always very clear that these types of endorsements from famous people were better than not having them. I would always say to my people when we were discussing these things, the fact that someone's a great footballer doesn't mean to say they know who the right prime minister is. They may know who the best football coach is. I was always quite ... not cynical about it, but aware of the fact that it was nice, but let's not kid ourselves.'

Noel Gallagher recalled the fabled gathering mostly-fondly, flattered that the prime minister of the day wanted to welcome him. But he regrets the picture with Blair and said he could still smell the cheese.

And Noel's publicist Johnny Hopkins felt the band – and the wider public – were excited and seduced by the idea of dumping the Conservatives and achieving revolutionary change. 'I believe they did feel used, after the event. No, I didn't encourage them to go. I was very concerned about how it would have impact on the band and the label. But I understand their impulse for going. We were all caught up in getting rid of the Tories, who had destroyed much of the North and other parts of the UK. The atmosphere of change and possibility was appealing. The fact that music could be a part of bringing about a change of government was definitely seductive. Inevitably much of it was an illusion.

Nevertheless, Noel got his revenge on Thatcher by, allegedly, scrawling a Hitler moustache on her portrait.'

Alongside Mel B, Sleeper's Louise Wener has talked of the sexism and misogyny of the 90s, which saw the explosion of magazines such as *Loaded* and *FHM* and a tsunami of lad culture, spearheaded by men like Chris Evans and Liam behaving badly. So did Blair worry about aligning himself with such a movement? He looked confused when I asked this, before responding: 'We'd expanded enormously the number of women MPs. There was this huge influx in 97 of women MPs. Women were starting to assert themselves much more strongly. And I read some things now where people look back on that time and think that it was a kind of wrong turning for women's liberation, but I don't think it was really. I think, at the time, people felt, why shouldn't women have a good time too?

'So I think you should be careful, because I think the problem is people forget how stuffy British society was at an establishment level before we came in. And the change was enormous, and the change then changed the Conservative Party too. I think we, as New Labour, almost personified the new wave of feeling and optimism and possibility.'

At the 1998 Labour Party Conference, Chris Evans broadcast his Virgin Radio *Breakfast Show*, which was attracting around 4.7 million listeners every week, live from Blackpool, and he invited me on as a guest to discuss New Labour, Blair and the PM's celebrity and wider appeal. Unthinkable today. It was something of a symbiotic relationship with Chris. He would talk and follow up stories I'd written in that day's newspaper and we would monitor his show and report newsworthy nuggets he'd spoken about on air. We promoted one another. His articulate and revelatory breakfast shows, at that time, were must-listens for a considerable constituency of young Britons. Evans would be tearing around London with his team, getting into scrapes with whichever friends he had at the time – Paul Gascoigne, Danny Baker and the like, often staggering into his radio show late and regaling listeners with his drunken tales and escapades.

Sometimes, his predecessor on early breakfast, Dave Pearce, would have to fill in and improvise until Evans made an appearance.

Dave and I have worked together for decades and he compiled a Dance Bizarre column for us in the 90s, to reflect the growing influence of club culture. He told me: 'On more than one occasion Chris arrived with a bright pink face and a slightly sheepish grin, glasses a little skew-whiff after a particularly harsh night out with the likes of

Danny Baker and Paul Gascoigne. I think its fair to say a fairly large quantity of booze would have been consumed in the process and you knew you were in for a particularly mad fun show. Everything was great but there were a few hiccups on the way.

'One morning when I was sleeping peacefully in my bed in Ealing, West London (I had moved onto my own weekend show by then) I got a call in the early hours of the morning from a BBC exec: "Really sorry to wake you but we have a situation." He then went on to tell me Chris Evans wouldn't be able to do the breakfast show that morning, and could I get dressed and come straight over to the BBC studios to do the breakfast show?

'I looked at my watch – the show was due to start in a couple of hours. I gulped: "OK," I said. "Will his full production team be there – we can run with some stuff and ideas they have been working on?"

"Should all be fine", he replied.

"When I arrived at the studios to my horror there was no production team – just a stack of the early editions of the newspapers and no team. My heart sank as I faced the prospect of broadcasting to 7.5 million listeners with absolutely nothing prepared. Luckily the producer of the previous show agreed to stay on and help me but I still have the odd nightmare where it all comes flooding back. It turns out Chris had taken his entire team out on a bender – great publicity stunt but not so great for me. If you are reading this, Chris, you owe me a nice dinner."

Evans was firmly on the New Labour fan bus and aligning himself with Blair. I would review the new PM's powerful Blackpool speech on the pages of the Bizarre column, which was unheard of and, perhaps rightly, ridiculed in *Private Eye* magazine. Can you imagine Garry Bushell appraising a Thatcher conference address or Piers Morgan dissecting John Major's oratory skills?

Later that day, at the Blackpool Palace nightclub, we attended a Young Labour event and hit the dance floor with Evans, the Secretary of State for Northern Ireland, Mo Mowlam, who was not only a scream but had recently brokered the small matter of the Good Friday Agreement, along with Deputy PM John Prescott – both sadly no longer with us. Prescott was actually a great mover. There is a rather cringeworthy photograph of us boogying to Abba but, silly as it is, that image does encapsulate both the insanity and the brilliance of the 90s in many ways. Senior heavyweight ministers strutting their stuff with Britain's number one broadcaster and *The Sun*'s gossip columnist. It illustrated the coming together of politics, entertainment and the media, with a modernised, colourful sense of freedom, vibrancy and fun.

I asked Blair about his view on such antics and the shift that had occurred in British politics. 'Politicians became more accessible at that point. You could argue today that they are almost too accessible but back then, and maybe people don't remember now in the Thatcher period, the Conservative Party was pretty old-fashioned, stuffy. And, to be frank about it, at that point in time, you could never have imagined the Conservative Party would have had a black leader. It just wouldn't have been thinkable. People would just have laughed at the notion.

'So, in a way, you and Chris Evans dancing with Mo Mowlam and John Prescott is a sign that people just opened up. Mo Mowlam was Secretary of State for Northern Ireland – you can imagine the absolute culture shock she was in Northern Ireland. She also very much represented that shift in zeitgeist. She was fun but also completely unstuffy and approachable. It's not to say the Conservative people were completely bad people. I mean, they weren't. There were people who wanted to do their best for the country, but you compare Peter Brooke, who's actually a lovely man, as a symbol of the UK, when he was Northern Ireland Secretary with Mo, the difference is pretty extraordinary.'

The New Labour leader had also aligned himself with football and the Euro 96 tournament in the run-up to the election, even rewriting the lyrics to 'Three Lions' in his 1996 conference speech, telling delegates: 'Labour's come home to you, so come home to us. Labour's coming home. Seventeen years of hurt never stopped us dreaming, Labour's coming home. As we did in 1945 and 1964. I know that was then but it could be again.'

'I think that was Alastair.' Blair chuckled. 'He'll tell you it was! That was a line given to me. Was it a bit twee?'

A few months before that, Blair had met with then-Newcastle United manager Kevin Keegan at a Brighton leisure centre, removed his tie and jacket and indulged in a headers session with the former England captain, his starched white shirt and loose-fitting black suit trousers billowing in the wind.

But it was a risky stunt, with a nervy Campbell, Blair's communications chief and former *Daily Mirror* man, looking on. 'The headers with Kevin Keegan were a big thing,' Blair told me. 'That registered, actually. I didn't even know I was going to do it that day until I went, but it was a crazy risk to take, because supposing I'm not being able to head the ball. But he was so good, he could land it back on mine. This is the thing that always happens in these situations. You spend one day on the beach and someone has a photograph and they think: "That guy's always on the beach. He's got a country to run." I remember Bill Clinton telling me – never get a picture with a drink in your hand, because otherwise they think all he does is sit around drinking.'

Blair was, of course, himself caught beneath a landslide, and elected overwhelmingly after winning 418 seats, the largest in history, becoming the youngest prime minister of the 20th century. This ended eighteen years in opposition, the first victory for Labour since 1974. The party memorably chose D:Ream's club anthem 'Things Can Only Get Better' as their campaign tune. Weirdly, I'd seen D:Ream perform this track, among others, live the previous year at a small West End venue and would later hire their keyboard player Brian Cox as *The Sun*'s Professor, as he had an unnerving ability to discuss and write about incredibly complex scientific subjects in a digestible way. The key to well-executed tabloid journalism, which fitted my paper's ethos perfectly. But the idea that such a band and their signature tune would become so ubiquitous and utilised in a political context was unthinkable. As was the fact that the skinny bloke on keyboards would become a world authority on life, the universe and everything. The song opens with the lyric: 'We're not scared to lose it all, security thrown through the wall. Future dreams we have to realise. A thousand sceptic hands won't keep us from the things we plan.' The band would support Take That on tour, after which the hope-filled song spent four weeks at number one from January 1994 and then re-entered the charts in election month – May 1997 – peaking at number nineteen.

I ask the country's most successful ever Labour leader, who has never spoken at such length and depth about this Cool Britannia period, whether he personally chose the dance-floor hit. 'I don't know who selected that,' he said. 'It wasn't me, but it was an inspired choice. It caught the mood, a catchy song and the lyric was exactly the lyric you would have chosen. It was all part of the same thing, but I still think people underestimate the degree to which it would not have been the same if it hadn't been for the concept of New Labour, that the New was important. This is because you brought a whole lot of people on board that otherwise wouldn't really have been on board. And I think Labour would have won the 97 election anyway as the Labour Party. But I don't think we would have had the landslide or the high percentage of the vote we got, and I think there are a lot of people that would have not really backed us but did. And so the New in New Labour was important, even for people who would probably consider themselves on the left but understood that the old Labour Party had its own cultural conservatism that they wanted to overcome.'

Interestingly, he stressed that he thought modern Britain had recently lost its way along with a sense of positivity.

'The country has lost that sense of optimism. Countries are like companies or football teams or any local community,' he told me. 'You've got to know where you're going and feel confident that you can get there. So let's see how the new government does with that. But it's for sure that the country is not, I think, very optimistic at present. You want to feel your country is on the up. You want to feel you're part of something that's going places, doing things, achieving things. We've just been through a very difficult time, as many modern developed countries have. And the most important thing that people want and felt they would get back then was that things were going to move. OK, now some bits you might like, some bits you may not like, but things were definitely going to move.

'The country was not going to be the same. And it's always important to communicate that and have that sense of uplift. Provided you keep your expectations reasonable, it was a big moment of change, hope and optimism. So, provided you don't exaggerate that and think we were living through some golden age where everything was wonderful, there was a much greater sense of possibility. People felt quite proud to be part of the country. And if you asked people whether the country was on the up, then they would have said, yes, we are on the up, I think. So, in the context of today, those are quite big, big things to look back on. And I think that's why it's actually quite interesting you're writing this, because I do think that some of it was completely time-bound, but there are elements of it which are timeless lessons about how countries do well. They do well when they have a sense of optimism and possibility. Well, at least when they're given a clear direction.'

The Sun's role in politics and its importance at general elections has been a subject I've been quizzed about consistently over the decades. You can love or loathe the newspaper, as I know many do in equal measure, but you can never ignore it. It has always been a publication, a living organism, that listens to its readers – their hopes, fears and aspirations – and reflects those views editorially, and in a powerful way. For many years, *The Sun*'s executive team would collectively travel by coach on weekend trips each year to meet large groups of its consumers, usually at holiday camps like Butlin's, in places like Bognor Regis or Skegness. It was typically a fruitful and vital information-gathering exercise – often rather fun.

When *The Sun* launched in 1969, it was a Labour paper and remained so until Thatcher came to prominence in 1975; it then backed her leadership in those trio of election victories. In 1970, *The Sun* had given her the nickname 'Maggie Thatcher – Milk Snatcher' after she withdrew free school milk while Education Secretary.

But on 3 May 1979, the paper officially switched to the Conservatives and, in a famous editorial still examined by journalism students today, wrote: 'We are proud to have a working-class readership. The LARGEST working-class readership of any daily paper. We are equally proud of the fact that we have more young readers than any of our contemporaries. Both young people and traditional Labour Party supporters tend to be idealists. And *The Sun* is an idealistic newspaper. Why do we advise a vote for the Tories? Because *The Sun* is above all a RADICAL newspaper.'

In 1992, the paper boasted 'It Was the Sun Wot Won It' – legend will tell you Murdoch hated it – following John Major's triumph, having wielded an aggressive campaign against Labour leader Neil Kinnock, infamously superimposing his head on a lightbulb with the headline: 'If Kinnock wins today will the last person to leave Britain please turn out the lights'.

But soon after – and questioning of that decision – readers and executives grew weary of the Tories under John Major, with economic jitters and his personality bypass. Times changed, as did editors, and, on 18 March 1997, six weeks before the general election, the front page screamed 'The Sun Backs Blair'. Some older figures, on a divided office floor, were uncomfortable with the endorsement, but us younger newsroom bucks were ecstatic, feeling the paper needed an injection of youthful energy and a reflection of the zeitgeist.

The *Sun* editorial stated that the New Labour leader is the 'breath of fresh air' needed by Britain and shouted: 'The Tories are tired, divided and rudderless. This is the election for the millennium. In six weeks' time, Britain will vote for a government to take it into the 21st century. The people need a leader with vision, purpose and courage who can inspire them and fire their imaginations. *The Sun* believes that man is Tony Blair.'

It was very much an endorsement of Blair personally, rather than of his party. In July 1995, he had accepted an invitation to address Murdoch and the News Corporation conference, on Hayman Island in Australia, which he described as the lion's den.

Blair felt the backing was monumental, with the pre-internet paper selling 4 million copies a day and boasting more than 10 million readers. '*The Sun* newspaper endorsement was of me, and New Labour for sure, not the Labour Party. It was massively important. Today, the media is much more fragmented, but at the time, you had a much more predictable and stable media environment in which the main newspapers and the main TV stations were enormously influential.

'And so *The Sun*, which had been vigorously anti-Labour, backing Labour was of huge importance to us. The way that Neil Kinnock had been treated was seared into the party memory. At one level, that made it harder to come to an accommodation because people felt it in some way a sort of betrayal. But I was very clear that, provided we stood our ground in the areas where we took a different point of view, there were things that *The Sun* should endorse because we were going to be New Labour, we weren't going to disturb the essential economic settlement of the Thatcher years, but we were going to be socially liberal, we were going to invest in the public realm and do it in a way that was modern and not ideological.

'None of the traditional media outlets has the same authority today, but *The Sun* still matters as a paper. And the media environment matters. I mean it matters in any country, but it's always mattered a bit more in the UK, because it sets a tone for the debate … In the UK media market, the media does have to keep in touch with its readers. It's highly competitive still. And so that media environment is more likely to be an accurate representation of where the country is. So, it's still important in my view and the fact that *The Sun* endorsed Labour at the last election was important for Keir.

'I think it was easier in those days because there was more of a shared experience culturally. It was not just *The Sun* with 4 million readers, but also the 10 o'clock news or 9 o'clock news – or whatever it was at the time on the BBC – would have been watched by 8 to 10 million people every night. I don't know what the figure is now, but it's probably less than a million. For me, it was just about what I felt. I never sat down and studied the zeitgeist. I just felt what I felt. That's why, for example, I was always strong on law and order. When I was growing up, if people were on the left, they tended to be quite weak on law and order and socially liberal. And people on the right would be strong on law and order and socially conservative. But I grew up in a situation where, by the time I got the leadership of the Labour Party, I had a very clear view, which was you should be really tough on law and order, but actually, if someone's gay, that's their right and that's fine. So you were breaking up some of those old alliances. There was a new generation that just thought if someone's committing a crime, we should go after them, but if someone lives their personal life in a different way from me – live and let live.'

I also ask whether he recalled *The Sun* front page that got me noticed, endorsing him for a third term by pumping red smoke through a Vatican-style chimney built on the roof of our East London HQ. 'I have seen it since but don't recall seeing it at the time. *The Sun* has always thought outside the box creatively.'

In May 1997, there was a genuine sense of optimism among hard-working young people like us that it was our time and we finally had a voice. London was flourishing and the arts booming. The Tories resembled inhabitants of a bygone era and looked as if they belonged in a 1950s black-and-white newsreel. Satirical TV show *Spitting Image* captured Major perfectly as his puppet was entirely grey, save for a Tory blue tie. One of the most memorable sketches showed a besuited Thatcher treating her cabinet to dinner and ordering steak. 'What about the vegetables?' asks the waitress. 'Oh, they'll have the same as me,' the Iron Lady replies.

On the night of the election – the result of which was a formality, just a matter of how big the win would be – me and the missus went to dinner at the rather swanky Oxo Tower to celebrate and raised a bottle of champagne in celebration, feeling a sense of euphoria that Britain was on the eve of transformation. What shameless champagne socialists we were back then. Alan McGee joined an invitation-only celebration at the Royal Festival Hall, just along the South Bank from where we were lording it, with celebrity endorsers and party workers. Noel was on the guest list but decided to stay at his home, Supernova Heights in Belsize Park, with wife-to-be Meg. They celebrated with champagne, brandy and cigars, playing The Beatles' 'Revolution' at deafening volume and upsetting the neighbours.

I want to know whether Blair sensed this elation himself on the actual night. 'At that moment I was thinking more of the reality of the scale of the challenge ahead and getting to grips with government. But if you compare then and now, you have to recognise that the country has been through a lot since that time – the financial crash, the turmoil of a succession of Tory PMs in a short period of time, the divisiveness and impact of Brexit, the pandemic – so it's a much more complicated picture than when I became PM.'

So how does he reflect on the cultural movement this book is about, a moment with which he is inextricably linked, when music, art, politics, football, the media, fashion and food exploded like a champagne supernova in the sky. 'For me, the term Cool Britannia emerged shortly after we came to government, although apparently it was used by someone before, in 1996. I never invented the term; I never spent a lot of time thinking about it, but I was just aware of it. It's better than many other things that could be said about a country, given where we've been in recent times. It was a moment of hope and opportunity.

'You were coming to the end – not just of a century – but a millennium. There was a feeling that the country, despite all the problems of the exchange rate mechanism, was doing better economically. There was a mood for change, socially. There was a new generation that felt empowered in a way by a sense of personal liberation. You had women feeling they could play a bigger part. There was an air of creativity about the country and an optimism, and I guess all of those things came together. And then New Labour, in a way, was a political representation of the same feeling. I wouldn't underestimate the impact of Princess Diana as well; she was a symbol for the monarchy. Sometimes there are moments in time and in history where a whole set of things come together, without apparently being organised but very much in harmony with each other. It could always happen again. But I do think that at the core of it is a sense of optimism. The cultural aspect was not something I was consciously trying to do, but the great resurgence of the British arts and music scene as New Labour came to power added a hugely important ingredient to the zeitgeist of the time.

'It was a rebellion against the part of Thatcherism that appeared to say there is no such thing as society, or appeared to be indifferent to those at the bottom of the heap, or represented a social conservatism that seemed out of tune with what people wanted, the opposition to gay rights and so on ... If there was a rebellion, I think it was as much against social conservatism, but not necessarily against the economics because people could see that the country, in one sense, was doing better. New Labour represented those times because it was clear we weren't going to rerun the debates of the 80s.'

New Labour had concocted the magic formula, shedding the party's far left ideology and appealing to centrists like us, who wanted a government of modernist grown-ups. Politicians with vision and backbone have to take the people with them and Blair did exactly that. It's something modern politics has lacked since and many voters feel vexed that the traditional parties seem to lack that leadership, inspiration and hope.

Diana's influence absolutely cannot be underestimated – and she was certainly a global force who represented Britain. Her death on 31 August 1997 devastated us all; nobody much cared much for showbiz columns and mouthy Britpop bands for quite a period of time after her passing.

Blair articulated the nation's desolation in what must be regarded as one of his finest examples of oratory. I asked him to recall those moments. 'It was a very difficult thing to do. I wanted to convey the devastation and grief that I felt personally, but knowing how the country had taken her to their hearts and would feel the same terrible loss, I thought it important to reflect that. That is how I came up with the "People's Princess". And as we saw in the following days, tens of thousands of people from here and around the world visited the palaces to lay flowers in her memory, a truly extraordinary and moving expression of how much she meant to them and how iconic she had become.'

So, was that the moment that killed off the Cool Britannia movement, just four months into the New Labour government? 'I don't know, I can't really judge that. Even though Princess Diana was such a big figure and icon and had been there for all of it, I think it carried on for quite some time after her death. But all of these things have their moment and then the moment passes by.'

Blair would serve as our prime minister for ten years until 2007 when he handed over control to his chancellor Gordon Brown. His legacy has, of course, been tainted by the war in Iraq following the 9/11 terrorist atrocity. Infamously, Alastair Campbell had prepared a briefing document in 2003 called 'Iraq – Its Infrastructure of

1996

Concealment, Deception and Intimidation', which became known as the 'Dodgy Dossier' in some parts of the media. It claimed Iraq was in possession of weapons of mass destruction and it was issued to journalists to justify the UK's role in the invasion of Iraq, with 45,000 British troops deployed in the region. A total of 179 British Armed Forces personnel or MOD civilians tragically died during the operation.

But what does Blair regard as his government's abiding legacy from that period? He is quick to answer. 'In political terms, obviously the Northern Ireland Peace Process, gay rights, National Minimum Wage and we started the work to ensure the highest levels of social mobility and the reform of public services, which led to the highest satisfaction rates for the NHS and transformed educational attainment. We changed the social fabric of the country – it was more open and optimistic and that chimed with what was happening culturally.'

Blair would go on to reward the man who had discovered Oasis, Alan McGee of Creation Records, with an invite to the prime minister's country residence Chequers in Buckinghamshire.

The 16th-century manor house has been provided to serving leaders as their weekend retreat since 1921 and visitors have included Richard Nixon, Donald Trump, Ukrainian leader Volodymyr Zelenskyy and George W. Bush. Blair even entertained Russian despot Vladimir Putin there in 2001. Happy days, indeed.

But there was another monster invited the night McGee and his partner Kate attended – the broadcaster and national weirdo Sir Jimmy Savile, who had made a number of sojourns while Margaret Thatcher was prime minister, claiming to have spent eleven consecutive Christmases there. Savile had continued his broadcasting work throughout the 90s, with *Jim'll Fix It* airing on the BBC until 1994. He hosted various regional radio shows until 1997 and co-presented the final edition of *Top of the Pops* in 2006, appearing on *This Is Your Life* in 1990, the Beeb's *Have I Got News for You* in 1999 and 2006's *Celebrity Big Brother*. After he was a guest on the 1991 BBC Radio 4 series *In the Psychiatrist's Chair*, its host and resident shrink Anthony Clare declared: 'There is something chilling about this 20th-century "saint".' When presenter Louis Theroux confronted Savile about rumours of paedophilia in 2000's *When Louis Met ...* series, he responded tellingly with the words: 'We live in a very funny world. And it's easier for me, as a single man, to say "I don't like children", because that puts a lot of salacious tabloid people off the hunt.'

Other invitees that evening included Dame Judi Dench, writer John O'Farrell and Home Secretary John Reid. Reid was later the subject of one of my favourite *Sun* front pages, which read 'John Reid's Brain Is Missing' and explained that a nationwide hunt had been launched to locate his 'walnut-sized' brain after another full jails fiasco. He was livid, apparently. Ironically, the man who should have been in one of his prisons was sitting just across the table.

Savile was placed next to Mrs McGee and began to hit on her, kissing his way up her fingers and arms. Her husband branded him a 'dirty old fucker' who behaved like a gangster. He was baffled as to why Savile had been invited and reflected that his presence spoke of the power of celebrity and its relationship to politics.

Savile would always play up his links with the royal family and politicians, and employ them as a threat to journalists who had the audacity to dig into his questionable private life. There had been constant rumours across Fleet Street's newspapers about his links to paedophilia and a predilection for young girls, particularly, but it was always troublesome to prove. A friend, who grew up in West London in the 1970s, just a few miles from the BBC, told me that, as a young girl, she and a female pal were warned about Jimmy Savile by the girl's nan. 'This was the mid-1970s. My friend was brought up by her grandmother and, whenever we went to the park to play, she would warn us: "If you ever see Jimmy Savile, don't talk to him – he looks up young girls' skirts." We were about ten years old and weren't that far from the BBC studios and thought of it as a wondrous place. We'd always see celebrities from the BBC around that area but the word was that Jimmy Savile was a dirty old man and that he should be avoided.'

There had also been similar talk throughout my adolescence and early career about Savile's BBC colleagues Stuart Hall and Jonathan King, Liberal MP Cyril Smith and singer Gary Glitter, but these went unproven for many years and, in the case of Smith and Savile, tragically did not fully emerge until after their deaths. What these men had in common was that they were all flamboyant, larger-than-life characters hiding in plain sight, who utilised their wacky on-air and public personas to privately prey on vulnerable young people. Those in charge seemingly felt afraid to challenge such rumours and behaviours for fear of losing such supposedly golden talent, seemingly intoxicated by their fame – and ratings. A report into the scandals by Dame Janet Smith later found the BBC missed opportunities to stop 'monstrous' abuse by Savile and Hall because of a 'culture of fear'.

It was the same with Michael Jackson. Come on – if a weird bloke moved into your street, built a children's petting zoo and funfair in their garden and invited a steady stream of handsome young boys for sleepovers, you'd be suspicious, wouldn't you? But because it was Michael Jackson, everyone seemed to think he was just a wacky famous person. I would meet Jacko, as his fans hate him being labelled, when he gave a speech, in 2001, at the Oxford Union. I had derided the singer in print after allegations of a penchant for young boys. Jackson was caked in white make-up and seemed quite distant – it was an odd speech by an even odder man, who looked out of it. As I left the Union building on foot to locate my car, I was ambushed by a group of Jacko-obsessives, who threw a bottle of liquid at my face. As I wiped away the (luckily) harmless fluid, one of them screamed: 'If you don't stop writing nasty pieces about Michael, next time it will be acid.' When Jackson died in 2009, I was in the office until 4am and the paper's sales went up 326,000 in one day. That figure is almost double the *Daily Mirror*'s total sales today.

Savile was certainly a brutal operator who had some of Britain's sharpest lawyers on speed dial. He was also in

1996

possession of an OBE for charity work, a knighthood and a papal knighthood, the pontiff having crowned him a Knight Commander of St Gregory the Great. Intimidatory and priceless weapons in the Savile legal arsenal.

Later, as *The Sun*'s editor, the paper was investigating alleged child abuse at the Haut de la Garenne children's home in Jersey in the Channel Islands. It became a huge story dominating TV headlines and the press for many months, ultimately sparking a lengthy and harrowing public inquiry.

One morning, I was presented with an original black-and-white photograph – taken decades previously – of a grinning Savile in front of the architecturally distinctive care home building, surrounded by dozens of youngsters. There had been many unwritten stories over the years linking the DJ to child abuse but none proven and Savile had a reputation for being highly litigious. But this haunting image placed him firmly in the exact location where allegations of systemic sexual criminality were being investigated. I told the news desk to immediately dispatch a reporter to speak to Savile at his Leeds home to elaborate on the photograph.

The journalist gently asked Savile about recollections of his time at the children's home and he exploded, demanding to know what we were trying to imply, denying he had ever visited the islands. When the reporter produced the original photo, which put him firmly at the scene, he claimed the image had been digitally altered and insisted it was a fake. He was clearly rattled and lying – this was an original black-and-white picture, no question. Savile threatened the reporter with legal action and, guess what, combatively emphasised his links to charities, the royal family and politicians.

When this was relayed to me, I sensed we might be close to something and that we may be able to prise open a story that had eluded the media for decades. I drew up a front page, hitting the picture big alongside the headline 'Tell Us What You Know, Sir Jimmy'. But when *The Sun*'s lawyer saw my draft scribblings, his face turned a strange shade of alabaster. He insisted that there was no way he could sanction such treatment of the story and that Savile had very aggressive lawyers, who would take us for up to £4 million in costs and damages, likely resulting in my dismissal. I explained I was simply asking a question of a man who was obviously not telling the truth, assuring him I was running with it. No matter what. End of.

A few hours later, the lawyer returned, with several sheets of paper in his trembling hand, and displaying an even lighter skin shade than earlier in the day. It was a predictably thunderous legal letter from Savile's lawyers, threatening libel proceedings and, again, flagging up his links to the royals, highlighting the millions of pounds he had raised for charity and his work with hospitals like Broadmoor and Stoke Mandeville. I reiterated that I refused to be cowed. The lawyer then sheepishly explained that if I went against his advice, he would have to flag up my decision to the chief legal counsel in New York, a powerful man at Murdoch's side. I was thwarted. It's a decision that has haunted me since. We did ultimately run the photograph, but the copy was diluted and heavily legalled, softening any impact. Had I splashed the story in a provocative and powerful way, I'm convinced that it may have prompted victims of Savile's abuse to come forward and speak out, perhaps bringing him to justice before his eventual death in 2011.

But Savile's relentless lawyers continued to threaten legal action, even after publication. A letter written on behalf of the presenter by Fox Hayes solicitors, an, interestingly, now-shuttered Leeds firm, once again emphasised the 'huge sums' that Savile's charity work had raised for children and demanded a prominent statement 'making clear that any visit to the home was entirely innocent'. We were also ordered to delete the article from the website and pay Savile compensation 'for the injury to his feelings and reputation'.

Savile's lawyers insisted child abuse was the 'antithesis of everything he has worked tirelessly to prevent'. Apparently, despite the photo, he did not remember travelling to see the children at the care home and that 'any such visit would have been unexceptional save for the pleasure it may have given'. And journalists get a bad rap for inaccuracies. I hope you can begin to comprehend the frustration and boiling anger such moments provoke within an editor's body and mind.

At the Independent Jersey Care Inquiry into abuse at the home, a note proved Savile had visited on 19 April 1976, but police said there was insufficient evidence for an investigation into him to proceed. The note described him doing a fun run with a teenage girl from Haut de la Garenne with details of the money raised. Despite denying ever having been to the island when we asked him, Savile was a regular visitor to Jersey and was the star guest at the Battle of Flowers carnival three times in 1969, 1972 and 2002, where he was crowned Mr Battle on each occasion, something you'd think he would have recalled.

Alas, it wasn't until after his death, aged 84, that he was exposed as one of Britain's most prolific sex abusers; he is thought to have assaulted hundreds of males and females between the ages of 5 and 75. One hundred and fifty-one alleged abusers were identified in the Jersey investigation following the three-year probe, but only seven were successfully prosecuted.

In 2012, Michael White wrote an article for the *Guardian*, which asked: 'Jimmy Savile: why didn't the tough tabloids nail him? Those who should have acted didn't, kids who dared complain weren't believed, and all in a pre-internet age.' My question is – so why didn't the *Guardian* nail him? In 2009, White's paper had described Savile as a 'prodigious philanthropist'.

The truth is that Britain's powerful libel laws make it increasingly easy for the rich and famous to hide and avoid scrutiny. And, with dwindling revenues, many publishers want to avoid a costly fight in the courts.

Unfortunately, this has had a chilling effect on investigative journalism – and free speech. That's why I applaud *The Sun* and the bravery of its Editor-in-Chief Victoria Newton in publishing allegations against another BBC presenter, Huw Edwards, in 2024, in the face of fierce criticism and legal threats. Edwards was exposed for paying a drug-addicted teen £30k for sex snaps. *The Sun* also revealed he had broken lockdown – for a liaison with another young man he met online – and used his power to try and make a junior employee come to his Windsor hotel room around the time of Prince Philip's funeral in April 2021. It also emerged that the Corporation had received a complaint about the ex-*News at Ten* broadcaster, amid the fallout over the Savile sex abuse scandal itself, as long ago as 2012. Edwards later avoided jail, despite three charges of making indecent images of children. Again, another BBC presenter seemingly being protected by the corporation and allegations and red flags missed – or deliberately ignored.

Such investigations are much trickier to execute in modern Britain and journalism is poorer for it. Sprawling bureaucracy and legal over-reach is combining to create a chilling effect on journalism and free speech, yet this is one of our planet's most precious commodities, a basic tenet of democracy. We must fight to preserve it.

Britain appears to be catching a chill from this global free speech freeze blowing in from, among others, America, Russia and China. Civil servants in the, ahem, 6,000-strong Government Communications Service now trawl social media to monitor 'disinformation' and the crafting of 'counter-narratives'. Brrr.

And, in 2025, UK police were making thirty social media-related arrests a day, this following the bungled armed apprehension of *Father Ted* writer Graham Linehan, who was nicked at Heathrow Airport for commenting on X about trans issues. Thankfully, the spurious case was later dropped.

This stifling and straightjacketing of the media and the wider public has contributed to a national feeling of suffocation, as if our every move is being scrutinised, logged and filed, something quite unthinkable back in 1996.

But fifty-five years before that, author George Orwell wrote in one of his most brilliant essays, 'England, Your England', of a nation of sleepwalkers, who were being numbered, labelled, conscripted and coordinated. His prescient words may have been penned in 1941, yet they appear even more pertinent today.

This goes to explain our ongoing quest for reminders of a less shackled time. It is certainly something which has been central in this book and contextualises the nation's current obsession with all things 90s, the dazzling decade which defined liberation and freedom of expression to my g-g-generation.

The Oasis Live 25 reunion tour came at the moment great swathes of the nation needed it most and, as I conclude my analysis of the 90s, and its 1996 zenith, it is worth travelling back to that memorable summer of 2025 and to frame it further, in a social and cultural context.

It was a certainly a magical period of joyousness and reflection for many of us where millions of normal, hard-working people communed and united across the kingdom to link arms and chant together, attempting to blot out what many felt was a burgeoning sense of unfairness and injustice seeping into British society.

1996

My Top Ten Memorable Quotes of the 90s

1. 'She was the people's princess and that's how she will stay, how she will remain in our hearts and in our memories forever' – Blair nails the mood of the nation after Diana's tragic death in 1997.
2. 'This is history, right here, right now, this is history' – Noel Gallagher chirps at Knebworth in 1996 and puts the event of the decade into perspective.
3. 'Girl Power!' – the Spice Girls lay out their manifesto in 1996.
4. 'There were three of us in this marriage, so it was a bit crowded' – Princess Diana on her relationship problems to BBC's *Panorama* in 1995.
5. 'No! No! No!' – the climax of Margaret Thatcher's House of Commons anti-European outburst during a debate on integration in 1990, just ahead of her resignation.
6. 'Daft as a brush' – England manager Bobby Robson's assessment of precocious talent Paul Gascoigne ahead of the 1990 World Cup.
7. 'Choose life. Choose a job. Choose a career. Choose a family. Choose a fucking big television' – opening monologue of Ewan McGregor (aka Mark Renton) in 1996 film *Trainspotting*.
8. '1992 is not a year on which I shall look back with undiluted pleasure. In the words of one of my more sympathetic correspondents, it has turned out to be an "Annus Horribilis"' – the Queen gives Guildhall

speech with depressing verdict on 1992 ... if only she knew.

9. 'She has the eyes of Caligula but the mouth of Marilyn Monroe' – French leader François Mitterrand's 1990 view on UK PM Margaret Thatcher.
10. 'I showed my bottom to Michael' – what Jarvis Cocker told comedian Bob Mortimer after being arrested for mooning at Michael Jackson during the 1996 Brit Awards.

CHAPTER 10

End of a Century

Make sure you enjoy the dash

Ten 90s Learnings from This Book

1. On no account ever attempt to engage in banter with Noel Gallagher in any form of nightspot after midnight.
2. Always give your toothbrush an extra rinse if you've been in the vicinity of a Liverpudlian England footballer.
3. Never go out with Blur's Alex James or Suggs from Madness unless you've heavily fortified your stomach lining and consumed a minimum of two litres of water in 90 minutes or less prior.
4. Beware of demented Michael Jackson fans carrying grudges – and concealed liquids.
5. Always volunteer to play 90s memory games with Shaun Ryder and Zoe Ball.
6. If in the vicinity of two or more Spice Girls, have ear plugs close to hand at all times and deploy in emergency.
7. When in the company of Liam Gallagher and alcohol, always be sure to wear waterproof clothing.

END OF A CENTURY

8. Avoid late-night encounters with follicly challenged prog rock drummers who harbour a deep dislike for one's profession.
9. When interviewing sake-quaffing, ageing punk legends, prepare to be insulted, intimidated, laughed at, prodded and roughed up.
10. Get out there, work hard, do stuff, have fun, meet interesting people – maybe your future partner – and you never know where life will turn.

'Am I the only black guy here?' boomed heavyweight champion boxer Anthony Joshua as he joined us in a hospitality suite at Wembley Stadium – scene of a string of his memorable bouts – to witness the final performance of Oasis's visceral five-night residency in August 2025.

The Olympic gold medallist was jesting, obviously, but his snap observation was a curious one. And I wasn't about to argue with him.

Of course, there were multiple ethnicities among the 90,000, but the concerts felt like not only a resurrection for the band but also the reawakening of a huge swathe of our society, many of whom had felt forgotten, marginalised and overlooked.

In a Britain where the air feels thicker with political tension than it ever did in the halcyon days of the glorious 90s, Oasis rampaged back into our consciousness, representing and celebrating our everyman and everywoman – the normal, hard-working ordinary folk, of whatever race or religion – who pay their taxes on time and want the streets to be safe for their children.

1996

They were back at the right moment with a not-so-Great Britain needing their 90s swagger more than ever before. It was reclamation of power from the unspoken and unrepresented. The Lad Dads, as later depicted in the 2025 John Lewis Christmas ad, were back with a voice.

Cavernous fields and arenas stuffed full of optimists and seekers, ordinary people that are like you and me, but worn down by a Britain where hard workers are penalised while others laugh in our faces and exploit our failing systems. People who know what's right, who believe in law and order and decency, this nation's moral majority – fun-loving, yet respectful and tolerant – but with common sense and a scepticism for wokery.

Fourteen million hopefuls applied for 1.4 million tickets for the seventeen shows across Britain and Ireland. Just common people, who are no longer certain whether it's safe to pull their mobile phone out in public or wear a decent watch or jewellery on the streets. Oasis are that timely reminder of the 90s, an epoch when the country still had a sense of not only self-assurance, wit, sparkle and bloody-minded resilience but also of safety and security, where it wasn't afraid of its own shadow and before it marched to the beat of political correctness. The effervescent stadia where I witnessed the renaissance in Cardiff and London were packed full of jubilant people with smiles plastered on their faces and who still know how to have a damned good time. We met new friends, of all ages, sexes and colour, we thronged and bounced up and down together like maniacs until our legs turned to jelly. We told our nearest and dearest how much we loved them and spilt beer over one another, carefree. Oh, and how we laughed and cried tears of joy as our choir sang those choruses side by side. This was pure, unbridled elation and many had forgotten how that had felt. These raucous assemblies were populated by the sort of people who want the best bits of the 90s back, soundtracked by a group, still burning bright and encapsulating the working-class spirit of Britain – loud, defiant and irreverent.

There wasn't any political posturing, no vile calls for murder from the stage, no balaclavas; just Oasis giving fresh hope and inspiration to generations young and old, who were feeling increasingly ignored and isolated. This Oasis tour was a reassertion of British values of fun, community, spirit, communal celebration and imbibement, throwing your arms around strangers and chanting blissfully into each other's faces. It is a reminder of what, at its heart, Britain is still about, something that may have been buried and lost in a world of artificial intelligence, TikTok, perpetual war and a repetitive cycle of post-pandemic horror and misery, served to us 24/7 via the phones in our pockets. Two powerful Gallagher-propelled fingers up to the party poopers who want to stifle and silence us and ruin our lives.

Our nation has been enduring an identity crisis and feels demoralised by a faltering economy, left weary by violence, everyday crime and small boat crossings. A country on the edge. The tough-talking Gallaghers and their forthright opinions could not be further from those of our spineless elected politicians.

1996

It's been more than thirty years of tabloid and celebrity run-ins, interviews, gigs, japes and scrapes all around the world. The Gallaghers and their cohort certainly played a part in my successful career as a journalist and broadcaster, but the 21st-century Oasis is more refined and professional, although never safe. There was definitely a little less laddishness this time around, no maybe about it. In 2000, when I saw the band perform at Wembley Stadium, the brothers encouraged women to expose their breasts for the big screens and leered at them. No, this was a more polished and less shambolic Oasis, and it was poignant to see the group's children in the audience each night, led by Noel's daughter Anaïs, whose love and pride for her father was beautiful to witness. She took some ownership of the revival, tenderly documenting her exhilaration online, and also celebrated with the Lionesses after their Euros triumph, which typified contemporary Oasis. The concept of an England women's football team being invited to one of their, or anyone else's, anarchic gigs in the 90s would have been unthinkable. The three closing tunes – 'Don't Look Back in Anger', 'Wonderwall' and 'Champagne Supernova' – combined to produce one of the most majestic and exalted trilogies composed by any individual in contemporary music. I'm not certain this euphoric holy trinity can ever be eclipsed.

And it is 90s anthems like these, globally bigger than they have ever been, that are the decade's true legacy. When civilisations collapse, all that's left is the art. These 20th-century hymns, which have become part of the national canon, will live for ever.

END OF A CENTURY

The chemistry between Oasis and fan is like no other. But this was no box-ticking legacy act; it was a celebration of the pre-eminent British songwriting catalogue of the last five decades, two hours where you could forget your woes and your mortgage, an experience that is, in many ways, the antithesis of right-on Coldplay and Glastonbury, and representative of a monumental constituency of this country, reflecting its true nature and soul.

The atmosphere inside and outside of these sonic cathedrals was like that of a World Cup knockout game – but with all 90,000 of us supporting the same team and we didn't have to weep at a penalty shoot-out. Packed into tube trains afterwards, we laughed, linked arms and sang together all the way home, banging on the carriage doors and ceilings, most knowing every word of the same thunderous council house hymns we had been assaulted with just hours before. It was like 1996 all over again.

This was certainly the biggest British rock reunion of all time. No question. The technological, media and musical terrain has shattered so significantly since the band split that I cannot envision any other act hereafter surfacing with such cultural and societal impact or significance, capturing the zeitgeist and stimulating a nation and its people in the same way.

The 2025 Oasis experience served to remind us all of a simpler 90s era, where life felt more colourful, less oppressive and more liberated, more of a laugh, as I hope I have shown in this book. Back then there was a political hope, a thriving economy and a capital city abuzz with some the world's leading wealth creators, restaurateurs and clubs, revolutionary fashion designers and unparalleled artistic geniuses. Real household disposable income had doubled in the twenty-five years up to 1996. Britons took more holidays than ever before, and more of them abroad, owning more consumer durables and many of them considerably better educated, with enrolment in higher education rising from 621,000 in 1970 to 1.9 million in 1995. Most of us were happier and braver, emboldened with a go-getter mentality, one of putting oneself in the right place at the right time and creating luck and opportunity (illustrated by my own early career). This is a mantra echoed by Blur's Alex James, who stressed to me the importance of just doing mad stuff and making things happen, an attitude that seems to have served him well. Again, that doesn't happen looking at a phone or playing *FIFA* in your bedroom all day.

Let's hope this 90s revival inspires Britons to harness their newly reclaimed power and voice, and strive to restore the country we love, sparking a revolution in political thinking and attitude, bringing back the sense of fairness and justice that has seemingly slipped from our democratic grasp since 1996.

Oasis helped put a spring back in the nation's faltering step. The brothers played a not insignificant role in shaping 90s British politics, media and my own career, even contributing to the ushering in of Tony Blair as Labour Prime Minister in 1997. And these Oasis paeans are Noel's glorious manifesto for a brighter Britain and fairer society, resonating now more than ever. What is beyond doubt is that if Oasis and Britpop were a political party it would represent the real Britain and retain power for many years, its rivals caught beneath a Blair-like landslide.

The journey to the 90s, and its apex in 1996, had been fuelled in the Ibizan clubs of the late 80s, by Margaret Thatcher – as a figure to hate but also as the architect of the Enterprise Allowance Scheme – by Gascoigne and his teammates in the Italian sunshine, by Manchester and Madchester, The Stone Roses, Paul Oakenfold and Andrew Weatherall, by the sudden deaths of Kurt Cobain and John Smith and the birth of Goldsmiths College's artistic alumni. And, as the clock ticked down towards the dawn of a new millennium, a cultural bomb detonated, its influence still felt today. A creativity and flourish, much of it fighting against Americanisation, and often powered by stupidity, drunkenness, wit and bad behaviour, whether that be Gazza's goal and dentist's chair celebration against Scotland at Euro 96, Blur's Alex James, Keith Allen and Damien Hirst on the terraces wearing women's underwear and then penning 'Vindaloo', or Noel Gallagher's booze-soaked and cocaine-powered songwriting.

When Paul Oakenfold popped his first pill, it helped trigger a cultural revolution; he would help fire the decade's starter pistol and then become synonymous with the era that followed, working with The Stone Roses and Happy Mondays, inspiring the Inspirals and their gifted roadie and, then, assisting U2 in the trifling matter of becoming the biggest band on planet earth, before amassing such wealth that he could afford to live next door to Cool Britannia's very own PM Tony Blair in London, our throbbing capital city a story-machine for a hungry journalist like me. But, as the millennium closed, Oakenfold would go on to compose the theme tune for reality TV show *Big Brother* which, in its own way, was a contributory factor in killing off the very 90s he helped to create. Such reality TV inventions, and the hunt for the new Spice Girls or Take That, began to dominate the mass media, unknowns replacing very-knowns, the public fixated on observing the evolution of nobodies into superstars and, because of advances in technologies, being able to play a role in their development or destruction, through online voting. MTV may have ushered in reality TV with its groundbreaker *The Real World* as early as 1992, but later *Popstars*, *Pop Idol*, *Big Brother* and *Britain's Got Talent* swallowed up record and TV company's budgets and newspaper space, guitar heroes and serious music seemingly less of a priority. The focus sharpened in on celebrity, as opposed to art.

The ghastly death of Princess Diana played a significant role too, traumatising the country and extinguishing much of the joy and hedonism of the time. The Britpop balloon was punctured, leaving media coverage of it deflated.

But the elder statesmen of British rock would profit from the movement as the century drew to a close, with many twenty-somethings discovering the music of The Who, arch lad Rod Stewart and his Faces, Paul McCartney and David Bowie – whose careers would revive, their work reconsidered, as the New Millennium dawned. But this is the final act for those pioneers as they eventually slip off this mortal coil.

Yet the phenomenon that was the Spice Girls triggered a pop explosion and a stampede of female wannabes, tipping the balance away from guitar-driven rock, indeed, and roll. Record company revenues began to decline too as Apple's iPod launched and took a bite out of physical sales of records, which, like print news, slowed. Labels and papers, whose budgets were being throttled by the internet, certainly wouldn't be paying for pen-wielding young upstarts to travel business class to Hotel Okura in Tokyo or LA's Four Seasons quite as often.

Yes, there was an ugly side to the 90s, an air of sexism, misogyny and laddism, as Mel B so eloquently explained to me. Liam, Gazza and Chris Evans led the way, alongside magazines like *Loaded*, which just could not exist in the same way today. The mainstream media had its moments too, with its jingoistic own goals around Euro 96, but remoulded itself, the tabloids becoming more inclusive, campaigning and developing a new-found conscience and intelligence. Technology developed at an unrecognisable pace, closing in on those viewing child abuse images, as outlined in the Townshend case. But the authorities were not swift enough to snare predator Jimmy Savile during his twisted life. The pervert was gracing radio and television throughout the 90s and beyond, still being wined and dined by hoodwinked prime ministers and politicians.

There wasn't a smartphone in sight at Knebworth, Mile End, Ally Pally, Maine Road or The Verve's triumphant homecoming show at Wigan's Haigh Hall, just a transfixed crowd focused on musicians and their craft, rather than through a small screen. Those same screens would change the face of British celebrity and clubland for ever – and for the worse. Many stars became less approachable, more reticent about venturing out, letting themselves go and behaving badly, for fear of their frivolities being captured for eternity by members of the public – nowadays, every one of them a potential journalist, photographer or videographer. Liam Gallagher has his moments on X, but imagine if he and his peers had access to iPhones and social media when they were in their early twenties. Media training seems essential in a contemporary digital world, those in the public eye – and their gatekeepers – paranoid of someone saying the wrong thing and being cancelled, pixel-preserved evidence for all to see and hear, as cast-iron proof of their guilty transgressions. Social media has created a risk-averse generation, afraid to vent honest opinions or make brave creative statements for fear of ridicule or cancellation, in stark contrast to the no-holds-barred, anything-goes and everything-bared mentality three decades ago.

Unlike my interviewee Tony Blair, I believe it very unlikely that a moment like Cool Britannia, and its zenith in 1996, could ever occur again. Perhaps impossible. Many have drawn comparisons with the 2024 election of a Labour government, the first since Blair and Brown's reigns, but one has to remember the euphoria that greeted the former's coronation. Technology has all but killed off that likelihood. A journalist, editor and newspaper can rarely capture a zeitgeist when it doesn't really exist any more. The death of a royal, a major football tournament or the Olympic Games perhaps still has the power to unite some of us, but we are all nose-deep in our own metaverse, consuming self-curated and bespoke content from all over the globe 24/7, leaving a fractured, splintered media and consumer landscape.

Since those glory days, when nearly 5 million newspapers could be shifted some days, circulation of print copies has dived and advertising has shifted to online platforms, which, of course, didn't exist in 96. Naturally, digital audience figures have risen in national – and local – news outlets as a result, but the majority of readers are not prepared to pay for access to such news online, in the way they did with newspapers. Advertising revenues for such outlets are also a fraction of those which had been celebrated in print, so there is something of a crisis, particularly in regional media where financial sustainability is a clear and present danger, with news brands also affected by the proliferation of the BBC's digital footprint across provincial Britain over the decades. This has created a series of media deserts, not just in Britain but across Europe and beyond, undermining local democracy, allowing councils and politicians to avoid scrutiny from journalists. Most of the press agencies I wrote to for a job back in 1990 sadly no longer exist. Just think of all the court cases and council meetings blissfully taking place unexamined and unchallenged, in the very same buildings I scoured during my early twenties.

This explosion of digital data and analytics at our fingertips has also reduced risk-taking and surgically removed gut instinct from much decision-making. Historically, some of the media's most memorable ideas, campaigns and headlines have been spur-of-the-moment hunches and lurches into the unknown, pushing boundaries of humour and, yes, sometimes silliness and absurdity, the hallmarks of our unique nation.

The Britpop bands inspired groups like Coldplay, Arctic Monkeys, The Libertines and the proponents of 'indie sleaze' to pick up their guitars and achieve success in the noughties – or should it be 'naughties'? – and beyond. And, yes, the Oasis and Blur reunions have restored a little of the spirit and joy of that glorious 90s decade, but many of the big beast bands of old have left the reservation. It is also alarming to consider that by 2026 we had lost members of Pulp, The Stone Roses, The Smiths, Happy Mondays, The Prodigy, Inspiral Carpets and Faithless, among others.

Proper bands have been displaced by a hyperindividualism generation, with wafer-thin over-produced pop collaborations featuring half a dozen or so artists, deliberately targeted and inorganically assembled to exploit social media algorithms and streaming platforms. A&R scouts sit in hostage to TikTok, rather than spending late nights stalking Camden's Dublin Castle or Glasgow's King Tut's Wah Wah Hut to hunt down a new, undiscovered breed of durable superstars. Labels then have to fathom how to expand and elongate said TikToker's 30-second snippet of muzak into a three-minute, radio-friendly slice and make it 'go viral', creating an immediate and short-lived generation of wannabes, destined to become neverweres. The current music scene feels stale, safe and unoriginal, while the joy and hysteria around Blur's and the Gallaghers' rapprochement proves a 90s legacy and indicates a dissatisfaction among the young with the state of popular culture, a swathe of society for whom Adele, Dua Lipa and Ed

END OF A CENTURY

Sheeran just don't cut the Colman's. It takes us all back to a simpler and less divided pre-pandemic era, before the proliferation of digital devices and the daily torrent of social media dented the joy of communal experiences – and the mass media's power and influence to chronicle and convey such events and movements.

The human relationship with music has become more transient. Today, it is a more casual interaction, less embedded than it was in 1996 and before. Technology means that some music is often quick to make and distribute and is then briskly consumed. Like fast food – tasteless and disposable. It feels as if much, not all, modern music has been knocked off in a hurry. There are far fewer troublesome musicians with naughty habits and expensive instruments and barely any bands, creating a music scene that is less meaningful. The new breed of controllable pop stars do what they are told and are seemingly less demanding of royalties.

Perhaps, at time of writing, that is why the last British rock band to reach the number one singles position in the UK was The Beatles in November 2023 with their farewell 'Now and Then', a reworking of a 1977 Lennon demo.

The ritual of saving up pennies and heading to a sacred record shop, those chapels of awakening and discovery, to hand over your pocket money for the vinyl equivalent of a Wonka bar, have all but disappeared. That real-world act and its touchable prize represented something – a physical product to be cherished, dusted, studied in depth and listened to, over and over again. Not just discarded and disposed of after a few inattentive listens.

1996

When an £11.99-a-month streaming subscription silently slips from our bank account each month we barely notice, so the music we consume comes to mean less. The digital distractions of scrolling and skipping mean we are less likely to dive in deep and long, thence becoming absorbed and entranced in the same way.

Like society, art has become colder, more distant, transactional and faceless, sometimes lacking the passion, humanity and profundity of what came before.

It is the same in TV and film. Tarantino and Danny Boyle's productions are intense, deep and human, with scripts refined and refined again over years, capturing memorable and absorbing dialogue, much of it quoted decades on. Modern technology means some, but not all, films can be hastily assembled and tidied up later in the editing suite, and that can neutralise the magic and sterilise what was natural and special, exactly the tactile the stuff humans love.

It's a similar picture in journalism. Artificial intelligence can knock you up a nuts-and-bolts piece of copy in seconds – even if you can accept that it will most likely be riddled with inaccuracies, it will probably be totally bereft of humour, spark, fervour, mischief and a genius headline, as highlighted in this book. Never Mind the Algorithm Bollocks, We're the Humans.

AI was nothing more than a colloquial northern English term of acknowledgement when my journalistic career started, a time when we were witnessing monumental transformations in media, technology, politics, discourse and popular culture when, serendipitously, my obsessions and fascinations seemed to chime with what an observant paying public wanted to read about and devour.

The 1996 Brit Awards on 19 February at London's Earls Court was the emblematic enthronement of Britpop – and the wider Cool Britannia movement that had flourished around it. As a nation, we were relinquishing that powerful American influence, which had started to make many believe that – as Blur once proclaimed – modern life is rubbish. Instead we started to look to these down-to-earth, straight-talking lads and ladettes from provincial Britain who were reclaiming the Union Flag from the racists, in celebration of our creative powerhouse of a country. This was vigorously promoted and celebrated through the vibrant pages of our highly competitive newspapers, some with eye-watering daily sales.

It was a sometimes choppy voyage of discovery that would ultimately lead me to one of the greatest – but toughest – jobs in journalism. Yet it was a dazzling and beguiling trip of a lifetime, one which would somehow usher me to Downing Street to audiences with six prime ministers, to Buckingham Palace to meet Queen Elizabeth, King Charles and Prince William, and to Margaret Thatcher's funeral; travelling around the globe to meet world leaders, many of the planet's sharpest thinkers and intriguing minds, and scores of musical and sporting heroes. Along the way, there were headbutts, hangovers, shoves, snubs and run-ins and Johnny Rotten, the bashing of a precious Oscar and a lager in Liam's lap. The only consistent and key requisite was ensuring I had jollity and laughter along the way, putting to sensible use my privileged position and the tumultuous life that had engulfed me.

Remember this. When we die, there will be numerical etchings on our gravestone, dates over which every one of us is completely powerless, namely our date of birth and the date of our death.

The simple dash between those dates is symbolic of what we can achieve during our limited time on this earth. For me it's namely love, friendship, family, laughter, successes, fun and joy.

Enjoying the dash was what the 90s was all about. Make sure you enjoy yours.

Acknowledgements

Love to my parents Michael and Deborah Mohan and their amazing record collection. To my sisters Michelle and Isabel.

Thank you to Tony Blair, Alex James, Mel B, Shaun Ryder, Paul Oakenfold, Johnny Hopkins, Chris Poole, Vernon Kay, Chris Briggs, David Davies, Jane Savidge, Stephen Street and Dave Pearce, for their interviews, insight and support.

Thanks too to Julie Crowley at the Tony Blair Institute, Anita Gillam, Louise Gannon, Rebekah Brooks, Victoria Newton and Dave Hogan for their assistance on this project too. And to Michael and Charlie Ingall and all at Versa Studios/Allied London for their support, Prue and Tom Onions of Daisy Green, Morgan Howell @SuperSizeArt, Mike Smith, Mrs Animation, Amanda Docherty, Robin Ashton, Jill Furmanovsky, Richard Jones and all at The Barbican Music Library.

To my publisher Katya Shipster, Isabel Prodger and Kate Neilan: thank you for your guidance and advice.

Picture Credits

Images courtesy of the author with the following exceptions:

P.1 (top, bottom left): JMEnternational/Getty Images; p.1 (top right): Mirrorpix/Getty Images; p.1 (bottom right): © Dan Towers/ The Sun/News Licensing; p.2 (top right): Avalon/Getty Images; p.2 (bottom): Alexander Hassenstein/Bongarts/Getty Images; p.3, p.4 (middle), p.5 (bottom left), p.6 (top, bottom), p.7 (top, bottom), p.8 (top): © Dave Hogan; p.4 (bottom): © Jayne Russell/The Sun/News Licensing; p.5 (top): Brittany Smith/Alamy Stock Photo; p.6 (middle): Patrick Ford/Redferns/Getty Images.